My Life as a Comrade

My Life as a Comrade

The Story of an Extraordinary Politician and the World That Shaped Her

K.K. Shailaja

with

Manju Sara Rajan

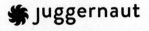 juggernaut

JUGGERNAUT BOOKS
C-I-128, First Floor, Sangam Vihar, Near Holi Chowk,
New Delhi 110080, India

First published by Juggernaut Books 2023

10 9 8 7 6 5 4 3 2 1

P-ISBN: 9789393986597
E-ISBN: 9789393986511

Typeset in Adobe Caslon Pro by R. Ajith Kumar, Noida

Printed at Replika Press Pvt. Ltd.

*This book is dedicated to those young social and political workers
whose work will carry the future of our country.*

— K.K. SHAILAJA

*To my family — those who remain and those that are lost.
We learn and form in one another's company. Always.*

— MANJU SARA RAJAN

Contents

A Kerala Timeline   ix

Preface   xv

1. An Intertwined History   1

2. Communism Comes Home   19

3. Winds of Change   35

4. A Mother's Love   49

5. A House of 'Parents'   57

6. The Eternal Balancing Act   71

7. The Call of Politics   95

8. A New Chapter Begins   127

9. Reviving the Healthcare System   149

10. A Flood of Disasters   173

11. Taming Nipah   179

12. A Deadlier Virus Strikes   207

13. The Kerala Model   243

14. Ministering to the Most Vulnerable   257

Epilogue: Onward 271

Notes 277

Select Bibliography 281

Acknowledgements 283

A Note on the Author and Co-Author 287

Index 288

A Kerala Timeline

1766–92: King Hyder Ali invades Kerala's Malabar region. The Mysorean occupation continues till his son, Tipu Sultan, hands over his territories to the British after losing the Third Anglo–Mysore War.

1792: Malabar becomes part of the Madras Presidency.

1793: There is mass resistance in the form of a farmers' movement led by Pazhassi Raja against British occupation of the region.

1805: Pazhassi Raja is killed by the British in the Wayanad region of Malabar. He remains a symbol of revolution and of Malabar's perseverance.

1820: The governor of Madras Presidency, Thomas Munroe introduces the ryotwari system to the Malabar region.

1879: One of the earliest attempts at tea planting in the state, the North Travancore Land Planting and Agricultural Society Limited is formed under J.D. Munro and A.W. Turner.

1920s–1930s: A phenomenon called kudiyettam takes place – there is large-scale migration from central and southern parts of Kerala to the Malabar region.

1939: The Communist Party of India (CPI) in Kerala is formed at the Pinarayi Conference on 31 December. Members include E.M.S. Namboodiripad (EMS) and A.K. Gopalan (AKG).

1941: Known as the Kayyur incident, on 28 March, a farmers' protest turns violent and results in the death of a policeman. Many are put on trial and four people are given death sentences.

1950: Twenty-two Party workers imprisoned at the Salem jail who protested the ill-treatment of prisoners are killed by police firing in the Salem jail massacre.

1952: Along with sixteen other CPI members, AKG is elected to the first-ever Lok Sabha held in India.

1956: Kerala becomes a state.

1957: The CPI wins the first assembly election of Kerala. The new government passes the Kerala Stay of Eviction Proceedings Act within twenty days of coming to power. EMS becomes the first chief minister of Kerala.

1957: Kerala's first education minister, Joseph Mundassery introduces the Kerala Education Bill, which guarantees free education for all, making public education the responsibility of the government rather than of private institutions and individuals.

1958–59: A series of protests called the Liberation Struggle takes place against the Communist government of the state.

1959: The CPI government is dismissed by the Centre and EMS steps down as chief minister. President's Rule is imposed in the state.

1964: The CPI splits into two factions: the Communist Party of India (CPI) and the Communist Party of India (Marxist) (CPI[M]).

10 September 1964–6 March 1967: President's Rule is imposed in the state due to indecisive election outcome.

1967: CPI(M) comes to power for the first time in the form of a seven-party alliance called the United Front. EMS becomes chief minister for the second time and his term lasts till 1969.

1970: The Kerala Land Reforms (Amendment) Act comes into force.

4 August 1970–3 October 1970: President's Rule is imposed due to no party obtaining majority in the elections.

1975: Indira Gandhi declares a nationwide state of emergency and many senior CPI(M) leaders are jailed, including AKG and Pinarayi Vijayan.

5 December 1979–25 January 1980: President's Rule is imposed in the state due to loss of majority.

1980: The KPCC joins hands with Congress-I to form an alternative government in an effort to prevent the CPI(M) from coming to power.

1980: Leader of the Left Democratic Front (LDF) alliance E.K. Nayanar is sworn in as chief minister for the first time.

1982: In Kerala Assembly's general elections, the United Democratic Front (UDF) led by the Congress assumes office with K. Karunakaran as chief minister.

1991: Kerala High Court upholds the Sabarimala temple ban – women in their reproductive years are legally forbidden to enter the temple's premises.

1996: The LDF government launches the People's Plan Campaign as an effort at decentralization of power and to give more control and autonomy to local governments.

1997: Kerala's State Poverty Eradication Mission (SPEM) establishes Kudumbashree, a poverty eradication and women empowerment programme, with a special focus on economic empowerment of women.

2007: The Kerala Medical Services Corporation Ltd (KMSCL) is set up to provide essential drugs and equipment needed by public health institutions.

2008: The Kerala Social Security Mission is created to formulate and implement social security programmes/schemes in the state.

2016: Pinarayi Vijayan of the CPI(M) becomes the chief minister of the state.

2016: The Kerala government launches the Nava Kerala Mission to address issues in health, education, agriculture and housing.

2017: The Hridyam Misson is launched as a website to focus on the management and care of children with congenital heart disease (CHD).

2017: The Aardram Mission is launched to focus on the primary, secondary and tertiary systems of Kerala's public healthcare.

2017: Cyclone Ockhi strikes Kerala.

2017: The Anuyatra campaign is launched to empower disabled people and make Kerala a more disabled-friendly state.

2018: Kerala formulates a cancer control strategic action plan.

2018: Kerala becomes the first Indian state to issue separate identity cards to transgender people so that they can avail government facilities and welfare schemes.

2018: Heavy floods hit the state. There are nearly 500 deaths and the total economic losses are estimated to be around Rs 40,000 crore.

2018: The state's health department launches Arogya Jagratha – a campaign to educate the public about communicable diseases.

2018: Nipah virus outbreak is first reported in Kerala on 19 May. Within forty days of the outbreak, the health ministry is able to control the spread of the disease in the state.

2018: The Supreme Court declares the prohibition of women at the Sabarimala temple as unconstitutional, although violent protests soon follow and the issue remains a contentious one.

2019: The Institute of Advanced Virology is inaugurated in Kerala following the Nipah virus outbreak.

2019: Varnapakittu, the first-ever State Transgender Art and Cultural Festival, is organized by the state's Social Justice Department.

2019: Under the 'Sadharyam munnottu' (Be brave, go ahead) campaign, the Kerala Women and Child Development Department launches one of its first major event – a series of Night Walks to help women reclaim public spaces, especially the ones that remain inaccessible to them.

2019: The Kerala government announces plans for introducing Smart Anganwadis in the state to enhance physical, mental and social development in children.

2020: The first case of COVID-19 in Kerala is reported on 30 January. By the end of the first lockdown in May 2020, the mortality rate is below 0.4 per cent in the state.

2020: Kerala's health ministry becomes one of seven in the world to be awarded for 'outstanding contribution' towards the non-communicable diseases-related sustainable development goal (SDGs) by the UN.

2021: The State Health Agency (SHA) decides to bring all government-sponsored healthcare schemes under one roof to bring down the cost of healthcare in the state and provide more equitable coverage to all.

2022: The State Health Application for Intensified Lifestyle Intervention (SHAILI) app is launched to diagnose and combat lifestyle diseases such as hypertension and diabetes.

Preface

Writing this book has given me a chance to take a bird's eye view of my life thus far. But it has also been an opportunity to look at much more. As someone who is part of the political world, I can only look at my own life in the context of the stories of those around me. When you're working for societal change, the present is a milestone to judge how far you've come from the past, and how much you must strive to advance further in the future. As the story of a humble social worker, my tale is also one of social change in the society that I am part of. The history of my place and its people will, I hope, offer an explanation for why Kerala itself is the way it is today.

We all know that when a person is subjected to unusual circumstances, they evolve so they can deal with such situations. The ordinary and extraordinary things that happened to my family and those around me have indelibly influenced my life. I will talk about some key incidents that took place before I was born and during my early life, connecting those threads together to show how they impact the present.

I was born in a small, lush village on the sidelines of the great Western Ghats in Kerala, on the western edge of peninsular India. That noble mountain range, stretching 1,600 kilometres through

Karnataka, Kerala, Goa, Maharashtra, Gujarat and Tamil Nadu, influences the lives of everything that lives in its nooks and shadows. The way small mountain springs spread throughout the Ghats, then come together to form large rivers before flowing into the Arabian Sea is a metaphor for our lives. The veins of water that snake through the region created opportunities for livelihood, birthing and moulding our societies in what is really one of the most beautiful parts of our country. For aeons the dense tropical forest cover formed a sort of blanket over these parts, cocooning people in their own little worlds. Till, at one point, the tremors outside erupted into the lives of our communities in the Malabar region of Kerala.

When the Thalassery–Coorg road was cut through the Ghats during the British colonial period, to ease the transportation of goods, people watched with amazement as places outside their realm opened up. Giant bridges came up above the rivers, offering a completely new way of interacting with nature and living in this region. The Iritty bridge, a feat of engineering crafted out of steel back in the 1930s to connect parts of Kannur district, still stands today over the Bavali river. Iritty – many historians believe it is a shortened form of the name Irattakadavu – stands at the confluence of two rivers, Bavali and Bara puzha (puzha means river in Malayalam). Just about 2 kilometres away from Iritty, in a place that must look like a tiny full stop from the sky, by the banks of Bara puzha, sits Madathil, my village. A string of such hamlets come together to form the larger administrative unit of Payam panchayat.

When my family first settled here in the 1930s there were barely any people around; it was mostly just forest. And even though many things had changed by the time I was born, our history still influenced our circumstances. It formed our beliefs and our affiliations. A combination of that geography and the socio-political structures that evolved through the millennia in that environment has shaped me and my life, both as a human being and as a politician. Writing down my story has been an opportunity to look back at those influences. Of course, all the incidents filed away in my memory can't be printed here. After all, everything, including a book, has its parameters. Which is why many historical incidents have only been hinted upon. Having said that, I hope readers find it interesting and useful to learn about the simple circumstances in which I was born and raised, and the incidents and inclinations of the people that influenced me. I would be very happy if this book helps its readers to better understand human nature and what drives us.

I recollect the words of the great Russian revolutionary and author Alexandra Kollontai. At the start of her book *The Autobiography of a Sexually Emancipated Communist Woman* (1926), she posed this thought that I can relate to: 'Nothing is more difficult than writing an autobiography. What should be emphasized? Just what is of general interest? … it is a matter of forgetting that one is writing about oneself, of making an effort to abjure one's ego so as to give an account, as objectively as possible, of one's life in the making and of one's accomplishments.'[1] And that shall be my effort here.

1

An Intertwined History

I come from a family in politics but not a family of politicians. Everyone who enters the political arena is a political worker but not all will become politicians. There are thousands of people out there who will work their entire lives without aspiring for personal gain. The heart and soul of our system is composed of such faceless individuals. They go out on the streets to fight for privileges they may never enjoy, they become prisoners to protest injustice meted out to others. It is not easy to understand what drives such people. Their stories get subsumed by brighter ones, more successful ones.

My life story is built on the history of many such people, including my grandmother and my uncles. I stand on their legacy. It is they who taught me about politics – what it means, why it's important.

I come from a small place; as a child, the village I grew up in was my whole world. Once you gain political awareness, when you realize that small changes can make a big difference, your horizons spread outwards. You stop thinking of yourself and think of the larger group, of us instead of I. To me this is what being in politics means. To use my position to leave a lasting impact. Once you are able to do something to make a situation better, the satisfaction can fuel you through many disappointments and lows. I find it addictive: in public life you are never out of a job, something always needs fixing. When I was a Party worker in a village, there was a limited sphere within which I could make a difference; when that village Party worker became a district-level then a state-level Party worker, and later an elected representative, the sphere of influence and change became larger.

For a communist, parliamentary and extra-parliamentary activities are just two aspects of public work. Every effort must lead to one thing: social change for the better. What that means for a communist is engaging in the class struggle to eradicate existing feudal–capitalistic structures that support class inequalities.

Today for some people success means popularity and popularity means power. For me, my political career has never been about power. I started as a simple Party worker who became a member of the Party's Central Committee, was given the opportunity to contest an election, and eventually got a job as the minister for Health and Family Welfare, Women and Child Development, and Social Justice. As each task or responsibility falls on me, I carry it out to the best of my ability. And onward I go … I am always conscious of the expectations that come with any role I'm given. I saw my berth at the cabinet as an opportunity with an expiry date, so the fixing of problems when I had the chance always felt that much more urgent. Do my best. Leave it better than I found it. Move on.

My journey into politics was made possible because of the socio-political milieu I was part of. I come from a family of people who get involved in problems, in struggles, who believe in working for change. But we had no clout, no connections, except for those forged on public battlefields. However, the structure of the communist Party, which has been our mainstay for generations, was egalitarian enough to nurture the rise of a dedicated Party worker, one rank at a time. Along the way, opportunities and encouragement from others, coupled with my tenacity and a belief that we can make a difference, have pushed me forward. This is my story. But it is also the story of the Malabar, and the growth of communism in Kerala.

When you travel from the southern tip of our state, where the capital Thiruvananthapuram is located in the erstwhile Travancore region, move to the business capital of Kochi, and then to the northernmost areas of the Malabar, while the landscape generally remains bountifully green and lush, you're traversing fairly different subcultures. In the fourteen districts that make up Kerala, every other place has a distinctive variety or twang of Malayalam, particular economic interests, and predominant religion and agricultural focus; the taste of the food changes, and so does the personality of the people.

North Kerala's Malabar is distinctive for the influence of some of the most diverse tribal groups in the country, alongside a varied population that's embraced Islamic, Hindu and Christian traditions throughout its history. The terrain varies as much as our people, going from the Arabian Sea on one side to the Western Ghats on the other, harbouring rubber, coffee and tea estates, as well as magical wild areas like the Coorg forest, Silent Valley, Attapadi and the Nilgiri Biosphere Reserve.

My family is from Kannur, one of the six districts that make up the Malabar region. We've been here since the time of my great-grandfather Madavalapil Raman Mestri, who worked on a British tea plantation in what became post-Independence Karnataka. The Malabar districts like Kannur, Kozhikode and Wayanad – boasting plenty of high-altitude areas with perfect temperate conditions – were prime locations for the English plantation experiments. Various crops, from tea and coffee to different spices, were tried and tested in parts of these districts. And because of the heavy capital investment needed to set up an estate, only the English could do it.

Raman Mestri's family was from a place called Kalyasseri in Kannur. In Kerala's caste structure, our family identify as Ezhava, which in today's parlance is an Other Backward Caste (OBC). By caste, my great-grandfather would have had few prospects other than agriculture. So Raman Mestri was, by the sounds of it, an unusual man. The suffix 'mestri' in local parlance signifies a supervisor. It was the early 1900s, when a job was a rare thing, a time when land and agriculture were the main markers of wealth. Because of a single circumstance – that he got a job in an English tea estate in Makkoottam, on the Kerala–Karnataka border – our family story unfolded in a particular and somewhat unusual way for those times. Raman Mestri's job gave him some resources, and it gave his kids the basic dignity that was denied to so many people around them.

According to family lore, Raman Mestri fell in love and eloped to marry his first wife, my great-grandmother Devaki, who they say was brave and beautiful. They had five children, the freedom fighter M.K. Ravunni, M.K. Kalyani – Ammamma, my grandmother – M.K. Damodaran and twins, M.K. Krishnan and M.K. Raman. Kalyani was born in 1917 – the same year as the October Revolution in Russia. It was also the year of the birth of the late Prime Minister Indira Gandhi. I am reminded of the late Prime Minister Jawaharlal Nehru's thoughts about the year 1917 in his book, *Glimpses of World History*. Writing to his daughter Indira on her thirteenth birthday, he said:

The year you were born in – 1917 – was one of the memorable years of history when a great leader, with a heart full of love and sympathy for the poor and suffering, made his people write a noble and never-to-be-forgotten chapter of history. In the very month in which you were born, Lenin started the great Revolution, which has changed the face of Russia and Siberia.[1]

Kalyani and her brothers were just teenagers when their mother Devaki died. Sometime after, the widower Raman Mestri married a woman called Parvati (Paru). As it happened, she was a widow with a son, Karunakaran. When these parents came together, they created a new family that till today remains an integral part of our extended relations. My grandmother always referred to her stepmother affectionately as Matte Amma, which means 'other mother' in Malayalam. In those times in Kerala, at least anecdotally, remarriage was a practical option among most communities, and families were made and unmade without all the social stigma this carried in other parts of the country. If a partner died young, it just made practical sense for a widow or widower with children to remarry. Sometimes they married siblings of their late spouses, or different families just came together, fathers and mothers fitting into the roles of missing partners. For my family, for generations, broken marriages, triggered by death or betrayal, became a pattern.

Raman Mestri was independent and foresighted, so after his remarriage and with the future of his burgeoning family in mind, he decided to build a new home for the children from his first marriage. Our family history would unfold along the 55 kilometre stretch of the Thalassery–Coorg road once he decided to build a new family home in Madathil in Payam panchayat. Raman Mestri had built a good relationship with the local landlord or jenmi, the head of the Kalliatt Nambiar family, which owned everything as far as the eye could see. They could gift land to anyone they wished to. Once you had their permission, you could just mark a plot with stone posts, get it approved and call it yours. There was no paperwork; the landlord's word was gospel. But, of course, that sort of largesse-based ownership wasn't really ownership. A family could be thrown out of their home if the landlord got cross with them for any reason.

Anyway, the Kalliatt yajamanan – people used the honorific yajamanan, which translates to 'master', for the head of the jenmi household – gifted perhaps 50 acres of land in Madathil to my great-grandfather. It was a heavily forested area without any agriculture. The plot was large enough that Raman Mestri could build a home and still had plenty of land left around it. In those parts at the time, most people lived in huts with straw roofs, not just because they couldn't afford pucca housing but also in deference to caste requirements, which dictated what kind of dwelling people could build for themselves; only a thatched-roof house was allowed for most. But Raman Mestri excavated laterite from the same property and built a house of stone; it must have seemed like a palace for this family and an extraordinary concession by the landlord back then. The house came up beside a little canal, on the flat side of a slight hill. There was no road to get there, other than a path cleared of overhang and shrubbery. To cross the canal a large hardwood tree was cut and laid across as a makeshift bridge, and every few years a new one would replace the old.

I do not know how my maternal great-grandfather came into his job but it ensured that our family history is entirely embedded in the Malabar region, and later Kannur district in particular. If we hadn't been part of Kannur, perhaps we'd have been very different people making very different choices. Kannur's small and big places along the Thalassery–Coorg highway – like Iritty, Payam, Madathil, where I was born, Mattanur, which I represent now as a Member of the Legislative Assembly (MLA), and Pazhassi, where I live – have defined the people we've become. Many of our areas border parts of

Karnataka so there is a constant movement of people back and forth, crossing state lines for education, work and the everyday living of life. If I could put a colour to my childhood it would be the green of our neighbourhood, teeming with trees and foliage, brooks and canals. The hillsides rang with mysterious sounds and calls you couldn't identify. Mythology, superstition and beliefs swirled over everything. If everyone believed something, that something could well be fact.

The Malabar region is also imbued by a rebellious and egalitarian sensibility, which played a major role in its embrace of communism – the philosophy by which I was anointed even before I was born. One of the greatest examples of that vitality is the legendary eighteenth-century ruler Veera Kerala Varma Pazhassi Raja, the Malabar's most illustrious warrior and a man who hasn't got his due in our national conversation. He was a prince in the erstwhile Kottayam kingdom, or Cotiote, that ruled parts of the Malabar till 1792. (This Kottayam has no connection to the district of Kottayam in central Kerala.) He was known by the name of his dominion Pazhassi, my current home town. The vast majority of his life was spent fighting against foreign rule over his ancestral region.

It began with Hyder Ali, the king of Mysore, who began incursions into the Malabar in the 1760s and occupied the region till 1792, when Hyder's son Tipu Sultan was defeated by the East India Company and its allies. When the Mysoreans attacked this region, most of the rulers of the area, including the Kottayam king, fled south. But Veera Kerala Varma, a nephew of the ruler, stayed, coming of age as the head of his small kingdom in 1774 in this era of battles. The Mysore occupation was also a major obstacle for the East India Company, preventing them from gaining full access to this verdant region, which was an important centre for the black pepper trade. At the beginning, Pazhassi Raja fought the Mysorean incursion with the help of the

British. When it became clear that the East India Company was looking to effect its own invasion over his home territory and seeing the tax burden they put on his people, Pazhassi Raja turned against them. In 1792, the British defeated Tipu Sultan in the Third Anglo-Mysore War, and he was forced to accept and sign the Treaty of Srirangapatinam. All of Tipu's territories in the Malabar were written over to the British, which brought the Malabar region directly under colonial administration in the Madras Presidency.

The change in authority over the region brought significant long-term changes to this agrarian society. Till the British took over, the Malabar's social structure, while being caste based and tremendously unfair, was at least symbiotic, each caste having a societal role that coexisted with another. The high-caste jenmi, which means 'by birth', were the Brahmin and Kshatriya groups who did not engage in agricultural activity, so the right to work the land went to other castes. Only the upper castes had the right to acquire knowledge, but since they couldn't grow food, the system of land tenure was based on sharing of the produce among all groups in this non-monetary society. The farmers, including those of the Ezhava caste, leased land from the upper castes, did agriculture and kept up to half the produce for themselves. And like that, every caste had what we call a kulathozhil, or inherited occupation.

When the English took over administration of the Malabar, they changed the land tenure system and fundamentally changed the region as it had existed for millennia. I am not exaggerating when I say that English rule of the Malabar set our region back by generations. The way the colonial administration drew up new land laws was based on a misreading of local customs. Ours was not a culture that wrote down its perceptions and systems, there were no prescriptions and tablets that a foreigner could simply read and absorb to learn about the place. In fact, the first comprehensive study of the Malabar region was written and published only in 1887 by William Logan, who was appointed as Collector here under the English administration. It was called *Malabar Manual*, and it surveyed the entire region, describing its geographical, social, cultural and economic structures in great detail. Logan took the help of local administrators and whatever documentation was available to create a storyline of the region from its earliest mentions till his time. It was compiled over many years; how much of it Logan wrote directly, how much was edited later, how much is simply written from hearsay – all this is difficult to tell now.

The British administration, applying a literal Western mindset, looked at a society that functioned on very nuanced rules, and drew up a list of self-serving legislation. Till then, farmers could not simply be dislodged from the land they worked on because of customs prevailing in the area; everyone was in some way dependent on the labour or protection of one another. Was it fair and egalitarian? No, it wasn't. But there was no formalized legal 'ownership' of land. Instead, tradition and customs offered a subtle understanding of rights and responsibilities. The rules of society were based on shared mythologies and beliefs, on the inherent acceptance that society functioned with the hands of many.

The English were interested in the Malabar for its natural providence, but knew it was far too complex in character and terrain for them to conduct the everyday affairs of administration themselves. Under the new land laws, the English declared the upper-caste jenmi the 'owners' of the landholdings, giving legal sanction to a hitherto customary societal role and turning much of the land in these areas into private property. In effect the English co-opted the upper castes, turning them into agents and administrators who could mop up revenue for the colonial administration from those lower down the chain. The symbiotic relationship between people who worked the land and the ones who were permitted by caste and tradition to function as landlords was shattered. What was a social construct now became legal authority. And so was born a new being, the capitalist, earning passive income on the backs of farmers who, bogged under taxes and levies, became akin to indentured labour.

In response, Pazhassi Raja led a decade-long farmers' revolt against the British. When the administration destroyed his palace, flattening it symbolically to build the Thalassery–Coorg road, the king and his band of loyalists melted into the thick forests around north Malabar's Wayanad region. From within its jungles they fought the East India Company for more than ten years in a series of battles now called the Cotiote Wars. It was the longest military campaign the colonial administration waged in India. You could say Pazhassi Raja was an early Independence fighter, waging a precursor to the First War of Independence of 1857. Known among his people as the Kerala Simham, or the lion of Kerala, Pazhassi Raja was murdered by the British in Wayanad on 30 November 1805. But the legendary king remains an important emblem of revolution in our parts, a symbol of the Malabar's obstinacy in the face of aggression.

With the death of Pazhassi Raja, the Malabar region was fully within the control of the British. The administration devised ever more intricate ways of ensuring regular revenue from here. In 1820, Thomas Munroe, governor of the Madras Presidency, introduced to the Malabar the ryotwari system – the land revenue collection structure similar to the zamindari system. Every person in any kind of activity now had to pay some sort of tax that would become a revenue source for the higher administration. Moreover, the English and the jenmis together nominated adhikaris, or administrators, to govern rural areas on their behalf. This was essential because many of the jenmis had no idea of the extent or scale of their properties; much of them were far-flung, and in those days, it was impossible to keep track of tenants and produce without some help. These administrators functioned like the present-day village officers. Today a village officer's position is a public posting, but back then the heads of important local families were chosen to be the administrators. They were responsible for measuring the jenmi's share of produce, collecting taxes and presiding over the area as judge and adjudicator on behalf of the landlord. Essentially, these administrators were sort of a local stand-in oppressor over farmers and labourers. They were often corrupt, using weighted measures and tricks to reduce the already minuscule share the farmer was owed.

There were three forms of leases. The first was the kanakudian, under which farmers gave jenmis remuneration to use the land permanently, or rather bought it from the landlord for a large sum of money. The second, more temporary, arrangement was the kuzhikanam, in which the farmer could pay the landlord a certain sum for using the land for fifteen years. The money was kept in a sheela or cloth, and called sheelakaashu, or cloth money. But that wasn't all. Much of the land wasn't completely arable when the farmer got permission to use it. To make farming feasible he'd have to clear it of shrubbery, undergrowth and tree coverage. For everything he cut or plucked off the land, even though it was useless rubbish, the farmer had to pay kuttikanam, a compensation. After fifteen years, the farmer would have to renew the relationship by paying for another fifteen-year term. But it was common for a jenmi to conjure up grievances about his lessee and change the terms of the agreement before the fifteen years were up, even though the farmer had paid upfront. When such situations came up, a farmer had no recourse other than to accept whatever the jenmi said.

The third tier of relationship between landlord and farmer was verum paattam, which translates to 'simple lease'. In this form, the farmer had the right to use the land for a very short period. The jenmi could get rid of him at any point. The farmer had to pay for the right to use the land by handing over a significant share of the produce he gained from working it.

Since most farmers didn't have the resources to buy land, they were either long- or short-term lessees. The landlord took as payment large shares of everything that came out of the vayal (paddy fields) and parambu (vegetable or fruit farm). The landlord's share of paddy was called vaaram, while his share of other crops – like coconut, pepper, banana – was called paattam. And of course, sometimes, the landlord took money.

The clauses, percentages and amounts – every element of this lopsided transaction was decided by the jenmi in his own favour. For instance, the vaaram was measured with a para – a wooden vessel that came in different sizes – brought by the jenmi's administrator. The farmers often called it kallappara, or 'false measure'. If the vessel had been tampered with, it stood to reason that a landlord would get considerably more than what was acceptable as a standard measure. And the farmer was left with far less than he'd planned for. The grain was harvested and dried in the sunlight to be readied to give to the landlord. But if the adhikari complained that the grains were slightly wet then the farmer was fined an onakkuvaashi, which translates directly to 'drying obstinance', as if the temperamental grain itself had refused to comply. In such cases, the administrator took more grain to offset the alleged weight gained by the wetness of the produce. In this way, the administrators employed many tricks to take as much as they could for the landlords.

There was no consideration in times of natural disaster, no force majeure clause to relieve the farmer of his burden in case of an emergency. The jenmis took what they wanted. Again, on festivals such as Onam and Vishu, lessee farmers had to offer a vecchukaanal, literally, a 'keep-see', which means that the farmer had to take some produce to the jenmi's illam (illam refers to an upper-caste household) and present it to the family as a 'gift' for the occasion. Those who didn't were punished for their insolence. Such forced contributions were the norm when any sort of celebration took place in the jenmi's house.

So it wasn't unusual for the farmers to end up with as little as one-tenth of what they'd harvested on a landowner's fields. Farming was entirely dependent on the monsoon and could only be conducted a few months of the year, so once the grain ran out farming families starved. The colonial administration has the ignominy of having ruled over several years of famine in the Malabar, all the way up to the late 1890s. In these areas you ate what you grew; there were no other options.

At the time, there was a saying in our parts: 'There's no rice to be had even if you give gold.' That line should give you an indication of how little food there was to go around. I've heard stories of people foraging for all sorts of roots and bark from the forest floor to eat, resulting in a deluge of cholera and dysentery cases and deaths, especially of small children. It was commonplace for a family to have ten or eleven children but the death rate was so high that only a few survived.

It was a form of slavery. Indenture was assured because these people were caught in a cycle of debt. Farmers were lucky if their families were left with even two months' worth of grains, while the jenmis' granaries were filled to the brim with provisions.

If a farmer dared to dispute any decision or refused anything asked of him, the landowners meted out their own brand of punishment. Even the most trivial infraction could get a person killed. It is said that near our area, in a place called Irikkur, there existed a jackfruit tree the landlord used to hang 'difficult' tenants and workers. This tree stood over a canal, and so when the rope was cut the body would simply float all the way to the Arabian Sea. From somewhere else there were stories of rudimentary gas chambers, where people were put into a small cell and choked with the smoke of burning grass; some particularly monstrous chieftains would even introduce snakes into the chamber. One group of people inflicting pain on another, sanctioned and aided by the prevailing system: this cruelty is etched in people's collective memory.

In my grandmother's youth, much of the area in Madathil was heavily forested; wild elephants, and even leopards, roamed there. The only farmland around was in the hands of two Nair families, Rairu Nair and Kunjiraman Nair, who had leased it from the landlord Kalliatt Nambiar for agriculture. In the early 1920s and 1930s, large-scale farming was only just beginning, as people from the southern and central parts of Kerala began moving to the Malabar region during the intra-state migration phenomenon we call kudiyettam.[2] Many of our neighbours had arrived in the Malabar from central districts like Kottayam and Pathanamthitta, which were then part of the erstwhile Travancore kingdom. The two regions were similar in some ways but quite different in others. The Malabar was linguistically attached to the other territories that would eventually become the state of Kerala, but in customs, beliefs and geography it was very unlike the south. Even the word kudiyettam has a different connotation in the southern regions of Kerala. There, it is tantamount to 'trespassing', whereas in our parts, it stands simply for migration. Economically, Travancore was rich but when it came to arable land, there wasn't enough for everyone. Some of the land had been converted to spice, tea and coffee estates, or was in the hands of a few people who were wealthy in resources, caste or connections. For agrarian families looking to cultivate on their own piece of land, there wasn't much scope. Which is why they undertook the arduous journey northwards to the Malabar – a region which to a southerner back then must have seemed like the badlands, full of forests, disease and critters, but with plenty of prospects.

There's a poem I read in a book called *Kudiyettathinte Itihasam (A History of Migration)*. Originally written in colloquial Malayalam, it went along the lines of: 'When Father hears of the Malabar / It's time to bring out the quinine …' These two lines have stuck with me because they give you a sense of the fear about the Malabar region in the minds of people. Back then quinine was a sort of cure-all medicine for many ailments of the tropics, particularly malaria. If somewhat facetiously, the poem underscored the dangers of a Malabar adventure. Yet, for so many people the dangers were worth the risk, because the landlords in the Malabar region were willing to sell land, or land was available for the taking in very remote areas. I've heard that large processions of people came, oftentimes half-dead from the long journey, with farming tools and sacks of seedlings of crops they wouldn't find in the north. They'd have started in places hundreds of kilometres away.

Whether they had initially set off by bus or train, much of the hillier parts of the terrain had to be traversed by foot. It's unlikely that these migrants had a specific destination in mind; rather, they were headed to a general vicinity on a wing and a prayer, as they say. Even if a person managed to buy some land from a landlord, to make such mountainous areas suitable for agriculture took quite a bit of time and effort. Once the land was cleared of forest cover, they often had to literally etch canals into the land to channel water from natural water-bodies in the area. Then it had to be protected from wild elephants. The men would stay up all night to stave off the animals while the women and children took shelter anywhere they could.

Most of these people who came from the south to the Malabar were Christian families, though there were Hindus too. In fact, the history of churches in the Malabar goes back to this very important period of migration. The arrival of these new residents also fundamentally altered the centuries-old hidebound thinking of people in our parts.

In Madathil, for most people, poor and illiterate, superstition offered the only rulebook for life. Anything and everything had a supernatural explanation. For instance, there was a little kaavu, or sacred grove, dedicated to a local goddess people called Bhagawati. Every year in the Malayalam calendar month of Meenam, people performed the pagan ritualistic dance Theyyam in this sacred grove. Residents there believed that once the date for the Theyyam performance was set, it was bad luck for women of the area to give birth in the neighbourhood. All expectant mothers were packed off to relatives' houses before they were likely to go into labour. Then a Christian man and his family moved to the area from Travancore, and his wife got pregnant. As always, the locals told him if his wife stayed on there and gave birth, the child would die, so she had to leave. Now, this family had nowhere else to go, the man had no one to send his wife to, so he simply refused to follow their advice. He told them, 'After all, my god is different from yours, so maybe we will be spared.' As it turned out, his wife gave birth to a healthy baby boy, and she went on to have seven more children, without any fear of Bhagawati's wrath. Every single child was robust and healthy. And that superstition faded away.

My grandmother Kalyani was about nineteen when she was

married off to a man called Karayi Krishnan; he was more than ten years older than her. From the stories we have heard of my grandfather, he was extremely kind and considerate to his young wife, and the two were deeply in love. I remember a family joke about the two of them: 'If Kalyani gets a headache, Krishnan would have one too.' She was very fair and he was quite dark, day and night opposites who came together and lived a short but happy married life. He was a successful businessman, and the family was quite well off, by the standards of that time. She had two children with him: Shantha, my mother, and Damayanthi. But like her father before her, Ammamma (meaning simply 'mother's mother') lost her spouse early and suddenly. And after a dispute with his family, the young widow and her two daughters, who were probably between six and eight at the time, moved back to the house her father had built for his children in Madathil.

My grandmother must have been about twenty-seven years old then. She'd left as a new wife and returned a young widow with two small children. But it was there in that home, with her brothers, that she would evolve into the politically active matriarch I remember. She didn't travel far throughout her life, she didn't graduate from school, she was from a mofussil part of our vast country, and she belonged to a generation of women who were expected to stand quietly on the sidelines of history. But she would do exactly the opposite: she participated, and she led a far fuller life than most people.

Whatever skills she had, she made full use of them to do as much as she could. Her father had enough foresight to send her to school till fourth form (at the time, graduation was upon completion of sixth form). But in a social set-up where there were no jobs for women, the only use she could make of that education was reading voraciously. She was always dependent on the fortunes of the men in her life. Despite her widowhood, initially she lived comfortably with the support of her father. She didn't have much money but whatever she possessed, she shared. If someone needed a bit of gold for a wedding, Kalyani would give away her own earrings. If a family found themselves homeless, she would invite them to take some of her land to build a home.

Before her father's death, he married my grandmother off again to one of his relatives, a man called Vasudevan. With him, she had four more children: Chandrika, Chandran, Sahadevan and Shyamala. But she continued living in the home her father had built for his family. I was born in that house and grew up there, nourished by my grandmother's stories that blended the historic, the mythological and the political tales of our region.

Ours has always been an oral culture. Our history is in our stories and my impression of the world, the role I had to play in it, everything I would eventually become, was based on the stories Ammamma narrated of our history. Major events outside our walls created smaller quakes in our own home, and in this way the stories of the Malabar intertwined with those of my own family. This home still stands today. More than eighty years old, it is now but a humble, ramshackle dwelling. It was the theatre of the most dramatic events that would unfold in our family, and the place I left in tears when I got married.

2

Communism Comes Home

Around the time of World War II conditions in the Malabar were particularly bad. The colonial administration was negligent at best and cruel at worst. The country was a hair's breadth away from Independence, but people in our corner lived the same oppressive lives they had for generations. The chokehold of the caste system was in many ways worse than in other parts of India. Local caste rules were heinous, spreading their tentacles into the most obscure corners of people's lives to make sure that every group stayed within the confines of its social placement.

There was a preoccupation with caste purity, an idea that became an obsession after the region came under colonial administrative rule in the late 1700s, and the elevation of the jenmi landlords under the ryotwari system. Untouchability was embedded very strongly, with complicated oppressive rules. There were diktats on what sort of dwelling a person could live in, rules even for where a person's shadow should fall, what a person could wear; lower-caste people were not to wear jewellery or dress in certain fabrics. Workers were fed in the most dehumanizing way that human beings could think up. Even up to the early 1950s it was common practice to pour rice and a curry into a hole in the ground patched with nothing but some banana leaves. After a day of work in the fields, people were expected to sit in front of such cavities that looked like a long dugout trough and eat out of them. It is said that when Swami Vivekananda travelled around pre-Independence Kerala and learned of the cruelty of the caste system as practised there, he wondered if our state was a 'lunatic asylum'.

The situation for women was particularly dismal. Women from lower castes had to survive the horrors of sexual exploitation and control in addition to everything else. I remember particularly the story of a woman called Cheriyamma of Kavumbayi village in Kannur district. I must have been about twelve when Ammamma first told me about her. According to one of the customary practices of the time, once a lower-caste woman got engaged to be married, she was required to visit the local landlord who had the right to take her virginity. It was a way to exert control over people, to ensure they understood that no piece of them really belonged to themselves. Cheriyamma had fallen in love with a fellow agricultural worker called Raman and secretly married him. Unwilling to subject herself to the humiliation of ritualized rape, she ran away before the landlord could find out about her wedding and hid in a relative's house.

The landlord was furious when he discovered what had happened and his people set out to find her. When they located Cheriyamma, she was sick with fever and her eyes were infected with conjunctivitis. That wouldn't deter the landlord who'd travelled all the way to a wretched little dwelling just to ensure he took what he considered his 'right'. Cheriyamma begged him for mercy. When she said her eyes were in a bad way and begged him to leave her be, the story goes that he laughed. 'I didn't come here to look at your eyes.' The man raped her. When her husband Raman arrived after work, he found Cheriyamma shivering and blood streaming from her eyes. She was blinded in the incident. But Cheriyamma not only survived that trauma, she went on to become an activist and a Communist Party worker who was part of the farmers' union. Cheriyamma often related her story of surviving a system that was designed to make her feel worthless. Her rebellion against the landlords was fuelled by her own experience. And it was the same for many in our region.

Ezhava women like my grandmother were not supposed to cover their upper bodies; at best they were allowed to don a kaachi, a rough cloth, as per caste rules. But Ammamma pushed back. She was always meticulously turned out in a white mundu and nerithu, or shawl. Her father brought cloth from the plantation where he worked, and with it she stitched blouses for herself; with any leftover fabric she fashioned rudimentary blouses, called rouka, and distributed them to other women in the neighbourhood.

One of Ammamma's constant companions was a woman we only knew as 'Karutha', who was from the Pulaya caste. She sold handmade mats for a living. Malayali readers will know that the word karutha means 'black' in Malayalam. It was a common practice back then for local landlords to be given the right to name the newborn of the poor in his territory. This was a task many of them undertook with sadistic pleasure. After birth, when a baby was taken to the jenmi he could name them anything he wished, and that individual would spend their life with that name. Depending on the frame of mind of the man in charge, a person could end up being named 'dry leaves' (Chappila) or even 'dust' (Podiyan). It was explicitly intended to humiliate, to demonstrate that those born of certain castes were not deserving of human dignity, or the right to make even the most basic choices in their lives. That they were less than human beings; they were property, to be treated and disposed of at the will and behest of those born with the right to decide the fate of their fellow beings.

Living in such a system for generations, many of these atrocities would have seemed normal to both oppressor and oppressed – each seemingly part of a system that was preset and reinforced over generations. But not everyone was the same, and people who stood out became totems of a different way of thinking. And so, over the generations, more and more people fought back. It entirely fits the Malabar's valiant personality that during the era of my grandmother, this region would become one of the key places that contributed to the growth of communism in Kerala. And with communism, my family would be pushed into the front lines of history.

Before I get into that I must pull back a bit and trace the way communism reached our shores. After the October Revolution or October Socialist Revolution of 1917 in Russia, through which the Bolshevik Party led by Vladimir Lenin established 'people's rule' in the country (which eventually led to the formation of the Soviet Union), many thinkers from around the world became curious about communist ideology. They made their way there to learn from the Bolsheviks and understand their experience. This included Left-wing intellectuals from India. It was a defining moment that would eventually lead to the establishment of the Communist Party of India (CPI) in Tashkent in 1920.[1]

But when these communists returned to India they were confronted by violent objections from the British colonial government. Many of them were hounded by false conspiracy cases; some of the famous ones are named after the cities where cases were filed, particularly in Kanpur, Meerut and Peshawar. The British wanted to completely block the spread of communism, but as we know they failed in their efforts. Instead, the movement took on another form. Those early communists decided that instead of officially organizing Communist Party units in India, they would remain within the Indian National Congress (INC), which was at the time the largest home-grown political organization in India.

In 1934, the Leftists within the Congress formed a faction called the Congress Socialist Party (CSP) in the INC.[2] So there were two contrarian groups within the Congress itself. Even founder-leaders of the Communist Party such as Elankulam Manakal Sankaran Namboodiripadu (popularly known as EMS) and A.K. Gopalan (AKG) were initially members of the CSP. In 1939 the members of the CSP congregated in Kannur district's Pinarayi area, also the home of Kerala's current chief minister, Pinarayi Vijayan, and took a collective decision to begin officially functioning as the CPI. In response to this, the Malabar Special Police (MSP), a paramilitary unit the British administration specially created to deal with unrest in the Malabar regions, began specifically targeting communists.

Our family's pact with Leftist ideology began with three of Ammamma's brothers: M.K. Ravunni, M.K. Damodaran and M.K. Krishnan. Ravunni, the oldest, was born in 1915 in Kalyasseri. I've heard it said in the family that Ravunni always bristled against injustice, even when he was a child. Perhaps it was a trait he inherited from his father Raman Mestri. In the 1930s he encountered Left-wing political thought through his friendship with three brothers from Payam called the Kallorathu brothers: K. Madhavan Nambiar, K. Gopalan Nambiar and K. Padmanabhan Nambiar.

These brothers were part of one of the three landlord families that owned most of the land around our region. One was the Kanakathidam family in Payam, then there was a family known as Keezhooridam Vazhunnavar – the latter word translates simply to 'the people who rule' – and the third was the Kalliatt family from

whom my great-grandfather got land to build our house. Many of
the first-generation Left-wing activists – such as the iconic EMS,
from the Elankulam Mana, and AKG from the Ayilathu Kutteri
Tharavadu – were from rich landed families themselves. And so
was the case with the Kallorathu brothers, who were part of the
Kanakathidam family.

My grand-uncles were also heavily influenced by author and editor
Ramakrishna Pillai, best known as the editor of the *Swadeshabhimani*
(*The Patriot*) newspaper and for his writings about the German
philosophers Karl Marx and Friedrich Engels and their book *The
Communist Manifesto*. Like many other first-generation Indian
communists, they were initially members of the INC and involved in
pro-Independence agitations. Ravunni was only in his early twenties,
his brothers even younger. At the time the socialist faction within
the INC was getting disenchanted with the organization at several
levels. In particular, there was a feeling that the INC had become a
party of professionals, with little representation of labour and farming
populations.

Once the CSP took shape, unions began forming among different
groups of workers, including farmers, who had for so long borne the
brunt of the landlords' irrational demands and the one-sided revenue
system. The CSP also created a volunteer corps of young people,
who were trained to oppose and fight the landlords. In 1938 the
CSP in Calicut organized a volunteer camp in which a gentleman
called Sardar Chandrothu Kunjiraman Nair served as trainer. He
had retired from the MSP. Sardar Chandrothu, with training in the
ways of the MSP, would prove invaluable for his contributions to
the CSP and eventually the CPI. This volunteer corps had three
chief goals: oppose the landlords' abuse of power, strengthen the
farmers' unions, and give assistance to society's most downtrodden,
particularly people who were sick with diseases like smallpox.

Ravunni and his brothers were heavily involved in the volunteer group. The brothers had the complete support of their sister, my grandmother Kalyani. And while their father Raman Mestri wasn't happy about his sons' activism, he was open-minded and didn't want to prevent them from doing what they wanted. To get his oldest child into a more stable occupation than politics, Raman Mestri set him up with the type of store we call a ration shop, which was popular back then. It sold rice, wheat, sugar and other everyday basics. For my great-grandfather, worried about the well-being of his son, a small business must have seemed like a safe, sensible option, but that wasn't the sort of thing that interested Ravunni. He stood out in every way: ideologically, in temperament and even physically. He was widely known as 'six-fingered Ravunni' because he had six fingers on each hand and six toes on each foot. When he had to go into hiding to evade capture because of his political activism, he was always easily identifiable because of this physical trait.

At a time when practising caste biases was just the way things were, Ravunni was an idealistic humanist. He wasn't interested in taking the easy route his father had planned for him. The young man was influenced by the messaging of communist stalwarts like EMS and AKG, and felt his life was better spent in the service of people. So, as you can imagine, the small business enterprise his father established for him was a disaster, and the family ended up mangled by debt.

Thinking back on it, through the eyes of a parent, my great-grandfather wasn't wrong to worry about his children getting involved in politics. And yet, how could those young men not participate? When there's hopelessness in the air, you fight or just give up. As human beings, we are led forward by people who refuse to give up. In the Malabar, the population had already been through several cycles of famine and unrest, and there was little to no improvement in people's daily lives, no matter what was happening around them politically.

Payam, in particular, quickly became an important centre for farmers' agitations, and in 1937 when a farmers' union was organized in its Keezhoor area, Ravunni was chosen as its secretary. He was a voracious reader and a convincing orator. At the time Keezhoor was ruled by one of the cruellest landlords in the region, a man called Kezhooridam Narayanan Vazhunnavar. Ravunni railed against the malpractices of the landlord family in a speech. Quickly thereafter a case was filed against him, accusing him of speaking against the landlord. According to the literature of the police case, the chief accusation against Ravunni was that he had denigrated the landlord by calling him a 'half BA', alluding to the fact that the man sat for his Bachelor of Arts exam but didn't pass. For that slight they arrested Ravunni and sent him to jail for six months starting from January 1939.

Led by the Kallorathu brothers, huge farmer demonstrations in Iritty protested against Ravunni's incarceration. On 1 February 1939 there was a massive meeting of farmers' unions. Farmers filed into Iritty from various places in small groups, coming together like a swarm. A local leader called Comrade Raman Nambiar presided over the protest, while senior Communist Party leader C.H. Kanaran spoke at the meeting. Thousands of farmers signed a petition to the colonial government in Madras demanding Ravunni's immediate release. When Ravunni eventually came out of jail after six months, he once again went back to his work in the farmers' unions.

The year 1939 was also when World War II began in Europe. The British colonial government declared that India would join the war campaign. There was considerable opposition against that decision which was taken unilaterally by an occupying government without any consultation with the people it would affect. Protests coalesced under an anti-imperial movement called the Samrajya Virudha Samaram.

On 15 September 1940, Ravunni participated in such a protest organized by the Kerala Pradesh Congress Committee (KPCC). EMS was the president of the KPCC and Mohammad Abdul Rehman Sahib was the secretary. In Mattanur, the protests brought together a heaving throb of farmers and there was a lathi charge against them by the police. Despite the brutality, people refused to leave the venue. In the confusion, a police constable called Raman was killed. In the aftermath of that incident – and speedily, because it was a policeman – the authorities filed cases against several people. Eight people were sentenced to imprisonment, including M.K. Ravunni, who was sentenced to four years in jail. Though he was able to survive the earlier incarceration, this second chapter would prove to be his undoing. As a political prisoner he was severely beaten in jail. By the time he was released in 1945, the thirty-year-old Ravunni was extremely ill. He'd sustained injuries to his internal organs. And in 1947, M.K. Ravunni died, leaving behind a wife and baby daughter.

Ravunni's story became a sort of legend in our family, and with my grandmother's telling and retelling of it, he remained a philosophical lodestar for us, pointing in the direction of what is right and essential. If our family had wealth, it was the principles that were enshrined in his sacrifice: we inherited it, we nurtured it, it fed us. This is what I meant when I said my family has been in politics for a long time but we are not a family of politicians.

In 1947 when India became an independent country, despite the fact that the communists were also a key part of the agitation for India's Independence, many continued to be incarcerated. Communism was still banned in this country at that time, and stalwarts like Comrade AKG celebrated India's Independence while in prison.

For our family, things would get worse before they got better. Ammamma's two other brothers, M.K. Krishnan and M.K. Damodaran, were also actively involved – as part of the volunteer corps – in the farmers' agitations that shook our region in the late 1940s. They participated in major agitations around Payam. One incident would change the course of their lives.

As I have noted, farmers were fighting for survival. Things didn't necessarily get better because Independence had been achieved. While many farmers' families starved, the landlords' granaries were swollen with grains, and so of course these granaries became the focal point of people's anger; the prize of rebellion was food and freedom. According to an old scheme set up by the erstwhile colonial government, farmers were supposed to donate all excess grains they had to consumer societies. When there was any sort of shortfall, these stored grains could be distributed by the consumer societies as ration among the general population, at least that was the idea. Of course, the farmers didn't have any excess to give away. Whatever they had mostly went to the landlords. So the farmers demanded that the donation to the consumer societies should be taken from the landlords. When the landlords refused to allow this, there were protests. In one instance, a group of protesters stopped a consignment of grains that was being taken by landlords; they demanded the grains be taken to the local consumer society office instead. When the landlords refused, the protesters distributed the grains to the starving farmers.

With farmers' groups refusing to back down, the strength of the protests increased; simultaneously in places like Payam, Pazhassi, Thillankeri, Karivellur and Kayyoor, there were violent reprisals by the authorities. Police fired bullets and the farmers fought back with whatever weapons they had. At the end, five farmers died at the hands of the MSP and their goondas; twenty-two farmer homes were also burned as retaliation. And in the case that was filed because of the firing, the police named my grand-uncles M.K. Krishnan and M.K. Damodaran as defendants. As the police came looking for these men, they went into hiding.

It was a complicated, difficult time: my grandmother often said those years were the worst. My grandmother's son, Sahadevan, was born in 1948. Ammamma's father, my great-grandfather, and her brother Ravunni were dead, and her brothers Krishnan and Damodaran were in trouble with the authorities. At that point, there were five children growing up hand to mouth in the house. My mother was a teenager, so was her sister Damayanthi, then there were Chandrika, Chandran and the littlest at the time, Sahadevan; Ammamma's youngest child Shyamala was born later.

The young mother and her brood mostly fended for themselves, making the most of the earnings from her husband's small business. He was based in Iritty, 5 kilometres away from the family home in Madathil, because he was unwilling to leave his sister's home and live with his wife. At a time when nothing was ever 'convenient' these kids had to go from Madathil to Iritty on foot, meet their father, buy supplies and come back home. It wasn't safe for the adults to go. The single road between these two places was always manned by contingents of the MSP on the lookout for communists. Damayanthi, my mother's sister – only about thirteen years old then – was quite brave. With some of her younger siblings in tow, she would take the back roads, sometimes even sneaking between police trucks, to get to her stepfather's place of work to bring home the supplies. On occasions when her baby brother got sick, it also fell to Damayanthi, herself just a child, to take him to the hospital. To be made responsible for carrying a small child for such a great distance, to get him care and bring him back safely – one can only fathom the fear and desperation that created such a situation.

The MSP frequently showed up at our house, searching for my grandmother's surviving brothers Krishnan and Damodaran. The back of the house bordered a heavily forested area that concealed an old quarry, the same one from which my great-grandfather had once extracted laterite to build the home. As a result of the extraction there was a wide hole in the ground, which the young communists used as their hiding place. The neighbourhood was filled with gossip and spies; if anyone saw food being carried to the old quarry, they would immediately alert the police or the MSP. My grandmother was, of course, a conduit for communication and supplies for the young rebels. She would hide food in a large pot covered with a plate of cattle feed, so that anyone who saw her would think she was off to feed the cows. Sometimes cow feed would leak into the food below, but it was what they had. She would wait till the fugitives had finished eating and then return home with the pot.

At the time, in our parts there was little support for communists or their sympathizers. The landlords propagated the idea that communists were godless and ensured that communist supporters were socially spurned. Having said that, my grandmother was very popular in the area. Many of our neighbours and acquaintances were people who had arrived as part of the kudiyettam process from the south of Kerala. My grandmother had directly helped many of them when they first arrived. Some had stayed in our chaayppu, or outhouse, for weeks while they set up homes for themselves. But, if she and our family got into trouble over our politics, many of these same people would simply look the other way. For one thing, most were Congress supporters. Even if some were sympathetic to the communist cause they would never publicly support them. (Because of the enmity between the Congress and the communists at the time, spies and whisperers were often called 'Congress goondas'.) And even more importantly, most people were united in their religiosity and, therefore, in their lack of sympathy for communists.

In one particularly frightening incident, a group of Congress workers and members of the MSP threatened to burn my grandmother's house to the ground to smoke out her brothers. To get to our house, as I had described, you have to walk over a bridge made of tree trunks; sitting on our front porch you could see people approaching over that makeshift bridge. My grandmother was expecting the crowd because someone had warned her that her home was a target. When she told us this story later, she'd talk about how she tried to get her neighbours to store whatever valuables she had at home, but they refused. They were afraid the police would become vindictive if they helped a communist woman. She hid them in the same quarry that also protected her brothers and other activists. A desperate woman's attempt to safeguard her meagre belongings.

Women were meant to be protected by men: that was the way people were raised, that was the way my grandmother had been raised as well. Her marriages were meant to be her protection, and yet there she was in charge of a house full of young children, living through the frightening consequences of the decisions of people around her. If her faith in the Communist Party hadn't been rock solid, the ordeal that day might have broken her. There's a porch in front of the house, the same porch on which she'd tell us her stories. That day she sat on that porch waiting for the crowd she believed would burn her house, and everything in it, to the ground. She'd tried everything and then given up trying. So she waited, listening. Like a swarm of bees, you could hear them before you saw them. There they were, the police and a pack of goons walking towards the house, egging each other on, buzzing with excitement and anticipation.

Just as the crowd neared, a representative of the local landlords, the Kalliatt family, ran ahead of them. The man told the police that Appanu Yajamanan, the Kalliatt landlord, forbade them from burning the house. 'This house was made by the trees of my forest,' he had apparently pronounced. 'I gave it to Raman Mestri and no one here has the right to burn it down.' In those parts at that time, despite the police and the laws of an independent country, the word of the local jenmi was final. There was no question of disobedience. The crowd dispersed, and the family was saved.

On another occasion, a constable of the MSP came to Kalyani's front yard and demanded she allow him into the house to search for her brother M.K. Krishnan. Ammamma was sitting in the veranda cutting jackfruit, so she had a knife in her hand. She said, 'No, Krishnan is not here. Is he a plate that I can hide him in my house? It is your job to find him, so you go do that.' When the policeman made to come inside the house to look, she got up and, holding the knife out, she said, 'Get out, don't enter my house. Go get the amshamadhikari's notice, and then come back to search my house.' The amshamadhikari was the equivalent of the village officer; he was the chief administrator of the landlords. The policeman retreated; back at the police camp he told everyone Kalyaniamma had threatened him with a knife. While they said they'd prosecute her for it, thankfully, they never did.

At any rate, my grandmother couldn't protect both her brothers for long. While Damodaran managed to elude the police, Krishnan was arrested and jailed first in Kannur central jail, and later moved to the notorious Salem jail near Coimbatore. At the time, the Salem jail was run by one of the cruellest wardens in the country. Political prisoners were regularly dehumanized, tortured and treated like petty criminals.

On 26 January 1950, when Home Minister Madhava Menon

Kozhipurath from the Congress government of Madras State (Kerala became a state only in 1956) arrived to inspect the jail, a group of Comrades submitted a petition to the visiting minister highlighting their treatment in the jail. In retaliation, the jail authorities moved the communist prisoners to an annexe building.

It was a single ward with a small entryway, now stuffed with too many people. The prisoners protested by going on hunger strike. The jail authorities, angered and frustrated by the situation, shot at the prisoners.[3] That day, twenty-two people died, and around a hundred prisoners were injured, including Krishnan. He was shot in the head, but stayed alive, protected by the bodies of his comrades who were felled before him. But even though he survived the shooting, Krishnan never recovered from the shock of that incident mentally, and physically a bullet remained lodged in his temple till he died. I remember how when I was a young child, my grand-uncle Krishnan would sometimes take my hand and run it over the bump on his temple where the bullet was lodged. The doctors had advised the family that it was too dangerous to operate and extract the bullet fragment. My other grand-uncle Damodaran continued as a Party worker all his life.

For the Communist Party, the Salem jail massacre stands out as one of the most heinous incidents in its battle-scarred history. Several important leaders and activists were lost there. Each one had been a participant in important agitations against some reprehensible aspect of the system back then. For instance, farmers sometimes took loans from the landlords by offering the land they farmed as guarantee. The landlords issued promissory notes as proof of such transactions, but often refused to return the promissory note even after the loan had been paid. This left the farmer in a vulnerable position because the landlord could block access to the land he worked on. It was those arrested in major agitations against such situations who had been incarcerated in Salem and lost their lives there.

At the end, it would seem that my great-grandfather had been right to fear for his sons and their political involvement. I know that my grandmother suffered greatly from the continual trauma of upheaval and loss during those years. She'd lived with their beliefs and worked to protect them for more than two decades of her life; to lose two brothers, one in jail and the other after long-drawn-out suffering, pained her immensely. My mother grew up directly affected by it as well, and she imbibed a sense of foreboding – the idea that anything could go wrong at any time. As the ones left over, I think they also felt some amount of survivor's guilt, in that they were able to make it to better days, while the men who had truly fought for a better tomorrow perished with the past.

Her experiences made my grandmother anti-police and anti-Congress to the hilt for the rest of her life. She particularly hated the men in khaki. She couldn't pass one without muttering something uncomplimentary under her breath. She never ever stopped seeing them as a symbol of state oppression. Later in her life, when she attended demonstrations, she'd goad them, saying, 'Come, shoot! But we will keep fighting.'

In the midst of her brothers' troubles Ammamma also lost her child Chandran, who died of typhoid. The emotional scars of that time remained with her throughout her life. The trauma ran deeper than she ever let on. In her telling, these stories always rose in a crescendo of triumph, but she was haunted by her losses.

3

Winds of Change

The political and social awareness in people like Ammamma and many others was nurtured by what they imbibed in the classes that Communist Party workers conducted back then in places like ours. My grandmother insisted her friend Karutha wear a mundu, even though caste rules forbade it, and the two of them attended Communist Party meetings together, like a pair of renegade girlfriends. Many of the upper-caste or savarna people in the area were angered by such everyday acts of individual freedom. Clothing was a significant public marker of caste domination: when anyone abandoned it, that threatened centuries of structural power of one group over everyone else. Perhaps my grandmother got away with it partly because of her father: the jathi or caste of the Makkoottam Mestri wasn't such a big deal for people. His work elevated him over his own lot and gave his family a degree of exemption.

My grandmother put her limited freedom and learning to as much use as she possibly could. She wasn't a political person as much as she was a social worker, and her instincts were finely honed by everything she learned from her brothers and the classes she attended.

I vividly remember the stories she told me about the smallpox epidemic that raged through Kerala in the early part of the twentieth century. It is called vasoori in Malayalam. Caused by the variola virus, smallpox could lead to death in three out of ten cases. But perhaps the worst thing about it was the fact that the disease manifested in a horrifying way. The body was covered with pus-filled warts, crawling all over, showing up on the palms of the hands, feet, and even the mouth and throat. Once the pustules spread to the throat, most people suffocated to death. When a victim died, the body was covered in coconut leaves and dragged away for cremation.

My grandmother had particularly horrible memories of it. When she was a child, her uncle, aunt and two children were all infected with smallpox. They were isolated in a barn near the family home. No one was allowed to go in or interact with them. She remembered hearing them moaning and wailing in pain through the night. She told us her mother would hold her and cover her ears with a bedsheet to shield her from the sounds. As each one of them died, she saw their bodies, people she'd loved all her life, being towed away to the funeral pyre. Those sights, its sounds and smells left an indelible impression on my grandmother. She fully understood the trauma of that disease on the people it infected and those around them.

One can only imagine the terror it wreaked on the population. In our parts, people – most of them poor, illiterate and caught in a turmoil of fear and confusion – interpreted the situation through superstition. They believed the viciousness of the disease was a manifestation of the anger of Kodungaloor Amma, or the goddess Kaaliamma. When she prowled the countryside for victims, no one was safe. If you consider that, even today, in the age of information technology, people believe things that are beyond the rational explanation of science and are factually incorrect, you can imagine how easy it was for people decades ago to believe that the supernatural had a role in their afflictions. And this heinous disease, with its physically distorting symptoms, made little sense to most folk. It seemed to arrive at random and ensnare anyone. It affected the landless, and it affected the landed. And so, it had to be other-worldly.

In our lush, wooded neighbourhood, superstition, religion and socialism were never at odds; you could believe in all those things at once, choosing the parts that worked for your own life. Ammamma, for instance, would often speak of the gods as though they were acquaintances, beings to be cajoled and chided. When her family went through difficulties, you could hear her telling them off for their cruelty, threatening them with her potential disinterest. With smallpox and its infection rate, people believed the only way to satiate the goddess was to leave an infected person to die; to let her take her victim. There was little public education about precautions, so people came up with their own. They said if someone had vasoori then no one in the neighbourhood should temper mustard seeds, or vasoori would enter that house. They called it the disease that shall not be named – yes, like Voldemort in the Harry Potter books. Just uttering the word vasoori invited the infection into the family. They warned children: 'Don't walk past a house with vasoori, or you'll get it.' Fear was the only deterrent that made sense to them.

When a person was infected, they were quarantined outside the house in a makeshift dwelling, and the family summoned the Devi's agent, or medium, a man we called komaram. He would perform a thoollal, a ritualistic dance mimicking a person possessed by a spirit. He always carried a bundle of turmeric powder and he always applied turmeric on the patient. In country medicine, turmeric was antibiotic, anti-inflammatory and everything in between.

Of course, caste had a role in this situation as well. The komaram

was always a poor, lower-caste person. He treated the sick, and if
they died, he had the right to take everything that belonged to that
person with vasoori. Often, this meant highly valued brass objects
like kinnam, a large spittoon, and a kindi, a tumbler placed on the
veranda of a home for people to wash their feet before entering the
home. It wasn't largesse, though. They gave it away to the komaram
because no one wanted the contaminated belongings of a smallpox
victim. The stuff was cursed in more ways than one. So they'd give it
to this poor man who'd take it home, clean it and use it or sell it for
basic necessities. Maybe because of the use of turmeric, a komaram,
they said, was rarely infected by vasoori. He always had turmeric and
ash smeared on his body. We don't know if that was what protected
him; perhaps it was.

Starting in the 1940s, the Communist Party held classes to teach
people how to deal with this infectious disease. EMS, AKG, Krishna
Pillai and N.E. Balaram frequently visited Kannur at that time and
spoke on the subject. The Party discussed vasoori in scientific terms,
as a communicable viral disease, and the possible ways to prevent
its spread. Party workers demonstrated the way to care for patients,
how to administer food and water, and how to take precautions while
handling clothing and other basic measures.

My grandmother attended these sessions and she picked up a lot
of information, which she then used herself. One anecdote she told
us concerned a twenty-year-old man called Koran, a labourer who
became infected with vasoori. When he got the disease, he was left
by himself in his makeshift hut. My grandmother decided to visit
him. Of course, everyone tried to dissuade her, but she was adamant.
When she got to his dwelling, he was lying on the floor. He had
warts all over his face, even his eyes. He looked frightening, she said.
He was moaning for water, suffering agonies, in the throes of what

people called villayattathinte moorcha, the pinnacle of the goddess's punishment after invading her victim's body; basically, it was what we know today as the critical stage of an infection. My grandmother told us she couldn't stop herself from helping him. 'My one foot was inside and the second one followed,' she said.

Ammamma put everything she'd learned from the Party's health classes to use. She took precautions to keep herself and her family safe, even as she helped him. To hydrate him, she dipped a small piece of cloth in some water that had been cooled after boiling and placed the cloth on his lips using a wooden stick, from afar, making sure not to touch him. He'd open his mouth so that the water dripped into his mouth. She sprinkled turmeric powder over his body, again making sure not to touch him. She told him she'd be back the next day. And she went, this time taking mashed rice gruel, which he could simply open his mouth and swallow. She applied more turmeric on him. On her way back home, she would bathe in the canal near our house, change her clothes and wash the clothes she had had on in the patient's house. She would never take these used clothes home without washing them first.

Slowly Koran's warts began drying and he could sit up. When he was better, she applied an ointment made from different parts of the pepper plant and bathed him in warm water. Once he was fully recovered, this man would visit our house, telling the story, over and over again, of how my grandmother had cared for him and saved his life.

She developed a reputation after that, and folks with sick relatives often called on her for help. She always went. If there was a death in the family, the relatives spent days in stupor and mourning, while neighbours ensured there was food in the house and everything was taken care of. Ammamma was everywhere in these situations, cajoling people out of their distress, sometimes chastising those who wailed too often or too loudly, otherwise feeding, tending and caring. Small places, especially, need neighbours like her, people who don't shy away from getting involved, who take the trouble of looking after near strangers.

Perhaps because she stretched far beyond social norms in so many aspects of her life, Ammamma also occasionally managed to step in between caste lines. Unusually for those times, several upper-caste Nair women were friends with my grandmother. These women were from landed families but in those days that meant only that the family had land and produce; individuals, especially upper-caste women, had no personal wealth. While my grandmother was considered the head of her household and lived in a home that her father had made in her name. In that sense, my grandmother was freer and more liberated than her friends. She was popular with the jenmi's family, which meant that while others of her caste were expected to use the back entrance of the landlord's home, my grandmother was allowed entry through the front yard. Though the landowning family were stingy with grain for most of the village, with her they would always share some. But there were limits to their consideration, and everyone understood that she was being treated as an exception without guarantees.

One of my grandmother's closest friends was a Nair woman called Chooliyat Kalyani. (Kalyani was a popular name around our parts. Every evening my cousins and I would play a game, where we tried to remember all the Kalyanis we knew: Edompalli Kalyani, Kottyampara Kalyani, Cholakandy Kalyani, etc.) One year, there was a big wedding in Kalyani's Nair household, and she invited my grandmother. Ammamma arrived at their house, dressed in her finery, a bright white mundu and nerithu bordered with gold kasavu weave, and looking better than any other woman at the wedding. Except that she wasn't like everyone else, of course. She was a lower-caste woman in the attire of a woman of higher birth. And others attending the wedding knew that.

At large Kerala weddings, everyone sat cross-legged on a mat on the floor and ate off banana leaves. When the time came for the sadhya, my grandmother took her place on the floor. After a while, she realized no one was sitting next to her. It seems the relatives attending the wedding said that if Ammamma sat with them, they wouldn't eat, because she was thazhnajaathi, or lower caste. Caught in the middle of this caste wrangle, Kalyani, my grandmother's friend, was extremely embarrassed. When Ammamma inquired what was wrong, her friend said, 'Let's go eat somewhere else.' My grandmother understood what was happening. 'I am hungry, I want to eat,' she insisted. As others got up to leave, she became furious. She said loudly, 'Look at you and look at me – what difference is there between us? I've worn good, clean clothes, after all. The most important thing for a human being is cleanliness, not caste. We should all try to be clean and neat.'

The Kalliatt yajamanan Appanu – the man who had gifted the land to my great-grandfather to build our home – was a guest there. Sitting on the veranda, he heard the commotion and asked what was going on. Someone said, 'We called Mestri Kalyani' – Mestri's daughter Kalyani, as my grandmother was called – 'but the ladies here won't sit and eat with her.' Then Ammamma came out and forcefully pleaded her case: 'You are the landlord – what is the right thing for them to do? I didn't come here without an invitation. They asked me to come and I came, but they won't eat with me. Don't you think it's time to end this system? I am as clean as the rest of you. I want to eat the sadhya here, with everyone else. It is not right to call me here and then insult me by not serving me food with everyone.'

Appanu yajamanan, who had always had a soft spot for our family, pronounced, 'This isn't fair. If you invite a person to a sadhya, you must feed them with the other guests in the venue itself. This is not right. You should not insult the guests.' And that was that. Once the jenmi made an observation like that, even if it mortified the others, they had no choice but to follow his directive. So they served my grandmother alongside everyone else. She had lost her appetite after the furore and didn't really eat much, but she had proved her point.

Such 'transgressions' might well have gone into the mix that ushered in a more egalitarian way of life in the state. And of course the sacrifices of many communists like my grand-uncle Ravunni cemented the respect for and faith in communist principles that people have in Kerala. Today, communism's influence has seeped into the psyche of most Malayalis, whether they identify with the Left politically or not. Every Malayali is a socialist in some way. I say that because most Malayalis consider themselves egalitarian, and are believers in education rights for women, and in the fundamental right to good healthcare. Labour rates are higher here, people have a right to their own piece of land. And because we built the state on the principle of giving people self-respect, today Kerala does not tolerate the kinds of caste-based atrocities still practised in many parts of our country. This is the direct influence of communism. As a population we have come to accept basic, simple, humanitarian principles, but it is important to remember that these rights were hard-won by many people who never lived to experience its benefits. We look upon those people who lost their lives in this fight as martyrs. Maybe martyrdom is an elevated status that families cling on to understand the deep anguish of their losses. But that's how it is for us, and so it is for families all around the country who lose their loved ones in this way. Our entire political fabric is woven with the threads of souls that fought for causes greater than their individual selves. So the title of martyrs is rightfully theirs.

On 1 November 1956, Kerala became a new state. Stretching from Wayanad in the north, to Thiruvananthapuram in the south, a series of Malayalam-speaking regions coalesced into a single entity. And then a few months later, in 1957, the state had its first election. In that unprecedented debut election, the CPI swept the polls with sixty seats in the 126-seat Assembly. In February 1957, the first Kerala state government was formed under the chief ministership of Comrade E.M.S. Namboodiripad, making it the very first time that a communist party had been voted to power democratically anywhere in the world. To go from being seen as criminals to members of the party in power was a dream transformation for Party workers like my family. They had been involved in election work and so they had anticipated the Communist Party would fare well, but they couldn't have imagined the mandate it got. My grandmother used to say they suddenly became important to everyone.

The Communist Party had won because of its agitation for equal land rights and reforming the education system in the state. So, within twenty days of coming to power, the new government passed the Kerala Stay of Eviction Proceedings Act as an ordinance, in order to prevent evictions of tenants by landlords. Excitement and anticipation ran high among the poor. There was hope that change had finally arrived, that their opinions and problems mattered, that centuries of caste oppression and systemized slavery would be eradicated. Having a piece of land to call their own was the ultimate stamp of dignity. In many places landless labour took over plots of land they'd been working on. The government also assured people that everyone would have at least a bit of land to call their own. Dignity and quality of life – these basic principles begin with having a home. The right to free education and reforming a system that was unfairly skewed in favour of sections of society were top priorities. But the revolutionary thinking involved in these very principles would make the communist government a target of interest groups and the Opposition. Almost as soon as the government came to power, there was a concerted effort to unseat it.

Till that first communist government came to power, the majority of educational institutions in the state had been run by Christian charitable organizations or upper-caste Hindus. In 1957, Kerala's first education minister, Professor Joseph Mundassery, introduced the Kerala Education Bill, which guaranteed free education to one and all, mandating public education as the responsibility of the government rather than of private institutions and individuals. But this very act, one that would eventually pave the way for Kerala's much touted status as India's most literate state, was, ironically, one of the reasons why the state's first communist government was brought down.

A series of agitations, demonstrations and a campaign called the Vimochana Samaram, or Liberation Struggle, began against the communist government. Various anti-communist groups came together against Namboodiripad's government. My uncle Sahadevan, my grandmother's youngest, was studying in a school in Iritty at the time. He said church bells would ring to summon people, who would then gather to participate in the Vimochana Samaram. There was a concerted effort to polarize people along communal lines, pushing the notion that communists are godless. In fact, at the time, the church forbade communist members from being buried in church grounds. The areas dominated by communities of people who'd arrived during the kudiyettam era were Congress strongholds for a long time, as I've noted earlier. Some years ago, I remember reading an article in *Frontline* magazine by journalist

A.G. Noorani, in which he recollected an incident from that period in Kerala. Congressmen from our state met then prime minister, Pandit Jawaharlal Nehru with complaints against the communist government and pressed him for President's Rule in Kerala. Nehru got irritated and reportedly burst out, 'communism, communism, you are always speaking about communism, but the bigger threat for the country is not communism but communalism.' An insightful prediction, but still, Nehru complied with his partymen's view.

On 31 July 1959, just over two years since the communist Party was elected to power, this popular government was dismissed and President's Rule was imposed in Kerala. In 1960, when the Congress government came to power, people who had taken over land from the landlords were forced off it. There were large-scale evictions across the state for various reasons. The way these evictions were conducted, the unfairness of the way displaced people were dealt with, resulted in considerable agitation among people.

On 3 May 1961, a battalion of 600 armed policemen, under the orders of the revenue department at the time, arrived at the village of Ayappancoil in Idukki to evacuate around 2,000 families. It was part of a land acquisition drive by the government for the Idukki hydro project. People were gathered into buses and sent off to a place called Amaravathi where the government had organized temporary shelters. In Kerala, we usually get showers every evening in early May as a precursor to the full monsoon that arrives by mid-May. As the conditions at this camp were terrible, everything leaked; there were no sanitation facilities or health resources, and little food. Comrade AKG, then Party secretary of the Communist Party, arrived in Amaravathi to support the villagers and went on hunger strike to protest the conditions in the camp.[1] When news of his agitation spread to other problem areas in the state there were protests against the government, which then became desperate to force him to end his hunger strike. A few days later, AKG was arrested and transported to the Kottayam Medical College, but he continued with the fast.

On 15 June, Prime Minister Jawaharlal Nehru instructed the government in Kerala to negotiate with the communist leader. The next day, the tenth day of AKG's fast, the government agreed to provide the villagers with compensatory land and so he ended his fast. More than fifty years later the incident is still celebrated by the people of Amaravathi. His stance proved to be an inspiration for many others in different parts of Kerala. In Kannur, in an area called Kottiyoor, people who had come as kudiyettakar – migrants from the south of the state – were being forcibly removed from land they'd occupied for a long time. The church leader there said, 'Go call AKG and bring him here. He cares about people. If he protests, they will stop the evictions.' AKG and Comrade B. Wellington, who had been a minister in the EMS cabinet, went there, demonstrated and stopped the evictions. And through a series of such populist actions even the church's stance towards communists began to change. People began to understand that communism was not against God; rather, it was for people.

For years after Independence, there was within the Communist Party an ideological tussle to decide the future stance of the Party. The aim of the Communist Party is socialist revolution, but what stage of that revolution had the country reached? After Independence was the country ready for a socialist revolution, or was it still working towards complete democratic revolution? What was the character of the state as governed by the Indian National Congress (INC)? There were multiple answers to those questions, but eventually out of the many, two distinctly opposing stances emerged about the stand the Party should take in the political future of democratic India. One faction felt that the country was led by national bourgeoisie; though they were pursuing a capitalist mode of development, it was time to cooperate with the new state and go forward. The other faction held the view that the new government was an organ of the class rule of bourgeoisie and landlords joining together under the leadership of 'big bourgeoisie', increasingly collaborating with foreign finance capital to encourage a capitalist type of development. Therefore, it was the Communist Party's responsibility to fight against the revisionist tendencies within itself.

At the sixth National Council of the Party held in April 1964, thirty-two members staged a walkout. Of these, seven were from Kerala: E.M.S. Namboodiripad, A.K. Gopalan, C.H. Kanaran, A.V. Kunhambu, E.K. Nayanar, V.S. Achuthanandan and E.K. Imbichi Bava. This group decided to organize the seventh Party Congress in Calcutta. In that Congress held from 31 October to 7 November 1964, a new programme was adopted for the Communist Party of India (Marxist), and that is how the CPI(M) came into existence; the other faction remained the Communist Party of India (CPI). The CPI(M) programme pushed for a people's democratic revolution in India. That idea goes back to the foundational thought that true democratic revolution can take place only after an agrarian revolution that results in the ending of caste discrimination and the feudal system as a whole. The Indian bourgeoisie was not ready to do that. So the CPI(M) decided that the next phase of the revolution in India had to be a democratic revolution led by the people, the working class.

Our family became part of the CPI(M). In the 1967 elections, the CPI(M) would form the government in Kerala.

4

A Mother's Love

My mother Shantha was the eldest of six children: four girls and two boys. Like her name, she was an extraordinarily peaceful and gentle human being in a boisterous, opinionated household. As often happened in those days, the eldest girl was the designated caretaker of all her siblings from the time she was old enough for the job. Her mother, my grandmother Kalyani, preferred reading books to doing housework, but of course someone had to do it, and it fell to my mother and her sister, Damayanthi. Together they were in charge of cooking and tending to the smaller children. They spent their childhood in two contradictory circumstances. When my grandmother's first husband, my grandfather, was still alive, the girls lived very comfortably, safe and secure. But one day, suddenly, it all collapsed. The two sisters weren't even ten when their father suddenly passed away of a heart attack. In the years after, as their family became targets for police reprisal and got buried under debt, my mother and her sister bore the brunt of their changed circumstances. These little girls often went without adequate food to eat.

None of the family had any experience of farming. I remember my grandmother telling me about the time a neighbour, Annammachettathi, gave her a yam so she could plant it. (In Kerala, the suffixes chettathi/ettathi and chettan/ettan are often used for an older woman or man, respectively, as a mark of respect.) My grandmother took the large elephantine root vegetable and covered it in a hole in the ground. When Annammachettathi came back and asked her how many cuttings of the plant she'd made, my grandmother showed the little mound where she'd buried the vegetable. One large yam yields so many sprouts that you can potentially plant even five cuttings from it and have a small crop of yam. Bury the whole thing in the ground and it'll just rot away. After that, Annammachettathi never suggested my grandmother plant anything herself.

But while they may not have been agriculturally inclined, the only money my family could earn at the time was from cultivation. They were deeply in debt and the men in the family were in hiding, in jail or just not doing well enough. Rather than take handouts from people, my mother and her sister decided to work in the paddy fields near our home. Those days they were paid for their work partly with grains and a bit of money. The field belonged to Rairu Nair and Kunjiraman Nair. They were sympathetic to our family, so at the beginning the young girls were allowed to take home pay even though they didn't work as much as everyone else.

But my mother and aunt were both fastidious by nature, and they learned the work. Planting and harvesting paddy require a person to be standing in slush under the sun for several hours at a time, pulling or embedding the plant by hand. The slushy soil protects the plant from too much heat and cold, and prevents weeds from taking hold. Since paddy crops are about the size of a bush, working in a rice field means you are hunched over almost the entire time. It can be literally back-breaking work. And in the heat of the Kerala summer, it is all the more demanding. But this labour was the only option for two girls who'd never completed their education. One step at a time, they persevered. The sisters were able to use the money from that work to buy some cows and hens, and with a bit of industriousness they managed to survive by selling milk and eggs. They also planted some cash crops like pepper, areca nut and coconut trees on their land. They didn't want to rely on anyone, so they did what they could and slowly improved their lives.

My uncle Sahadevan grew up amid this hardship, so he gave up the idea of studying further after high school. The trade he got the opportunity to learn was tailoring and so that was what he did. Once he was doing well enough, his sisters quit their work in the paddy fields, and by tying together their various bits of income, they managed to carve out a turning point in the family's fortunes. They would slowly pick themselves out of the debt pit they were in. But for my mother, things would prove to be difficult for quite some time.

It is always astonishing to me that when I think back to those days, I can't remember Amma showing even a hint of self-pity or rancour. She seemed to grasp a situation and work out the simplest and most practical way of dealing with it. When she was twenty years old, her marriage was decided as nonchalantly as the way most people make a small purchase. My father Kundan was twenty years older than her. A good-looking man from the Koothuparamba area in Kannur, he used to come to Madathil for business. He had a few acres of land on which he did some farming; well dressed and elegant, he must have seemed like a dignified person – a good catch. My mother's uncle Damodaran met him somewhere and they became friends. Being the eldest male in the family at that time, whose responsibility it was to secure a good match for his niece, Damodaran got the idea that Kundan should marry Shantha. Normally a marriage is arranged after a great deal of what you could call 'investigation'. All sorts of people are asked for a reference. But in this case, so enamoured was he by the idea that Damodaran didn't ask too many questions and presented the proposal to my grandmother. By the time my mother learned of the proposed alliance, the marriage was a foregone conclusion. My parents met for the first time on their wedding day at the venue.

Perhaps because of the vast age difference between them, I've heard it said that he was very kind and loving to my mother at the beginning. Her mother, my grandmother Kalyani, wasn't very keen that her oldest child leave and set up home with her husband in his home town, so even after she was married my mother remained in her mother's house. It does sound strange, but people had ideas like that back then, especially when it came to women. Your life was like that of a puppet; someone else held the strings and you moved this way and that depending on others' whims and fancies. Some sections of Malayali society still practised matrilineal systems at that time, so I suppose it wasn't entirely out of the ordinary for a woman to remain in her family home even after she was married. But it certainly wasn't presented as a choice to my mother. She would end up going back and forth between places, and my father would come stay at his mother-in-law's. That evolved as their system. Five years into their marriage, I was born.

At some point, my mother – in that way women can intuit such things – felt her husband was having an affair. Perhaps they had a falling out over this, but around the time I was five, my father just stopped coming to visit us. To me it was as though he'd disappeared. For a while there was no explanation or discussion about it. Then a lady and her child came to my grandmother's home claiming to be my father's first wife and daughter. He denied it of course, but my grandmother was suspicious, and finally made the background checks that should have been done before my parents' marriage was arranged. It turned out he had a partner and child back in his home town, from before he married my mother. They were not legally man and wife, so my mother was his only 'wife'. My grandmother felt my father's other family was not at fault for his actions and therefore welcomed them into our fold, even asking them to come and stay in our home. While my mother sympathized with the other lady and her child, I remember her anguish very distinctly. At night, lying next to her, I could hear her muffled sobs and sense her despair at the reality she was living through.

Then my mother took the most forceful decision of her life and resolved to legally end her marriage. Back then few people ever went to court over family matters such as these, but our family did. The court decided that my father was obligated to look after us, and I would inherit his property after his death. Since his other child wasn't born of a legal marriage, she wasn't recognized as an heir.

My father, in the way that many people do, wanted redemption just before he died at sixty-eight years of age. I was in college at the time and went to see him when he was in hospital. I remember clearly, how in almost literary Malayalam, he said to me, 'Forgive me, I couldn't step up to my role as a father or a husband. I strayed.' I said it was fine, things happen. It was too late for anything except compassion. And after all, he was my father. My grandmother ensured that part of the inheritance I received after his death was shared with his other family. My father's two families have remained close all these years, each having overcome the shock of discovery and rancour many years ago.

Though I grew up never wanting for anything, one of the greatest disappointments of my life is the loss of my father's presence from a young age. It is an inexplicable vacuum, a loss of something I never even really had. I was exceptionally lucky that there were always people around me who looked after me with so much intention and love that they fulfilled one person's role even better than he could have. I had plenty of role models. My mother, peaceful and strong, my uncle, who was active in local politics and insisted on taking me to every meeting and demonstration; there was never any impression conveyed that as a girl, it wasn't my place. And of course, my grandmother, who seemed to me the queen of the neighbourhood, a leader in every sense of the word. But the loss of a parent at a critical age in your life can leave an indelible mark, something that only you can identify.

Further down the road, as I became involved in politics and social work, experiencing that vacuum would help me understand and empathize with people who'd had similar experiences. In our society, such stories are rarely discussed or are glossed over, but I wanted to relate this for two reasons: to be able to say that we should not be marked by the actions of others, even a wayward parent, and more importantly, as an ode to my mother, whose strength and resilience deserves so much praise and respect. I am proud of the decision my mother took, I am proud she didn't capitulate to the norms of society, that she chose self-respect over patriarchy. Through all of this, no one really asked my mother her opinion or discussed how she felt. But I know my mother's heart broke when she realized her marriage had been a lie. I know she felt abandoned and unconsidered.

My mother and grandmother eventually came to live with me, my husband and family in Pazhassi, and were with us for a long time. Kalyani, the feisty communist, passed away in 2002 at eighty-three in my home.

My mother Shantha became great friends with my mother-in-law Kalyani, who was also living with us. I'd hear them both at night, chatting away about the old days, talking about people they knew, their old lives, giggling like schoolgirls. Both had been abandoned by their husbands, had lived with extended relatives, led exceptionally hard-working lives, and survived it all. They took care of one another when they were sick and had an almost enviable understanding of each other. My mother passed away in 2016, a few months after I took the oath as Kerala's health minister. About a month after she died her sister Damayanthi also passed away. With the death of each of the women who'd spent their lives caring for me – my grandmother, mother and aunt – there was a tremendous feeling of loss, of longing.

Even though you become an adult at eighteen, if the people who've raised you are alive, even the middle-aged have occasion to be children sometimes. Whenever I went back home, when these three women were around, I reverted to being their child. And even in their old age, when I was the one taking care of them, it was easy to slip back to childhood in their company. Through political upheaval and the daily strife of public work, if I closed my eyes and remembered my grandmother and heard her voice, saw my mother busy at work around our home, and that old frenetic house of ours, I'd immediately feel a sense of calm. If they are remembered, I still tell myself, they remain.

5

A House of 'Parents'

My official birth date according to documents is 20 November 1956, but that was one of those intentional clerical 'errors' made in order to make me eligible for school a year earlier. I was actually born on 15 March 1957, only a month after the communist government took charge in Kerala. I am extremely proud of the fact that I was born so close to such a singular event.

On 15 March, believed to be an auspicious day for Pooram festival celebrations in the month of Meenam according to the Malayalam calendar, my mother started to have labour pains. A lady named Malaya Maathu, a doula whom we called Maathuettathi, was called to assist in the childbirth. Women from the Malaya caste were responsible for assisting in childbirth and for years it had been Maathuettathi's job to deliver children in our area. She had a system: she'd start by massaging the pregnant woman's belly with warm coconut oil, and with that pressure over a period of time, gently push the baby out. And so I was born right into Maathuettathi's hands. As communists, my family neither believed nor read horoscopes but Maathuettathi's favourite thing to say about me was that as I was born under the

57

Pooram nakshathram (a star sign in the Malayalam horoscope), I was destined to be brave.

At the time our area had no doctor; the only qualified medical professional was 20 kilometres away in Mattanur. I remember my grandmother telling me the tale of a woman called Mariyam and her quadruplets. As you can imagine, there was no ultrasound system to determine and prepare for the number of children a woman was pregnant with. Whether there would be more than one was predicted based on the shape of the woman's belly and the wisdom of midwives. When Maathuettathi went to deliver Mariyam's babies, one child popped out, and then another. But the lady continued to be in a great deal of distress. Someone decided to call my grandmother there. When she arrived she said a doctor needed to see Mariyam immediately. The woman was in so much pain that my grandmother was worried she'd die. Her neighbours requested the jenmi for use of his car so they could go call the local doctor. The doctor arrived in time to deliver a third and a fourth baby. Unfortunately, the last one was stillborn. Mariyam was then stitched up and the doctor left. But even a week later, she continued to be in pain. When the doctor returned for a check-up, he was forced to undo the stitches to check what was wrong – only to realize that a piece of bloody cloth had been left inside the new mother! My grandmother used to say the only reason Mariyam survived that ordeal was because she was fated to live. Can you even imagine the turmoil of this woman undergoing what is one of life's most fundamental rituals? But such was the rudimentary condition of most things in the early 1950s, including medical facilities.

I was my parents' only child, born after five years of marriage. And by the time I was five years old, my father just stopped being a part of my life, as I've recounted. Since we lived in a joint family with my mother's siblings, though I sometimes felt a vacuum I hardly ever felt lonely. Together with my grandmother and mother, my mother's siblings, Damayanthi, Sahadevan, Chandrika and Shyamala – who were a part of my growing-up years – felt like additional sets of parents in my life. I also had a readymade set of friends in the vast circle of young cousins who were also part of the household.

Sahadevan – whom I called Kunhammavan, or 'younger uncle' – was born in 1948, in the middle of the family's worst crisis period. He was largely looked after by my mother and her sister Damayanthi; though they were his stepsisters really, they raised him like their own son. The other son in the family, Chandran, died of typhoid when he was eighteen, and so at sixteen Sahadevan became the only man in the family. There was just a ten-year age difference between us, but Kunhammavan became a father figure for me. He would eventually become a catalyst for my joining politics and a role model in my early years as a Party worker. By the time I was in the first grade, Kunhammavan had already started working at his tailoring job. Like the other senior members of our family, he joined the Communist Party; but unlike them he continued to work because he couldn't afford to forgo a regular income.

Then there was my aunt Damayanthi, who was about three years younger than my mother. An extremely beautiful woman, Damayanthi was married shortly after my mother, in almost the same circumstances. At the time, families with girl children felt a sense of near desperation to get them married, and with that sort of an attitude, she was paired off with a man who was entirely unsuited to her. After her marriage, she had a daughter, Shalini. When Shalini was three years old she became ill with cholera. My aunt wanted her child to be taken to the hospital, but her husband refused. So she picked up her little girl and walked the 6 kilometres from her house to our family home, but it was already too late. Shalini died shortly afterwards. I still remember Kunhammavan had bought two matching dresses – patterned with small flowers – for my cousin and I. Shalini was wearing her dress when she was taken away for her funeral. After her daughter's death, my aunt refused to go back home to her husband. She changed as a person after that, becoming angry and short-tempered with everyone, except me. I became a stand-in for her daughter and she treated me like her own. At the end of her life, when my aunt Damayanthi also came to live with me, I had the opportunity to repay her for the kindness and care she'd given me throughout my life.

The person closest in age to me at home was my youngest aunt Shyamala, who was only five years older, so she was like a friend. She was a very quiet and loving person, whose favourite pastime was gardening. Every day, she'd plait my hair and, picking out the best rose of the day, affix it to one of my braids, before sending me off to school.

It was a lovely feeling to be at the heart of the universe of these wonderful people. Even as each of these individuals were going through their own personal crises, the face they showed me was continually one of love and care. What more can a child ask for? That world is lost to time, really, because so much of how we function has changed since then. Anything from an era before technology now seems like a mirage.

By the time I was born, the family's financial troubles were mostly over, and even though we were by no means rich, I felt like the queen of my kingdom. Our house – the same that had been built by my great-grandfather – was governed by my grandmother Kalyani; my mother Shantha and her sister Damayanthi were her deputies, so to speak. Where we lived, our horizon ended where the roads finished; our view of the world was shaped informally through teachers, neighbours, family and friends. In my childhood there were a few buses around, but otherwise you had to go everywhere on foot. Our world was largely contained in the distance our feet could travel. Imagine a time like that, of that level of familiarity and self-containment. When one of us got hold of something nice, we shared it; all of us had at least a bit of it. A family couldn't survive on its own. It took neighbours, friends, sometimes even tradespeople you saw only a few times a year, to keep life going. That is one of the reasons I remember my childhood home as a hive of activity, where people gathered every evening to listen to Ammamma's stories, where neighbours landed up with their woes – and I got to watch a wise woman try to patch up the wounds of her world, in whatever way she could.

My childhood was full of stories and unique people. I've talked about the starring role superstition played in our world then. Superstitions, communist thought and religious faith comingled, bringing both order and chaos to people's lives. Most people had very little; some didn't even have a piece of cloth on their backs or a roof over their heads. It was still a time when for most the circumstances of their birth dictated their fate and place in the world. Things went wrong for many people because they had little to no control over their lives. To explain the randomness of their fate, they believed in spirits and demons, the 'friendlies' and the 'unfriendlies'; each set had to be kept happy and placated.

Even our house had a superstition surrounding it. People believed it stood near the spot where there was once a Brahmin illam. Illam is a word that pertains particularly to a Brahmin home. The story went that the family that lived there was killed during Tipu Sultan's military campaign in our area. They said these brahmarakshassus still haunted the area. Brahmarakshassu was a term used only for Brahmin ghosts. At night, particularly on slightly windy ones, there was always a kind of swooshing sound in the air, sometimes punctuated by a tap-tap noise, like a cane lightly hitting another. People would shut themselves in their homes, believing the sound was made by a prowling brahmarakshassu strolling around with a cane in hand. The sounds certainly were real, but of course the noisy ghosts weren't. It wasn't supernatural at all. Our neighbourhood was bordered with tall, thin reeds of riverside bamboo, which made a soft whistling noise when a large clump of these plants moved with the wind, one branch occasionally hitting another to go tap-tap, tap-tap.

Since people believed in spirits there were also those who lived off getting rid of them. Like one local pujari, whose expertise was chasing away lost souls. Once he had captured the lost soul through a puja, he trapped it in a bundle of palm leaves and set fire to it to release the soul. You knew the soul was trapped because everyone watched this agitated bundle of leaves hop around madly. So of course people assumed the man knew what he was talking about. My grandmother, a great purveyor of djinns, spirits and magical creatures of all kinds, later revealed the trick. The pujari would catch a little frog and trap it in between these leaves, tying the whole thing with string and holding it. Once the puja was over, he'd lay the leaf-covered object on the ground. Feeling the heat of the fire, the poor frog within would start hopping desperately, trying to get out. Till of course the soul of that unfortunate frog was snuffed out by the smoke and the movements ceased. My grandmother never revealed the man's secret to anyone. She'd say, 'Let him make a little money, it is a matter of his daily bread.'

That was the way. Everyone and everything had its place. We understood that people are complicated, they have good and bad habits, and within a realm of behaviour people tolerated quite a lot.

If neighbour Varkeychettan was a drunk then he was a drunk. You could hear him singing the famous Christian hymn 'Entathisheyame deivathin sneham' (God's love is such a wonder) from miles away. My grandmother would say, 'He's coming in hot.' Then she'd fetch some water and get ready. If he ended up in front of her, mumbling excuses, she would dunk his head in cold water and leave him on the veranda to sleep it off and sober up. When he came to, he'd go on his way. His wife Marychettathi and their children were a part of our lives. And that was that.

No one had money to curry favour or hire help; if you did for others, they did for you. Everything took a lot of effort, so there was little anyone could accomplish without the help of friends and neighbours. We were all living in a sort of barter system, I suppose. If you had muscles then you offered your strength, and you were paid back with a portion of what the other person had.

We had a huge jackfruit tree in our front yard. In the summer, when the jackfruit blossomed, it was Varkeychettan's job to climb the tree, like a Malayali Superman. He had abnormally long hands with fingers that touched his kneecaps when he stood straight. It was just a happy coincidence to know a man with very long digits who could shimmy up a jackfruit tree. Jackfruits are delicious but they are a lot of work. The largest fruit in the world, sometimes weighing more than 10 kilos, it has hard, craggy skin, oozing sap, and sticky insides. Once you cut into the fruit you couldn't stop till the whole thing was extracted and either cooked or eaten; since no one had a fridge it couldn't be stored. So from start to finish, there was a sort of assembly line – a human chain to process the fruit. All the adults in the neighbourhood would be involved, cutting, cleaning, shredding, boiling. The other children and I ran around the front yard while the elders did the labour. For the effort of harvesting the fruit, each person got a little jackfruit mash at the end, and a portion of the fruit to take home with them. A small square of banana leaf with a handful of boiled jackfruit, and a glass of tea. We didn't have enough milk or sugar to give everyone, so the tea was always bright orange, with smidgeons of milk and jaggery in each glass.

Many of these scenes – especially of everyone working together, sharing, playing – are etched in my memory, and I still replay them in my mind. Like the first time I saw a Petromax lamp. With the help of our neighbours we'd harvested some tapioca. As with jackfruit, readying it to eat was a celebration of labour and community. The tapioca was harvested, and then all of it had to be skinned, cleaned and cut into chips the same night – which we did by the light of the lamp. By morning it had to be dried in the sun. It was a way to process the whole root and save it for difficult months like the monsoon season when the dried tapioca became our staple. This was a community labouring for one another's benefit.

With my grandmother's propensity to get involved in the problems of all and sundry, there were always people around the house. Some of them were just biding their time for their lives to get better. Like the midwife Maathuettathi who had delivered me. Her husband was a drum beater; his instrument was the local chenda. He beat the drums on various occasions, even to announce movie releases. The couple and their two children lived in a tiny thatched-roof shack in the purampokku area – the community land on the riverbank. One monsoon their hut got swept away by the river, and they were left homeless. My grandmother offered them our chaayppu till they could get another home. It turned out to be a great boon for us kids. Kannettan, the husband, was allowed free movie tickets for his promotional services. And he'd take all of us, so we went to the movies for free. It's true that we didn't always get seats, but we got to watch the films, sometimes sitting on the floor or standing in the gallery of that thatch-roofed theatre. The family lived with us for almost one year. Later, when land was distributed among the landless, this family also got a home for themselves.

The three older women of our house – my grandmother, mother and aunt Damayanthi – spent a great deal of effort making sure I was safe. They'd been marked by the death of my cousin Shalini at just three years of age, and as a result they were obsessed about my health and well-being. They called upon whatever gods they had to keep their child safe. If I went out in the sun, they thought I'd sweat too much and catch a cold; if I got wet, that was the end of it. My grandmother would come at the other kids with a stick if I played outside too long. Mind you, I was a healthy, vibrant little girl, but my protectors were convinced that if I went out of their sight, horrible things would happen to me.

While their overattentiveness often annoyed me, I didn't mind most of the restrictions and usually found a way to bend the rules. But one stricture that was particularly frustrating was that I wasn't allowed to eat the school lunch like the rest of the kids. At the time, our standard midday meal was this very yellow, thick upma we called 'American upma'. As part of a scheme called the Food for Peace programme, the United States donated excess cornmeal from their farmers to other countries, and through the central government's distribution system it made its way to my little school in Madathil. Since it was made of American corn the dish was a bright cheery yellow. Most families around us often went without adequate food, and the rice in the ration shops was a cheap white variety that would congeal and remain uncooked at the centre. So for many kids in our school, the yellow upma was their main meal of the day. My family was better off, and my mother and aunt were convinced I'd become sick if I ate the American stuff. So every day at noon, they'd come and take me home for lunch.

But I loved that upma, its colour, texture – everything about it. And I couldn't have it. My favourite teacher at the time was Janaki Teacher; my grandmother had convinced her that I needed extra care because I was 'very sick', which of course was not true. She just wanted the teacher to keep an eye on me. It worked out to my advantage. Janaki Teacher knew how much I loved that upma so when I got back to school after lunch, she would be waiting for me in the teachers' room with a little bit of upma kept aside for me. It was an overcooked bright mash, but even today I can still taste it in my mouth. Over the years, I've tried so hard to replicate it, with turmeric and sooji, and of course it has never tasted the same.

In Kerala homes, in the evening, a coconut oil lamp was lit and children in the house were expected to chant kirtanas. Imagine the peace of a neighbourhood in the evening back in the 1960s/70s, before television serials and Netflix. The silence would settle in, a vast quiet over a whole neighbourhood. Then we kids of the area would race one another, trying to read faster than our friends. And because it was so quiet, you could hear each of us, outshouting each other through the routine: 'Rama Rama Pahima, Rama Pahima . . .' We'd do it at such breakneck speed sometimes that the whole thing would be elided into 'mara mara mara . . .'

After the reading, my grandmother, bathed, her oiled wet hair left loose, would sit on a mat on the ground, beside the oil lamp. It was my grandmother's evening durbar, or sadasu, as we called it. Neighbours, cousins, house guests, anyone and everyone would gather to listen. Religion, political affiliation, nothing mattered there. I remember a Muslim lady called Kadeesuma listening to Ammamma's tales from the Ramayana and Bhagavad Gita. Parvathy, Paramashivan, Raman, Sri Krishna – she presented the gods as though they were our friends. I enjoyed these stories tremendously and my love of the grand myths has stayed with me: to this day, I remain a fan of stories based on the Mahabharata and Ramayana.

I can picture the scene vividly in my mind. Varkeychettan, Marychettathi, Karutha and all the other main characters of the neighbourhood are in attendance. The stage is set, the soft orange glow of the oil lamp not yet casting its shadows as the grey-blue evening sky still provides some light. There is absolute silence as Ammamma speaks. You can hear every little thing around – even the murmuring water in the canal near the house. Only the birds, hurrying to nest for the night, dare break the magic. As the sun departs, as the day goes to rest, Ammamma's stories unfold, going back and forth in time like an accordion.

Tales of the first communists, of the MSP's atrocities, of her brothers' troubles, of how her parents fell in love, of the agitation for land: her stories were political, personal, social, moral. Very importantly, sitting at her feet we received an unparalleled education about the world. When she finished, I'd plead with her to tell us another story, and another, till 8 p.m., when we had to go study. On Sundays, though, she was very generous: storytelling filled the whole night.

It was from her that I heard the story of the Kayyur martyrs of the 1940s, Appu, Chirukandan, Kunjambu Nair and Abu Bakkar. These four young men lived in Kayyur village in Kasargod. All the rice and produce the farmers grew and harvested were being taken away by the Nileshwar landlords of the area. People were increasingly frustrated by the practice. The farmers' association, led by communists, organized a protest march to the jenmi's mansion. A police officer called Subbaraiah was called to disperse the group. The protesters marched on without heeding the police officer. It seems the policeman – no one knows how it happened – fell in the river and drowned. Even though Appu, Chirukandan, Kunjambu Nair and Abu Bakkar had nothing to do with it, as leaders of the march, a false case – that they'd caused Subbaraiah's death – was filed against them. They were taken to Kannur central jail. In fact, the late Comrade E.K. Nayanar, the three-time chief minister of the 1980s and 1990s, was also arrested but he was underage, so eventually they released him. But the others were given the death sentence.

The case was so obviously false that Mahatma Gandhi pleaded for the death sentence to be overturned. But the British government refused. When they were taken to be hanged, the men were asked to state their last wish. They said, 'We are getting set to die for our land, you don't have to hide our faces. Our last wish is to be reborn in Kayyur and come back to fight to alleviate the misery of the poor. Inquilab zindabad!' When the Kayyur comrades died, people gathered outside the Kannur jail, shouting, 'Martys are immortal!'

As Ammamma presented this story with all its verve and passion, every single one of us had tears in our eyes. Our hearts burst with pride for those men.

It was so sublime – this kindergarten of my life that eventually led me to politics, where privacy and silence are always in short supply. My grandmother's style of living, the people she invited into our lives, the stories she fed me at that impressionable age: she prepped me well.

I got a lot of sympathy because my father wasn't around, though I personally hardly felt the absence of a father. I have talked about how my uncle Sahadevan stepped up to the role in a way my actual father could never have done. His encouragement and belief in my capabilities would be the impetus I needed to fulfil a future I could never have foreseen. But everyone felt sorry for me, so I was spoilt silly – to the point that the slightest criticism from anyone reduced me to tears.

My mother's sister Chandrika had married and moved to Madras. Once a year when she came to visit, it was like a festival. The first time I saw an apple was when she got one from Madras. Apples were still not available in our part of the world at the time. And it was from her that I got my first bar of Cadbury's chocolate. She'd get off the red mail bus coming from Thalassery, with huge bundles of things: toys, sweets and so on. Seeing the bus arrive, we knew lots of goodies would be coming our way, including tantalizing stories of movie stars from the Tamil cinema world.

One year she decided I should get a haircut with bangs, just like Baby Jayalalithaa – the child star who would grow up to serve several terms as the chief minister of Tamil Nadu. No one in our part of the world had ever seen a real person with that type of a haircut. My school friends teased me relentlessly, saying, 'Rats bit off her hair last night.' There was just one person, Achhamma – a teacher who was quite stylish – who understood I had a trendy haircut. Everyone else thought I looked ridiculous, and I hated it. I'd return home from school crying every day, but there was no help for it. I'd cry to my aunt Shyamala, my constant companion at home, about the cruelties of my school friends and she'd placate me: I just had to wait for my hair to grow out.

Rather than rebel against my family's overprotectiveness, I was at pains to relieve them of worry, to reassure them, so I became quite docile. People who've known me from back then have often commented that I seem like a completely different person today. Who we become is also a matter of opportunity, I reckon, and how we use it. That 'new' me would emerge eventually.

6

The Eternal Balancing Act

In many parts of our country back in the 1970s and 1980s, a girl's education was thought of as an extravagance – as it is even now in certain parts. In post-Independence Kerala, the majority of the population agreed that girls must be educated. Education was considered a fundamental right for females – but up to a point. And fuller freedom was a rare luxury.

In 1974, when I cleared the Secondary School Leaving Certificate (SSLC) exams, the equivalent of the tenth grade exam, I realized most of my girlfriends would not be attending college. For many women of the time, their education would come to a screeching halt after they completed 10th grade, and they'd get married early. But I was lucky that my uncle and grandmother wanted me to study. The closest option for college was the Pazhassi Raja NSS College in Mattanur, which was around 20 kilometres from our home. And that is where I went from 1974 to 1979. There was no one who could offer any advice on the right subjects to study; there were no counsellors and no one else had the experience of higher education. I loved science subjects, so I decided to go into the science stream, which offered

the combination of biology, physics and chemistry. I completed my
pre-degree in 1976, and then my Bachelor of Science degree in 1979
with chemistry as my main subject of study, and physics and maths
as subsidiaries. During this time I joined the Madathil branch of the
CPI(M), officially becoming a Party member.

It was a time when my head was full of ideas of Marxism and
ideology, and Marx's focus on scientific evolution as a way to improve
society really spoke to me. Maybe because of the place and the way I
grew up, surrounded by superstition and unexplained mysteries, I was
especially fascinated by the very opposite premise of these subjects.

Among my grandmother's many fantastical tales was one about
how the world was a spinning top, sitting atop Bhoomidevi's head. In
these tales, lightning and thunder occurred when the god Devendran
got angry and swung the vajra sword back and forth. Rain was the
tears of people watching this in fear. Learning the logical explanation
of these natural phenomena in school, flashes of understanding would
go off in my brain. Aha! Now I get it, I'd think. The facts never erased
the magic of my grandmother's creative explanations; if anything, the
two polar opposite ways of understanding the world equipped me
with a great deal of empathy.

College offered a chance to learn everything at a deeper level.
Zoology was one of my favourites. The only impediment to truly
enjoying my special subject of study was the practice of dissection. We
had to dissect all sorts of creatures, particularly frogs and cockroaches.
The day I had these practicals, I wouldn't eat. But I loved everything
else, particularly the practice of keeping journals. I learned more about
our world and understood it better with that learning. Physics was
my second love. The more I learned, the logic and reasoning behind
communism made more and more sense to me.

I was lucky to be part of a communist-principled family, but even so, my grandmother – the head of our household – still held on to some of the feudal patriarchal notions of those times. She was a bundle of contradictions, one part rational, but with a sprinkling of religious, superstitious and gendered ideas that she couldn't fully cast off. For her, some things changed, with some things remaining as of old. For instance, she had strict rules when it came to engaging with the other gender. She'd tell us in the mysterious, mildly threatening way of elders: 'Don't stand too close to boys.' What she meant was that we should never allow interactions between the two genders to go beyond friendship. I understood her diktat to mean that if there was a whiff of impropriety I'd be in trouble. The parenting technique of the day was to instil fear, and she was very successful in this. I was very careful to never do anything that would upset her and my mother. This was especially because I understood I had more freedom than most of my female friends and relatives. I was allowed to do everything I wanted – within reason, of course – in college and outside of it.

As a young Party worker there was no question I'd have to interact with men, and Ammamma wouldn't even think of restricting that, but everything depended on my decorum and 'reputation', as we say. That pressure on women and the sexist assumption that women are responsible for how men behave – much of that remains the same in our conservative society. I know it is difficult for people to comprehend how a society that educates its women can also harbour outdated notions of propriety and decorum, but it is pervasive and puts an undue amount of pressure on women, while largely giving men a free pass.

When I was in my twenties, that attitude meant most women were simply not allowed the opportunity to be present in many situations. There were hardly any women at Party meetings, or in political life in general. So of course I stood out, reluctantly conspicuous, for I was quite shy and retiring by nature. Still, the environs of a Party office, Party meetings, conversation and debate were not new to me. I was comfortable there. And if there was work to be done, I knew my way around and felt I had a purpose. At the same time, I was extremely aware of my place in the cradle of my family, as the only child, as the centre of attention of the three women who adored me – and I was grateful for and appreciative of their care.

My life then was focused on learning more – and more. I knew there was a world out there but how I could grasp it, and contribute to it, wasn't yet clear to me. I was doing what was possible within the community I was part of. At the time of my studies at the Pazhassi Raja NSS College in Mattanur, I was involved in multiple Left-oriented local organizations, such as the women-focused Mahila Federation and the youth-oriented Kerala Socialist Youth Federation (KSYF). In 1978–79 I was elected to the KSYF's Jilla or District Committee.

At the KSYF we were a group of energetic and idealistic youth, maybe about thirty-five-odd people. Out of these, only four were women, because those who wanted to be active in political work needed permission from home, which they often didn't get. I remember M.V. Govindan Master, now the CPI(M) Politburo member, was then the jilla secretary. He was a highly inspiring leader and organizer at the time. I should explain the usage of the word 'Master' here. In the Malabar, we usually refer to schoolteachers as 'Master' for males and 'Teacher' for females, even if they are no longer in the profession. The affectionate nickname 'Shailaja Teacher' that I earned later in life is another example of this term of respect.

Among our contemporaries at the youth federation was the schoolteacher K. Bhaskaran Master. He was the KSYF's area secretary in Mattanur and, like me, a member of the CPI(M) Mattanur Area

Committee. There were occasions when the two of us were sent for district meetings as representatives of our committee.

As youth representatives, our mission was to go into those parts of our local communities that needed help the most – places where women faced domestic abuse, children couldn't get to schools, unemployment and alcohol abuse were rampant, and health facilities were lacking. We had to try to understand the problems better, educate people on their rights as citizens, and get them to participate in citizen-led initiatives. We were also responsible for increasing the Party's membership and therefore creating Party units in different places. This meant helping people understand communist philosophy and trying to get them to adopt a more scientific way of thinking. All this canvassing meant that I'd started speaking more and more on public platforms. I wasn't brilliant at this, but when there was an opportunity, I worked hard to do a good job.

On one occasion, my personal and professional futures aligned in a singular place and moment. I was invited to speak at the Pazhassi Reading Library, and I was quite nervous about it. Reading Libraries are a network of small rural public libraries set up to encourage book reading and boost the state's push for total literacy. A speech to such an audience meant I needed to speak with a sense of literary and cultural authority. And that is far more difficult than railing against prevailing conditions and the world in general. When they offered me the opportunity, I was quite hesitant to take it up, but when I spoke of it to Bhaskaran Master, he advised, 'Just prepare well and present it. After all, it is only a half-hour speech.' So, despite my reservations, as usual I didn't want to not try, so I said I'd go.

The inauguration of the library was to be done by someone else, and I was tasked with giving the main speech. I remember I spent every bit of time I had the next few days preparing. I read through the speeches of social activists and thinkers like Sree Narayana Guru and Swami Vivekananda, who'd said we would have salvation when Dalits and women come to power. I also read the works of social reformer V.T. Bhattathiripaadu, the poems of Edasseri Govindan Nair, and Sree Narayana Guru's shlokas. I had an armful of notes prepared on everything, and after tons of practice and preparation I, the first woman to speak at that venue, gave a forty-minute speech. The organizers were very happy. There were no obvious glitches, nothing left out, and I felt a tremendous relief when I got through it.

When the time came for me to leave, Bhaskaran Master came to see me off at the bus stand. Abruptly, in the middle of our quiet walk, he said, 'You spoke very well.' Then: 'I have something personal I want to say. If you agree, I would like to marry you.' When I first heard him say the words – the change in tone and this sudden proposal – my reaction was fear, to be honest. I was quite upset. Even though neither of us had done anything wrong, just hearing him ask me a personal question, involving the idea of love was more frightening than thrilling. I felt like I'd broken my grandmother's cardinal rules just by standing there. Yet, I had always known I would never agree to marry a stranger, chosen by others. My grandmother and mother had both walked into such traps, and it had turned out so very badly for them. I was sure they'd never want that for me. So I responded to Bhaskaran Master: 'I don't have a problem, but I'll only get into a marriage that my grandmother, mother and uncle are fine with. Please consult with them.'

On the way back and at home, I was very disturbed. I felt a mixture of confusion and worry. My mother, always sensitive to my moods, could make out something was wrong. I used to tell her every little thing. But I didn't tell her what had just happened. I was scared, thinking, 'What if she doesn't believe my version of the story? What if she thinks I've broken their trust?' Back then, the term 'love marriage' in our society immediately conveyed some notion of disobedience. So, it was very difficult for me to talk about this innocent and very respectful encounter with my mother. I knew I'd never marry anyone they didn't approve of, or that I didn't want to. Holding fast to these two ideas, I kept quiet and waited for a natural resolution of some sort. And it arrived about a week later. A fellow comrade from the Iritty unit of the Party came to the house and spoke to my uncle Sahadevan about a marriage alliance between Bhaskaran Master and me. When my uncle told Ammamma about the proposal, her first question was, 'Is theirs a Party family?' Indeed, it was.

In fact, Bhaskaran Master's family had also experienced many of the same travails of family life and the relationship upheavals that mine did. His parents, Mammen and Kalyani, were complete opposites, married off to one another by the decision of others. They were even physical contradictions: Mammen was a tall, imposing man, while Kalyani was tiny. Incidentally, as I would learn later, Mammen, a communist, was also injured in the same Salem jail firing that incapacitated my grand-uncle M.K. Krishnan. Kalyani's father, Chaathampalli Kunjamboo, was a strong and wilful character with a good amount of land and resources. And as had happened with my mother, he refused to allow his daughter to go stay in her husband's home. Similarly, again, Bhaskaran Master's mother would later learn that the man she had married was already with another woman, and as a consequence of her being unable to live with him, Mammen would eventually abandon her and their three children completely. In fact, he had five other children besides my husband and his siblings – a sister, Leela, and brother, Chandran. So, Bhaskaran Master was raised and looked after by his uncle. He became a schoolteacher at the age of twenty-two.

Usually, with arranged marriages, both sides expect the other to have the perfect gene pool with perfect histories – or at least they pretend to. For Bhaskaran Master and I, there were no such issues. Both families were politically aligned, understood the vagaries of life and circumstance and both, from lived experience, accepted that family histories can be imperfect. There was no question of judgement or rancour on either side about these aspects.

In 1979 I finished my degree, and as soon I was done, I went to study for a Bachelor of Education degree at the Sarvodaya College in Coorg district of Karnataka. Even though the college was across the border, it was close to my home in Madathil. Once our wedding was fixed, Bhaskaran Master and I would write letters to one another when I was away. Everything to be said had to fit into an Inland Letter those days, and there was always a period of waiting between one letter and the next. But that's how it was. He always kept me up to date about everything happening politically back home. We'd have discussions on paper, back and forth. Unlike me, he always delves deeply into subjects, he researches and investigates. He has a fantastic memory for history and dates, and all of this put together makes him a great raconteur. Even though I'd never allowed myself to envisage any specific sort of individual I would marry one day, knowing that my marriage had been fixed to someone with such an ideological similarity made me feel very content, I remember. Like a huge decision had been made and dealt with, to satisfaction.

Bhaskaran Master and I were married on 19 April 1981.

It was the perfect wedding of two communist idealists. No temple. No rituals. The proceedings took place at home. We invited the neighbours, friends and family. There was no exchange of jewellery and certainly no dowry. I had on a simple gold chain, earrings and a pair of bangles. A pandal was set up in the front yard for the sadhya.

I wore a simple blue georgette sari, with white embroidery on the border. The one aspect of a traditional wedding ceremony I retained was the thali (called mangalsutra in north India). Usually, there's a picture of a god on it; in my case I had it engraved with the first letter of Bhaskaran Master's name: 'B'. I remember going to a meeting with representatives of the Students' Federation of India, where some girls asked me why, as a communist leader, I was wearing a thali. I showed them his initial on the thali and said this was a token of love. 'You give gifts to one another when you like someone. Well, this is similar. But it is made of gold, so it is strong. It'll never change colour and will stay with me for as long as I live.'

With marriage I knew my life would change forever. Leaving my mother behind would be the hardest part. She was the person I talked to about everything, she was a soothing spirit in every way. We used to sleep on the same bed, and lying there with her made me feel so loved. Sure, I was already going around the countryside giving speeches and working in a political party, but at heart I was just my mother's child. The idea of leaving my family's embrace was debilitating for me. My grandmother, uncle, aunts, cousins – we'd all lived together in this small, joyfully cacophonic world. The thought of stepping out of that circle of love felt unbearable – like I was breaking a lucky spell, destroying the charm forever.

I was heartbroken. I don't think anyone will believe me entirely when I say this, but I cried for days in the lead-up to leaving home on my wedding day. Bhaskarettan chided me back then, saying, 'You're acting like you're going somewhere you don't want to, with someone you dislike!' (After our wedding I switched to 'ettan' – the suffix used for an older male – to refer to my husband.) He still reminds me, and we laugh about it. But I couldn't stop. The day I was leaving home, I cried the entire 20 kilometres between our two homes, which is just about an hour's journey. I felt like I was leaving the country even though I'd come to Pazhassi many times before. My mother and grandmother, aunts, uncles, cousins and my best friends, Vilasini and Ravi – they were my world at that point. It was an illogical feeling of being ripped out from all that I was familiar with.

Bhaskarettan had moved out of his uncle's house to one nearby with his mother and siblings. It was not very big, but it was spacious and gave us a sense of a new beginning. His sister was already married by then, and living nearby. The first thing I remember my mother-in-law saying to me is, 'Bhaskaran has said you are a Party worker and you will be going out.' I said, 'Do you mind, Amma?' She was emphatic: 'Not at all. We are also involved in Party work, so I don't mind at all. My father was in jail. And my grandfather also. Like Bhaskaran, you should go; you must.'

While I took some solace in what she said, I felt the weight of expectations on me. No one had expressed them, but all my life I'd seen women run homes and here I was, essentially a twenty-three-year-old graduate girl who'd rarely done a chore in her life. I didn't know how to cook. Even after college, I'd lived without any responsibilities in my joint family home. Moreover, I had two exams to finish, which meant I needed to spend some time studying. It was an odd position for a daughter-in-law to be in back then. In this new home, I didn't think it would be right for me to simply appear at the dining table at mealtimes, eat and leave. For one thing, there were no servants; everyone pitched in to get the household chores done.

Bhaskarettan's mother was an extremely hard-working woman, who laboured on her own rice paddy fields as diligently as the workers she hired. She'd raised her kids living in her younger brother's home, which of course came with its own compromises and hardship. So how would it look if I just got up every morning and went about my

own business? I vividly remember my first morning there. I didn't
know what to do. There was this anxious confusion. So many women
go through a similar feeling – this sense of displacement.

I asked Bhaskarettan, 'What should I do?' He said, 'Just help in
whatever way you can.' So I picked up a broom. The first chore of the
morning in most Kerala households is cleaning the front yard. The
entrance to a home should never have dried leaves and such lying
about, and there was no technique involved in this after all, so I swept
it. By the time I finished, my back hurt. Who could I tell? Feeling
achy made me even sadder.

The only chore I had done at home was grind coconut on the stone
grinder. Whenever my mother was unwell, this was the one bit of
help I used to give her. So I told my mother-in-law I could take over
that chore. My grandmother had taught me how to do it properly on
a traditional granite grinder which we called ammi kallu. It is like
the sil batta used in northern states, but in Kerala it's quite a large
accessory and built into a portion of the kitchen. Lifting the heavy
pestle and pounding something to a fine paste did require a degree
of technique. Ammamma had a reputation for her grinding skills:
she could turn desiccated coconut into the finest paste. That paste
is the base of many curries but it needs many other ingredients of
course, like turmeric or chilli, and I had no clue how much of either
needed to go into it. I was so embarrassed the first time I had to ask
Amma, my mother-in-law. But one day I made a switch that would
have made a great slapstick sketch. I'd decided to make some curry,
and instead of chilli powder, I added a heap of turmeric. The paste
was so yellow I had no option but to throw it out and do it all over
again. Amma knew what had happened, but she didn't say anything.
In many households such innocent goof-ups would have been the
beginning of a battle between mother-in-law and daughter-in-law.
But my mother-in-law was very understanding.

I don't know anyone who cooked as a 'passion' back then. It was an essential part of home life, so one did what one had to and moved along. There were no gadgets to make things easier. We didn't have a mixie yet or a washing machine. The process of stone-grinding a chutney once is enough to kill even a desultory interest in cooking as a hobby. People like to think that cooking and cleaning come naturally to women; they don't. We pick them up and learn these skills because we're expected to. Even as we hate the tasks, we perform them. Watching the hard-hitting film *The Great Indian Kitchen*, I was reminded of all these things and the absurd pressure on women to keep working till the very end of the day, when you clean everything in a kitchen for one last time, take a shower and blank out.

When the exams got near, my mother-in-law refused to let me do any more chores. She said, 'You need to study.' She insisted I concentrate on studying till my exams were over. She wasn't educated herself, and she could just as easily have refused to give me a break, but she wasn't petty. Our bedroom was on the first floor of the house, and I'd sit up there studying, though sometimes I'd fall asleep. I'd get chided by Bhaskarettan if he saw me napping. 'If you fail everyone will think it's my fault, so please sit up and study!' he'd say.

Once I passed the BEd exams, I got a job at the Shivapuram High School in 1981. That's when my world became a haze of hectic activity. Physical exertion was an unavoidable part of life back then. Every day, whatever had to be done, your hands had to do it. Like washing clothes. There was a canal called Moolathodu near the house; it had a good gush of water and that's where we washed our clothes every morning. That had become one of my chores, my first before heading to work. By the time I finished with the clothes and got back home, it was usually around 9 a.m. already. Amma would keep lunch ready, so I could pack it and put it in my bag, and I'd walk – usually run – to school.

The school wasn't too far away; it took about twenty minutes to get there, but since there was so much to do in those days, the walk felt like an hour. If I left home at 9 a.m., it could even have been a leisurely stroll. But I usually started from home at 9.30 a.m., or even 9.45 a.m., and then I'd be stress-jogging my way to work. I can never forget the anxiety I had about being late. The headmaster, K.T. Chandran Master, was a comrade who was very strict about punctuality. Everyone feared him. He'd be standing on the veranda of the school watching us. Whenever I was late, I'd avoid direct eye contact, hurry into the staffroom, sign the register and get into class. The first period was always difficult as my running/walking and stress would tire me out; the mid-morning break came only after two more classes.

I tried to do my best as a schoolteacher, but unlike most of my colleagues I was juggling many things at the same time. After school finished, I'd be at the Party office at 5 p.m. There was always something that needed attention, either a meeting, or someone in need of help. It was considered an essential part of our work so I couldn't avoid it; political activities also ate up all our weekends. So the preparation for my school lessons usually occurred late at night. By nature, I'm fastidious – a perfectionist. I wanted to teach well, so if it seemed like I wouldn't get through a lesson plan properly, I'd often pause my Party-related work and focus on the class. I tried to balance things and do my best, but there was always a sense that something or other was getting short-changed. House and family–school–politics: I was working by rote, going from one thing to the next from morning till evening.

I felt guilty all the time, as though I was falling short in the performance of all my duties. There was always a checklist of things to do, and I felt like I never did them well enough to deserve an A grade in anything. I was drowning in a tide of guilt: guilt I wasn't the best teacher I should be, guilt I wasn't doing enough in my political work, and guilt I wasn't doing enough housework either.

Amma never said anything to me, though. In fact, my mother-in-law and I were very friendly. At the end of my helter-skelter days, the one routine I looked forward to was sitting with her in the kitchen sharing our dinner and telling her about all the people I had met that day and all sorts of stories about the world. She was always very curious and wanted details about everything. Talking to her, I was always watchful for her disapproval or unhappiness about the things I was doing. It was my way of taking the temperature of our relationship. When she seemed fine and chatty, I was relieved. If she clammed up for any reason, I'd try to understand why and figure out some way of getting back to our normal affable footing.

On 6 March 1986, my first son, Shobith, was born. I remember my grandmother saying that it takes two months for a baby to smile. But I always felt like Shobith smiled at me from day one. I'd spent a month before his delivery in hospital because of some health complications, but holding my baby for the first time, every anxiety till that point melted away. My second son, Lasith, was born just a year after that, on 6 April 1987. Lasith was a cute little fellow, born with a thick head of hair and a reserved temperament. We'd waited five years to be parents, and it had felt like a lifetime. And then within the space of just one year, there were two babies in our home. Suddenly, our world was complete. The two grandmothers wanted a little girl also, but of course that wasn't to be. I remember telling them that they needed to wait and eventually daughters would be part of our family. When my boys grew up, Shobith married Sinju and Lasith married Megha, and that balanced out the gender equation in our home perfectly.

Once the kids were born, as a new mother, I took a bit of a back seat in the Party arena. I stopped going for meetings on weekends, and didn't take on any responsibilities in committees, though of course I felt bad about that too. At one point my sister-in-law and two children moved in with us while they were building a house nearby. So the house was full to bursting! Then Bhaskarettan suggested we build a small house and ask my mother if she would come stay with us. I wasn't sure my mother would come. She was the soul of her own home back then. Still, I asked her, confiding that I was finding it all too much, and she acquiesced. My uncle Sahadevan was quite unhappy about the arrangement. He saw her as his own mother and was extremely close to her.

After my father passed away, I received an inheritance that we shared with his other wife and child, as I've mentioned, and there was some land left over in my name, which we sold to buy a 34 cent plot in Pazhassi. Once this new home was up and running, the responsibilities of the house fell on my mother, I must sheepishly admit. I helped when I could, but I was then involved in political work in a more intense way.

Political work is extremely demanding. You're either fully in it, neck-deep, or you're not. Most women come to a point in their careers where they must fully commit or leave the arena entirely. I never had to make such a difficult choice. And that is because of Bhaskarettan. He's been unwavering with his support but, even more importantly, his support has been unconditional. Back then many women Comrades I worked with faced exceptional problems at home. They were always looking at the clock, worrying about being late getting home; and more often than not, the source of criticism at home wasn't a mother-in-law but a husband. Bhaskarettan on the other hand encouraged me, pushed me forward. I've never felt for a moment that he resented my successes, and he's never placed a restriction or obstacle in the way of my work. I was often absent for long periods of time from home. He has never said 'Don't go'.

Bhaskarettan reads a lot, and whatever he reads, he discusses with me. If he gave a speech somewhere I'd be the first person he'd relate the details to. He has beautiful handwriting and his notes are delightful to look at as much as to read. I remember many local leaders remarking on notes he's written for their use. On the other hand, I can't memorize someone's else's words. So though my handwriting is terrible, because I can only give a speech on what I have written myself, I have to make notes all the time. It must be my own voice. During my BEd education, a teacher used to tease me, saying, 'Looking at your handwriting one would think you're studying for the MBBS. Your handwriting is as unreadable as a doctor's!' Bhaskarettan and I also spent a lot of time teaching, taking Marxist theory classes throughout the district. He'd say, 'Even though you don't prepare so much, you present really well so everyone enjoys your class.' In hindsight, I realize how much my political thinking matured as a consequence of our marriage. If he'd been another type of person, I doubt I'd have been able to evolve as I did.

At a point in our political journey together, we both had to choose. When Pinarayi Vijayan was CPI(M) jilla secretary, they asked Bhaskarettan to become a full-time political worker since only full-timers are given responsibilities for committees and higher work. He was not in a position to do that. We had some revenue from agriculture but at the same time we had a lot of commitments and really needed a monthly pay cheque. Bhaskarettan worked at a government-aided school at the time, and he decided to keep the job. His decision meant that even though he is more politically aware, better read and a far more hard-working person than I, his

political career plateaued at a certain point. He was part of the State
Committee of the Democratic Youth Federation of India (DYFI)
and an Area Committee member of the CPI(M), but couldn't
progress to the district level. At the same time, he encouraged me
to play a more active role. And so, in 2004, I decided to join politics
full-time.

Eventually I became more senior in the Party committee hierarchy.
In our patriarchal, chauvinistic culture, such situations can become
crisis points. If Bhaskarettan had shown any kind of displeasure, I
would have had a very difficult time. Perhaps I would have persevered,
or perhaps I would have given up in frustration. If I had continued
without his full support, it's likely the family would have broken up. For
many women, those are the common fallouts of simply pursuing their
life goals. I am grateful that Bhaskarettan practised the egalitarian
theories we had learned about. It would have killed me to lose one
side of my life for the other. He loves the Party, he trusts it, and he's
proud of the fact that I am working for our society through the Party.
In front of our home in Pazhassi stands a chenkodi, the red flag of the
Communist Party. You see that flag before you see the house; it is the
soul of our home in every way, the backbone of our relationship, and
the foundation of the life we've built together.

Even if a husband understands the absence of his wife, children
shouldn't be expected to understand the absence of their mother.
Yet, that's what happened in my case. We'd waited five years to
have a child, and then when my sons entered the world, in quick
succession, they were born into my political life. They were part of
it, yet outside it, looking in. Without directly asking for help, I got
plenty of support for their care – from my sister-in-law, my mother-
in-law and my mother. But I was their mother, and I admit I still feel
a tremendous sadness that somewhere in their preteens, my career

took me away from my boys more than was reasonable. I first became an MLA when the children were in grades 5 and 6. Till fourth grade they were studying in the school that Bhaskarettan taught at. Just as they were ready to join the Shivapuram High School where I was teaching, I had to take leave from my teaching job to be a full-time MLA. When they realized I wasn't going to be there at school every day, they were heartbroken – and so was I.

And even worse, when they came home from school every day, I wasn't there. My son Shobith was a calm and quiet boy. Our favourite ritual together was bath time, when I gave him a bath beside the well at the back of our house. We loved this time together when he'd tell me everything about the plants and trees he could see. But I wouldn't have the time to do this every day, and that was one of the things I felt terrible about. I was hardly ever around to hear the stories my boys would tell as they tumbled home from school, bursting with excitement. If the Legislative Assembly was in session, I was hundreds of kilometres away from them. Sometimes these memories still upset me and bring tears to my eyes. In my absence, the boys' aunt and grandmothers stepped in and raised them. As a mother, I was both grateful and tortured by it.

If anything untoward happened to either of the boys, my guilt went into overdrive. Once when I came home at night, my younger son Lasith, who must have been about six at the time, kept pointing to his nose and saying, 'In my nose.' I could see it was difficult for him to breathe, so I looked to see if there was anything obstructing his nostril. There seemed to be some sort of fleshy protrusion inside the child's nose, which we thought was a nodule. Bhaskarettan and I took Lasith to an ENT doctor the next morning. After examining him, the doctor put a tweezer in and pulled something out. It wasn't a growth; it was a manjadikkuru, a little red seed that is seen as a lucky seed in some parts of the world. Children love collecting these hard, red-coloured inedible seeds, and somehow my son had gotten one stuck up his nose. It had probably been there a while because the outer red skin of this little thing had withered off and the inside bit looked somewhat flesh-like, which is why we thought he had a small swelling there. Thankfully there were no repercussions but that incident shook me. I blamed myself of course, and then I imagined all the other horrible things that might happen to my children in my absence.

The children were always running around bumping into things and hurting themselves. When she was home alone with them, my poor mother couldn't possibly take them to a hospital or doctor on her own if an injury occurred. So Amma would put some Ayurvedic ointment on the wound and manage. Every time I got home and saw a raw wound, I'd make up my mind that I was staying home from then on. But eventually, I'd come back to my conviction that I have a responsibility, and for as long as I could manage it, I needed to keep going.

Was it ambition? I don't know. If I thought of it as my ambition, I'd have felt even worse, I think. Society tells us women aren't supposed to be ambitious. A professional life is positioned as a luxury in a woman's life, as though it is a perk or an allowance offered by the kindness of those around us. And if we feel within ourselves that we have something to offer to the world, we're conditioned to feel guilty for it. I felt very strongly that I was doing important work, making my community better, using skills that I had. And given that I had such a supportive system at home to back me up, the guilt and emotional warfare in my heart didn't always make sense – but it was with me throughout.

Bhaskarettan and I had grown up surrounded by talk of politics, lathi charges, police and arrests swirling over our heads. What may have seemed unusual in another family has been normalized in ours for two generations now. My boys, even though they were growing up in the 1980s and 1990s, also experienced some of the tension and ambiguity that came with their parents' politics.

It must have been the late 1980s. I'd just returned from school, and there was someone waiting to tell me that Bhaskarettan had been injured in a lathi charge and taken to hospital. I knew there had been a big demonstration in Mattanur to protest against a minister in the Congress-led United Democratic Front (UDF) government who was pushing for the privatization of the education sector. Without saying a word to my mother, I rushed over to AKG Hospital in Kannur. There he was, his back criss-crossed with marks created by the cops' batons. His body was in bad shape and he had to stay in hospital for more than two weeks.

Another such incident was in 2003. During the Muthanga Adivasi demonstrations to protest the UDF government's delay in allotting land to the Adivasis, the police fired into the crowd, killing one person. The CPI(M) organized demonstrations to protest the killing. I participated in such a gathering in Kannur. We were face to face with the police, shouting slogans at them. We didn't do anything else, but the police got very aggressive. They were trying to chase everyone away, so we plonked ourselves down on the ground. Suddenly I felt blood streaming down the side of my head and that's how I realized I was hurt. I think they'd hit me on the back of the head with a lathi, and the area became numb from impact. As the bleeding was getting worse, soaking my clothes, people helped me up and took me to the hospital. I got six stitches on my head from that incident. I remember my kids visited me in hospital and I could see the tension on their faces.

When they got older, in high school, we'd tell them before heading to a protest or demonstration. They'd ask why, they objected on occasion and asked us not to go. I doubt if asking them to see the larger picture helped them understand the situation better in any way, but still we tried to explain the circumstances as far as possible. I'd always say, 'I'll be back soon.' As they got older their trepidation slowly reduced, we were able to discuss things in a deeper way. Because of the milieu at home, they were anyway very politically aware – even as teenagers.

As far and often as I could, I'd try to help the boys with studies when I was around, but while Shobith would sit at his desk for a while, my younger son Lasith wouldn't at all. I was quite worried about him. At the same time, for most of their school years they'd managed their studies entirely on their own. When he finished his Kerala board exams, Shobith wanted to study engineering but Bhaskarettan was quite set against it. He didn't think his children should pursue 'bourgeois' streams of learning like medicine and engineering. He wanted the boys to go for a general degree in a college. Such are the feelings of a comrade! But my son was adamant and we felt we needed to support his plans for his own life. Shobith is an extremely diligent, hard-working individual, he always has been. And unlike me, he's very handy in the kitchen! When he'd visit my quarters in Thiruvananthapuram when I was an MLA, he – along with my personal assistant Pramod P., who was a former student and like one of the family– would get right in the kitchen and cook for us. And I'm glad we weren't obstinate in our ideas about what Shobith should do; he secured a ranking that was good enough to earn him a place at the College of Engineering, Trivandrum, the state's premier institution for engineering education, to study electrical engineering. Even though he got an offer from an international IT company during their campus selection process, he felt he needed to stick with the branch of engineering he'd studied. Eventually he took a lower-paying but more satisfying job as an electrical engineer with a company in Kochi. Today he works in Abu Dhabi and lives there with his wife, Sinju, also an electrical engineer, and their five-year-old daughter Niral.

My younger son Lasith, on the other hand, wanted to go to a polytechnic college after school, and though we were keen to send him to college we eventually supported his decision. I'd worried about him the most, believing he wasn't serious. As it turned out, I was completely wrong. Lasith also took the engineering route and eventually got a scholarship to study MTech, earning a higher qualification that any of us. He liked to understand his subject deeply and master it on his own terms. A few years later, he wrote the exam for a job at the Kannur International Airport and got through. He'd found the opportunity, written the test and got the position all on his own. Today, Lasith and his wife Megha, an MBA, are parents to four-year-old Ifeya Jahnara.

I am especially grateful that for two boys whose parents have been in public life, they've always been careful to never put any burdens on us. Both the boys always fended for themselves; they've never suggested we use our connections or influence for their careers and so on, and so we've never had to say no to them. Both my sons are of course Communist Party workers as well, and that is a matter of great pride for their father and I.

When they were younger I worried endlessly that we weren't close enough as mother and sons, but that was unnecessary. In fact, as I'd predicted, I have been lucky enough to gain two daughters as well. Sinju and Megha have been more like my own children than just my sons' wives. Today, my children are my biggest supporters. We discuss everything, making sure to speak to one another at least once a day. They're always tracking what I'm up to out in the world, and they're always vocal with their support and praise. What has helped, I think, is that even though we weren't home together as much as many other families, the times we did get together, we spent well. We talked and debated; we argued but never failed to stay engaged with one another.

I am also lucky I can make up for the time I lost with my boys by spending time in the sparkling company of their two daughters. I might not be a 'traditional' grandmother, and they were both born when I was busiest in my career, but thanks to technology and intention, my little granddaughters, Malu and Ippu (our nicknames for Niral and Ifeya) and I are very close. When I hear them call me 'Achhamma' – father's mother – I feel a sense of joy and accomplishment.

I am so grateful for the quality of my family's bonding. My political life was only able to progress alongside my personal one because of my family's support. I grew up in the midst of plenty of love, so I always wanted that in my marriage and with my children. Society has built up many stereotypes around women who pursue their career. What is indeed unfair is when women are asked to choose one or the other, instead of being offered real partnership. I am lucky I had that in my life.

7

The Call of Politics

In college I had been an enthusiastic student which had also made me a bit circumspect about being politically active. I was a staunch Leftist but didn't like the idea of cutting classes to attend demonstrations, even though I'd gone for many with my grandmother. But coming from a family whose political antenna was always hyper-tuned, I was soon sucked into that arena.

I was – and still am – definitely an idealist, extremely interested in the theory of politics. I've always been curious about the systems that brought our society to where it is. I had skated over the principles of Marx but I thought I needed to understand those better. He spoke about dialectic materialism, where the pursuit of material wants causes conflict between opposing forces of nature. He believed we need to be catalysts for good. Marx said we must struggle for rights; it was right to do so. And we'd watched it play out in our world, with the feudal system. When tenant farmers became desperate about their broken lives, they fought back. In 1957 feudalism lost its power in Kerala, legally and symbolically, and that loss proved that struggle provides results. The most precious gain from that fight was the passing of the

Stay of Eviction Proceedings Act and later the Land Reform Act. I understood that change can come from action, and that was a deeply inspiring thought. The idea charges the most important feeling a human being needs to wake up each day: hope.

The early 1970s were quite a tumultuous period. For the Party it was a defining moment, when the youth wing of the Party in particular was extremely active. The current chief minister, Pinarayi Vijayan, for instance, was a student leader of the Party back then. He was seen as a heroic figure who stood up to the violence of communalist forces, particularly the Rashtriya Swayamsevak Sangh (RSS). There were plenty of orchestrated problems which may have escalated without the intervention of youth leaders like Pinarayi back then. I remember one incident in particular from 1971. Communalist forces started a rumour in Thalassery that somebody sitting inside a Muslim-owned restaurant had thrown a chappal at a Hindu procession. And as a result, this beautiful little town, where Hindus and Muslims had coexisted peacefully for ages, was suddenly on edge. The RSS was threatening to retaliate by hurting Muslim families in the area. AKG called upon communist activists to protect Muslim families, and that is what Pinarayi and other Comrades did. The result of their willingness to stand in harm's way to save others was that they created a lasting impression in the hearts of people. They were the sort of political workers because of whom a party's reputation lives on for decades. Such people become urban legends in their own right.

My uncle Sahadevan was also very active in politics at the time. While he never entered full-time politics, he was a dedicated local worker who spent a great deal of time canvassing in difficult places. At that time, there was very little support for the Communist Party in the mountainous areas of the Malabar where communities had settled during kudiyettam. Communist Party workers were not welcome in many of those places; residents were known to throw stones and attack workers in other ways to discourage them from going there. But there's no impact if you don't persevere and Party youth were nothing if not relentless. My uncle and Pinarayi knew one another quite well, since they were both from Kannur and worked in the same areas. And the current chief minister wasn't a man to shy away from a difficult situation, not then and not now. He asked my uncle – his peers used to call him Sadu – to accompany him to a place called Aralam near Iritty. The Party had decided to set up a branch in that area, which had a significant population of kudiyettam residents. So, they knew it wouldn't be an easy enterprise. At any rate they hired a jeep and off they went. The men got to Aralam and could see groups of resentful residents watching their every move. But they still had a meeting, finished their work and set out to return home.

On their way back on the same road they'd taken to Aralam, a tree trunk was now blocking the road. It hadn't been there earlier and it looked strategically placed, in that obviously no one had attempted to clear this obstruction from what was quite a small road. As they got nearer, half a dozen glowering men had gathered near the tree; instead of trying to clear the block, they were simply staring at the oncoming jeep. It was obvious that their intention was to attack the people in the vehicle. Pinarayi told the driver, 'As we get closer, slow the jeep when I tell you.'

When the jeep stopped, Pinarayi got out of the vehicle and stood there looking resolutely around him. My uncle told us Pinarayi hitched up his mundu, rolled his sleeves and called into the jeep, 'C'mon, let's move that out of the way.' The onlookers seemed a bit surprised and nervous at his willingness to come out in front at them. They stood aside. The Comrades moved the obstacle, ran back into the jeep, and drove away. My uncle asked Pinarayi, 'We didn't even

have a stick to defend ourselves, so Vijayetta, how were you so brave?'
He replied, 'If we'd showed we were scared, they'd have beaten us up.
You show them we're moving forward no matter what, they'll just go
away. Instead of running from a problem, it's better to face it.'

I was in college, between my pre-degree and degree courses, in
1975, when Prime Minister Indira Gandhi suddenly declared the
Emergency on 25 June 1975. The Allahabad High Court had issued
a verdict convicting Indira Gandhi of electoral malpractices and
barred her from holding any elected post. In reaction, her government
cracked down on civil liberties, arrested Opposition leaders and
imposed censorship on the media.

It proved to be a very difficult year for my family, as it was for most
Communist Party members and sympathizers. Many senior leaders
of the Party were jailed: AKG was arrested, Pinarayi was beaten up
and arrested as well. In 1976, while the Emergency was still in place,
there was a protest meeting organized by the CPI(M) in Iritty town.
Shortly after the meeting began, the police got there and bundled my
uncle into their vehicle. They didn't even say why they were taking
him away. My grandmother, who was also there, started shouting
slogans against them.

We eventually found out that they were accusing Sahadevan of
setting fire to a public bus. Several such eruptions were occurring all
over at that time and the police had no clue who was responsible. In
fact, at the time of the incident he was being blamed for, my uncle was
attending a wedding at a Congress partyman's house. The wedding
host actually went to the police station to provide Sahadevan an alibi.
But they wouldn't relent. In order to elicit a false confession, they beat
my uncle and another comrade, B.K. Kadar, who was my uncle's best
friend. Trying to turn them against one another, the police tortured
them both. My uncle often spoke about how they were strung upside

down and beaten on their feet. I remember him talking about how his friend had needles pierced between his nails. Even though the men continued to protest their innocence, and despite the fact that there was no evidence against them, the cops registered a case against these two and nine others. Some of them were sentenced to life imprisonment while my uncle got two years as punishment.

I had just started my BSc degree – the first person in my family to have reached this stage of education. It should have been a time of joy and celebration. Instead, our home went suddenly quiet, as though someone had died. For Ammamma, after all she'd been through with her brothers, losing her remaining son to the police was more than she could bear. She was angry and sad, frenetic and scared. This history being replayed – and now involving her child – was very hard for her; the fact that he was completely innocent made her rail against the police even more. Sometimes I'd hear her chiding the gods, as was her wont at such times. 'Where were you when the police caught my son?' she'd mumble angrily. In retaliation she refused to light the evening oil lamp. She'd sit on the veranda, lamenting, 'All you had to do was take care of my house and you didn't.' It was heartbreaking to watch.

Till then the stories of my grand-uncles' difficulties were just that – only stories. Now, I was watching one play out in front of me. I started going to college, but there was no excitement, no joy. Kunjummavan had worked harder than anyone to get me there. With his earnings, his sacrifice of his own prospects for an education, he was responsible for creating the circumstances of my growth. And he was in jail. A year and a half after his arrest, he was found not guilty by the court. There was never any proof against him anyway. By the time he was out, I was almost in my third year of BSc. After his release, things slowly got back to normal at home. To this day Kunjummavan suffers from back pain that started because of that police assault.

Still, we were one of the lucky ones. Many families lost their children during this time, sometimes in the most randomly cruel way. I want to tell you the story of one young man, a brilliant student called P. Rajan, who was studying at the Regional Engineering College in Kozhikode at the time of the Emergency. He was a very talented singer and actor as well. On 1 March 1976 when he returned after participating in an intercollege arts festival, the police raided his home and arrested him. They claimed that Rajan had criticized the government during his performance. He was never seen again after his arrest. Much later, due to the efforts of his father T.V. Eachara Warrier to understand what had happened to his son, and because of a court order by the Kerala High Court, the police were forced to admit the young man had been tortured and killed in custody. It was revealed that he had been held at a local police camp where the cops executed terrible atrocities, hitting him on the spine, kicking and beating him. They also tortured him with something called uruttal, or rolling, wherein a heavy wooden log is rolled repeatedly over the victim's body. Rajan died as a result, whereupon the police got rid of his body, which was never found. His father, a college professor, wrote about their family's experience in a book called *Oru Achchante Ormakkurippukal* (*Memories of a Father*), before he passed away in 2006. It is impossible to read that account without crying.

Thus, the Emergency strengthened my resolve to enter politics. Watching the injustice of many intellectuals, writers, politicians and others being incarcerated, the attack on India's democratic and federalist ideals, made me aware of how fragile our system was. Observing the events of that year, especially my uncle's ordeal during that time, and becoming more aware of the inequity of power and resources around me, communism and Marxian thought started to make even more sense. For me, witnessing first-hand my uncle lose his freedom for nothing, under false premises, was a tremendous shock. The unfairness of it hit hard. Deciding at that moment that politics was going to be my way forward, I became a member of the Madathil CPI(M) branch in 1977.

Around that time, I attended an area-level meeting of the Kerala Students' Federation (KSF), and they asked me to take part in a discussion. The late CPI(M) Politburo member Kodiyeri Balakrishnan was then the leader of the KSF. At this meeting I spoke about the problems students faced, the price rise of books and some other issues, in what was my very first public discussion. I was a pack of nerves. I was probably not very good, but people were kind and encouraging. It's wonderful to be told after you did the thing that scares you the most that your performance wasn't half bad.

My uncle, however, wasn't happy with this level of engagement for me. He was adamant I should be more involved. If anything, his time in jail had increased his resolve and dedication to the Party and its politics. My grandmother was equally keen on this and supportive of his notion that I had to do more. I, on the other hand, was very sceptical about being in any kind of leadership position. I was happy to go for meetings and do back-end work, but anything that involved the limelight left me petrified. But perhaps I just needed someone else to believe I could do it and give me a push, because eventually I agreed to become the secretary of a Mahila Unit. Once I was secretary there was no choice but to participate.

The CPI(M) is the vanguard of the working class of the country. Its faith in democratic centralism and inner-party democracy ensures it is a strong and disciplined cadre-based organization. This allows it to effectively mobilize the public through class and mass organizations. In the structure of the Communist Party, the smallest unit at the very root tip of the hierarchy is called a branch, consisting of nine to eleven selected members. If you remember, I had joined the Madathil branch. A group of branches from an area collectively forms a Local Committee, and a group of Local Committees forms an Area Committee. Then comes the District Committee and then the State Committee, leading upward to the Central Committee at the national level, and finally the Politburo, which is at the highest level of the Party. At the branch level, active Party workers are formed into an auxiliary group. For one year, these workers are trained in Marxist ideology and informed about the process and the intention behind organization building. Depending on their performance, some become candidate members, and then from this lot a group of permanent members is elected. A Party branch includes both candidates and permanent members.

When I first understood this structure, what impressed me most was how the whole system was built on egalitarian principles and the fact that it was performance oriented. These ideals may seem simple to us now, but in those days, the muddy gore of feudalism and caste clouded our world. Most things seemed to function on the basis of family connections and/or caste calculations, so to enter a world where growth based on merit was viable meant there were possibilities for someone like me.

At the local level, Party work is a euphemism for all sorts of functions, big and tiny. At our Madathil branch there were eleven of us. The branch level is the grassroots, and it is the biggest place for learning. It is where the work happens. We were responsible for organizing people into groups, such as women, youth, agricultural workers and children. I was asked to organize women's groups in our area. What that means is finessing the art of canvassing. In those days, most people in our region were either apolitical individuals who lacked any political awareness or Congress supporters, and given the

region's history of anti-communism, people would turn their backs
– literally – on anyone who seemed to be a Leftist. Moreover, we
wanted women to join and that made the job doubly hard. At the
time, everyone – including women themselves – considered females
the lesser gender, the second sex. If the world was difficult to negotiate,
their own homes were even harder. Most were reluctant to attend
political meetings because their families wouldn't allow them and
society didn't approve of it. Trying to scale such cultural barriers is
hard work, even if you are the same gender.

I had not seen much gender imbalance in my own home. Our
household was ruled by a woman and she went where she needed to
go. In fact, on days when I knew I was going to visit a particularly
difficult household, I took my grandmother along as moral
support. I knew they'd be persuaded knowing I was Kalyaniamma's
granddaughter. With as many canvassing tricks as I could conjure,
I went from house to house, encouraging the ladies to attend Party
meetings – even if they came for just a few minutes – get involved,
learn about issues, but even more importantly, understand their rights.
I'd say, 'Come, we're making a little area unit, there's nothing to do,
just join.' In the vernacular of our area, there's this word vendappa –
which approximates to 'please, no'. I heard that a lot. Sometimes you
call a hundred people and only twenty actually show up. Since I was
merely a college student, they were more easy-going with me, and I
persevered. When you're working at that level, you are trying to make
small, hopefully incremental changes, and you are fuelled solely by
belief. To be able to get a group together and have a district-level
woman leader speak at a gathering felt like the grand prize.

Slowly, we were able to sign up women, many who'd never gone
anywhere without their husbands or families. We were able to
speak to them about women's education, how they had a right to

expect more from life than just domestic duties; we listened to their problems – such as difficulties with abusive husbands, pay disparities and the lack of education opportunities. At that time, the eldest daughter of the family would probably never be sent to study, ending up caring for their younger ones. We gave these women a place to talk about their lives.

I particularly remember a discussion when Susheela Gopalan, one of the founders of Leftist women's organizations, came to a zonal meeting. She spoke about how in Soviet Russia women had the option of dropping their kids off at a state-run creche while they worked. This was something we found novel and unbelievable at the time. In fact, I didn't realize how common such childcare units were in the Union of Soviet Socialist Republic (USSR) till much later. It was a really important issue that many of our women flagged. What do we do with our children when we go to work in the fields? We needed a reliable but simple and sustainable solution.

Our answer was creating a society called the Mahila Samajam, under which we started Balwadis or daycare centres, where women labourers could leave their children every morning. The Balwadis were overseen by retired teachers. The national Integrated Child Development Scheme, which was launched in 1975, had still not made its way to our part of the country. That scheme, which allows for one rural childcare centre, called Anganwadi, per 1,000 people, fully covered my district only by the time I became an MLA in 1996, when 253 Anganwadis came into being. The Balwadis we ran were informal and managed with donations from the community. The meagre amounts we raised were used to feed the children and keep them safe. Our solution was simple but effective, and it took into account local conditions and realities. It was certainly a better option than taking children to work. Many women were forced to bring their children to a field while they worked. They'd have them within watching distance, sometimes with a rope around an ankle and tethered to a post to ensure the little ones didn't simply crawl or walk away. Today the Anganwadi system addresses this same issue for millions of people.

I've dwelled on how superstitions were part of the air we breathed. People of my grandmother's generation accepted them unquestioningly, and many people like the pujari, the komaram and others benefited from being the middlemen in this 'system'. But sometimes these beliefs became life-threatening, and in a modern world they had to take a back seat. Many of the classes the Party held then were aimed at educating people to rise above blind belief. Sometimes people preferred to take their sick to a shaman instead of a hospital. If someone died in difficult circumstances, people believed their souls stayed back on earth to haunt everyone. Then there was all the fuss around a woman's period. Even in my communist house, I was not supposed to touch my mother when she was menstruating. If I was desperate, I had to use an iron rod to touch her! Till the fourth day when she'd go to the canal and have a bath, she was considered too tainted to engage in the normal activities of the household.

As Communist Party workers, we spoke out against these things. Perhaps one of our most radical pieces of advice was on marriage. We said families needed to seek the agreement of young women while choosing a partner. Of course, most marriages were arranged, but it was essential to ask the girls' opinion of their suitors. If we heard a family wasn't sending a girl to school we'd go and check on it, speak to the families, and ensure the girls were sent to school. As young Comrades we felt we were doing the essential work of improving our community, of giving people information they didn't have or had no way of getting. And there were results. We saw increasing numbers of women join the Mahila Association. We watched more and more girls going to school, joining college and entering the workforce. People slowly moved beyond superstitions and accepted simpler explanations for things around them. Today it would be very unusual to find a Malayali woman being ostracized during her period. The area where I worked was a microcosm of the rest of our state, and this work of social reform and education was at its peak all over Kerala in the 1970s and 1980s.

As for me, within five years I went from the local unit to the village-level and area-level committees. I also became president of the KSYF unit at that time. When I completed my bachelor's degree in 1979, my grandmother and mother were overjoyed. I considered joining law school, but my family had just worked its way out of debt and studying law wasn't financially feasible. Even though I felt somewhat disappointed at not being able to pursue law, I eventually settled into the idea of a BEd degree, which was just a one-year course back then. The college was close enough, even though it was in Karnataka, and there was a hostel. My engagement and marriage would take place within a two-month period in 1981 when I was home for vacation and there were still two exams to be taken.

After my degree, I became a schoolteacher at the Shivapuram High School. I taught physics, chemistry and, occasionally, English. Looking back, I realize my experience as a teacher left a lasting impact on me. Working with children engenders a great deal of empathy. Some kids respond to positive reinforcement, some need a firm hand, others just need someone to listen to them, but the mix of all these different types of personalities, and dealing with so many together, prepared me well for life in politics. To many teachers I knew, teaching was about more than just relaying the syllabus. They approached their work like social reformers. I remember Shobha Teacher whom all the kids loved, because she interacted with them more like a mother than a schoolteacher. There was a student called Gowri in one of Shobha Teacher's classes. The child came from a very difficult home with little to no parental care. Her mother suffered from a mental illness and the father was an alcoholic. She therefore came to school with soiled clothing, and at one point, she had lice. The other children in the class refused to sit near her. Shobha Teacher got a doctor's prescription for the lice shampoo and spray, and made sure Gowri used it. She'd even go and check on her at home. For me, it was inspiring to watch the way she worked, her sheer dedication.

I learned the art of cajoling, and cheering, as a teacher. I also had the chance to channel everything I learned from Ammamma. Even in a school environment, there was a lot of superstition. Any type of behaviour that deviated from the so-called 'normal' – anxiety, depression and of course serious ailments like schizophrenia – were all slotted into the realm of spirits and evil. My grandmother had always been the go-to spirit chaser in our area. People would call her if someone was having a psychotic episode. Perhaps it was just good timing, maybe it was her presence, but I've heard that she was able to calm such people down. One rural antidote in her arsenal was to threaten the 'spirit' with a rather unusual punishment: that the person would be forced to consume urine. Let me reassure you, though: it was only ever a threat, it was never done. It seems the threat itself was sometimes enough to bring people out of the trance. I realize this sounds ridiculous, but it was one of the many beliefs that held sway during that time. In telling and retelling these stories, and with the strength of belief of the many, these ideas felt absolutely real to most people.

One time, in my school, a teenage girl became feverish just before an exam, turning unresponsive and behaving erratically. A colleague came to me, whispering that she thought the child was possessed and warning me not to touch her. The girl had an empty look in her eyes, blankly staring in front of her. When I went near her and tried to touch her forehead, she pushed me away. But I kept talking with the teenager, slowly put an arm around her, and told her she was running a fever. The girl told me a tale involving a cemetery and spirits. It turned out that she passed a cemetery on her way to school every day and some kids had scared her about the place. Together with anxiety over her exam, she'd had a sort of breakdown. As she spoke, she began breathing calmly and returned to her usual self. I remember feeling proud to be my grandmother's child.

In that milieu where people turned to superstition to explain their lives, I found solace in science, as I've noted earlier: its logic appealed to me. And also ideas about scientific socialism, of the importance of scientific progress. The idea that societal change is based on moving things forward interests me. Don't discard anything. History exists to teach us, and offers a foundation that can be built on. Our society in Kerala has changed so much. Both in ideas and physically. I am old enough to remember how things used to be. For example, there was this lady called Edwompally Kalyani who made this superb kattankaapi, or black coffee, with jaggery. We'd go to her house just to drink that lovely coffee. But it was barely a house. Walls of woven coconut palm leaves were stacked like a house of cards, with a thatched roof on top. In the rainy season, her house was full of water, the roof giving in completely sometimes under the weight of the rain. To get inside this dwelling, you had to bend almost double, because the awning was so low. Now, all that is gone. Where her little hut once stood, there's a concrete building that looks like a mini castle. A big change built on the foundation of an old entity. But I digress.

At the time, even though I was very active in area politics, I saw teaching as my career. The political work was more social work than anything else. I had no idea where I'd go with it. None of us had any goals for higher office, no dream of getting a ticket to fight an election. Most of us didn't even know it was something we could aspire to. Things have changed now, there are more opportunities. In my day you did the work because you believed in what you were doing. For every person who goes from grassroots-level political work to a ministerial position there are thousands who never get there. They are the foot soldiers of our democracy.

For me, the biggest hurdle I faced in entering public life was my own reticence about public speaking, which I've written about a few times already! But it is one of those things that improves with practice. I was lucky other people realized that and pushed me to silence my inner monologue of doubt. Among my early turning points in this respect was in 1979 in Iritty. At a meeting, the main speaker for the evening was delayed, so a local committee member, Comrade Chathukutti, suddenly announced, 'Shailaja will speak.' Then he turned to me and said, 'You say what you can.' With that prompt, I went in front of the mike. Now, one thing I've realized is that if you put me in front of something, my instinct is to do the best I can. 'Comrades,' I began, and spoke of my experiences working with people, the problems they faced, and issues the prevailing government wasn't paying attention to. It was unprepared but seemed to meet Comrade Chathukutti's approval, and I took that as a win. Later, in times to come, I'd learn about preparation, understand how to speak keeping the audience in mind, and think about structure – that 'the content should have a beginning, a middle and a conclusion', as the author Sukumar Azhikode once put it to me.

From 1981 till 1994, I never stood for any elected office. Then in 1994–95 there was a Jilla Council election, where representatives for local district governments were being selected. I was living in Mattanur at the time, and the Mattanur division seat was reserved for women. At that point I had been an active and popular Party worker there for almost twenty years. So, when the election came around, many people assumed I would be the candidate, but then another name was suggested by the higher committee. When this gave rise to a discussion in our Area Committee favouring my candidature, Bhaskarettan and I said that we should accept the opinion of the District Committee. I announced I would not contest. The other candidate was from another area. It was a strange situation, something I'd never found myself in before. This possibility of an election ticket coming out of the blue and then disappearing just as quickly. Naturally when there's a chance of moving to a different job, one gets excited, but when it doesn't materialize one has to accept it. For some time, I thought, 'Why not me, why couldn't I have stood for this election?' But my mind always dials back to my original purpose: What am I? I am a communist. I am a comrade.

Then in 1996, it was the year of Kerala's legislative election. There were discussions in the Kannur District Committee about candidate names for the ten Assembly constituencies in the district. Since I was not in the District Committee I was not aware of what was happening. Two days before the nomination deadline, the district secretary called to inform me that the Party had decided I should file my nomination papers for the Assembly election from the Kuthuparamba constituency, which was about 8 kilometres from where I was living at the time. I was about forty years old. Suffice to say, I was shocked. I lived in a constituency where the Congress usually won. Whereas Kuthuparamba was a stronghold of the Communist Party, from where luminaries like Pinarayi Vijayan and M.V. Raghavan had stood for elections. I didn't think a simple Area Committee member like me would be asked to contest from such an important constituency.

The fact that I wasn't from the area added to my nervousness. Of course, a person can contest from anywhere in the state, but it makes a difference when the voting public is familiar with your work. But this was the Party's decision. Bhaskarettan, who is always supportive in everything I do, was very happy. When I expressed my doubts about making it work there, he said, 'The Party has decided, so don't worry.' And so, I filed my papers.

At the time, the area secretary at Kuthuparamba was a man called M.O. Padmanabhan, popularly known as Pappettan. He was a senior comrade, very strict and disciplined. He'd insist people remove their footwear before entering the Party office and such. I was nervous about the turn of events, and so was he. Pappettan wasn't sure how he could shepherd a greenhorn like me to victory, and the area's Party workers were worried about the public's reaction to the nomination of a young woman from another constituency. After one round of campaigning, Pappettan told me he'd been worried about my level of involvement but now he felt reassured. 'Everyone agrees you are the right choice,' he said. 'They will accept you. You've got their hearts and minds, we're not afraid now.'

An election campaign is a humbling, intense experience. As a candidate, you're the leading light, with all the attention on you, but the real powerhouse is this massive chorus of people behind you. The 1996 legislative election was my first election campaign as a nominee. I was a rookie in every way. The day before submitting my nomination papers, I was called to the Kuthuparamba Party office. At the time, there was a custom you had to partake in before embarking on an election campaign. Candidates were taken to the homes of elder Comrades and martyrs' families to seek their support. It was a way to show respect to the long road the Communist Party had taken to get to that point – the lives that had been lost, the work that had been done to get us where we were. This simple gesture gave candidates an understanding of how far we'd come, from an era of witch-hunting to respect. A veteran leader, Comrade Chanduettan, accompanied me on that outing.

After the nomination, election committees – from local to booth level – were formed to create a plan for the campaign. There are two types of campaigns: one is personal, the other is a broader approach. A candidate is expected to visit all the major parts of the constituency, going from homes to offices and businesses, meeting and seeking votes directly from people. The second format is more impersonal – and loud. As a candidate you're perched atop a vehicle and speaking through a microphone; the dramatics of it means you leave an impression on the voters' minds. On any given day leading up to the election, there were almost twenty programmes to attend and speak at. Not everything is long-form. In many places, another speaker would warm up the crowd and then I would make a short, five-minute speech.

This was all new to me. I'd watched these scenes from the wings before but to be that individual at the heart of the hurricane felt traumatic and thrilling at once. Two decades of working in the public arena had prepared me very well, though. Constituencies are political demarcations, but people in a single district face very similar situations. I knew the issues to be addressed. At the time, my own home had no electricity connection. Almost fifty years since Independence, and we still functioned with a kerosene oil lamp. The road to my house was not tarred and during the monsoon it was pockmarked with pits of water and slush. I understood what the people faced, and what I didn't know, I ensured I learned before giving a speech. Local leaders and Party workers spent a great deal of time bringing me up to speed. Then there was the election manifesto – the backbone of each candidate's speech. With all that information, preparation and tremendous support from the Party cadre, I thought the first round of campaigning went well.

My heartbreak lay at home. My children were only ten and eleven years old at the time – fifth and sixth graders. I was leaving home early every morning; rarely was I back even to put them to bed. After the public events of the day, candidates often have to participate in smaller meetings to canvass for support. By the time all the talking and meetings and discussions were over, and I was finally home, it would be at least 11 p.m. Then by 7 a.m. I was back on the trail following the agenda set for the day. And it was that way throughout the one-and-a-half month-long campaign. I felt extremely guilty, and this gnawed away at me. Unlike now, when technology has made it possible for video calls and conversations at will, it wasn't possible then for the children to feel like they were part of this process in any meaningful way. It was a part of the job and I understood what I had to do, but it was a terrible feeling to know I wasn't there for my kids.

At the same time there are legions of Party cadre working selflessly for the singular goal of making you win. To not be present with them in that moment, and do whatever it takes, is simply not an option. It is difficult work. There is no minute to oneself for the candidate or anyone working on the campaign. Kuthuparamba was an easy constituency, but I didn't want the margin of victory to drop from the previous election. It was extremely important that I create a connection with the voters and that meant engaging with as many people as I could.

The CPI(M) won the Kuthuparamba constituency in 1996 by

more than 16,000 votes, which was higher than the margin of victory in the previous election. Pappettan, in particular, was extremely happy and he remained a tremendous support to me till his death a few years later.

I was an MLA. When that realization first dawned on me, I couldn't quite grasp it. People talk of achievements being a dream come true but some ideas are too fantastic for you to even dream of them. That's what this was like for me. I hadn't plotted my life in that way. I was just doing what I could. The fact that all those small tasks and incremental wins would lead to Kerala's Legislative Assembly felt like a revelation. I remember entering the Assembly for the first time ever. Taking the oath in the presence of Bhaskarettan, my children, our family and Party leaders from the Kuthuparamba constituency was the high point for me. Nothing can compare to that first time with all of them there. I personally took an oath that I would do everything I could for the people of my constituency. For twenty years I had been someone presenting people's problems to the government, now I had a bigger responsibility: to solve them.

Our administrative system is complicated. There are provisions and ways to get things done but you have to acquire a deep understanding of them. While I had good intentions, I wouldn't be able to fulfil any of them without knowing the long, complicated process of securing funding, for instance. I decided to learn. I wasn't shy about asking people for help. I watched those who knew the system and how they made their way through it, I talked to senior bureaucrats to understand provisions and paper trails, I spoke with more experienced MLA colleagues to understand how things worked in the Assembly. If you allow the insecurity of being new to the role to overwhelm you, you miss the chance to learn and become better at your job. I wasn't trying to prove anything to anyone; my intention was to be effective. And

I approached it the way I'd approached my studies: with a sense of inquiry and tenacity.

One of the first major requests I received was for a bridge. The Vengad panchayat in my constituency sent an application for a bridge across the Iripakkadavu river. There were two villages on either side of the river without direct access to each other. People had to traverse the entire circumference of each village to get to the other bank. And during the Kerala monsoon the force of the river meant the villagers couldn't even take a boat over to the other side. If there were floods both these villages were totally cut off from the mainland. These people had a genuine need, and they'd prepared their request properly. The only problem was that I didn't know how to make it happen for them.

At the time, the Public Works Department (PWD) office in Thiruvananthapuram was headed by a very diligent chief engineer called Joseph Mathew. I went to see him and spoke very frankly with him: 'I am the Kuthuparamba MLA. I want to get a bridge made in my constituency. But I don't know the procedures. Can you help me?' While he couldn't have said no, he could have fended me off with excuses; instead, Joseph Mathew decided to help. He explained the process involved in getting such a large project done. We had to make a plan and estimate for construction; after that we needed administrative sanction from the finance and public works ministries, then we had to create a drawing; when that was approved, we needed a technical sanction. Once that came through, we would tender the project and it would then get under way.

This administrative process can take months, and if some element within the many layers of such a proposal puts up a hurdle or objection, it could even take years. But with the chief engineer's help and assistance from the supportive panchayat presidents in the area, we had a plan and an estimate within three months. Armed with that, I went to see the Public Works Minister P.J. Joseph and explained our need to him. He gave us the administrative sanction we needed. The next hurdle was to get the approval of the finance department, for which I approached Finance Minister Sivadasa Menon and secured his permission. And like that, in six or seven months, the work order was passed, and within a year of embarking on the process, we were able to lay the foundation of the bridge. This gave me a lot of confidence, and it also reassured me. It showed me that if we were straightforward and passionate, bureaucrats would help and we could achieve much.

During my first five-year term as the Kuthuparamba MLA, we constructed seven big and small bridges, several roads and buildings for Anganwadis, and completed many other development-related works in my constituency. But for every one project that happens, ten others don't even start because there is a limited amount of money and resources. There are many needs, but there is only so much one can do. Still, I was thrilled to be part of the development of my region. That is the magic of public life. If you make a genuine effort as a public servant, the impact you can create is tremendous.

As I wrote earlier, the area where I lived didn't have an electricity connection. After my election the electricity department offered to extend a line from the main road to bring power to just my house as a special privilege. Bhaskarettan and I refused the offer. At the time the 240 families in our area had already submitted a Minimum Guarantee work proposal to the electricity department. 'Minimum Guarantee' is a private–public partnership type of arrangement where the families that would benefit from a project are required to furnish a small portion of money as their contribution; the government would make up the rest of the cost. So, if our proposal was approved, everyone would benefit. I pushed to get this passed instead of accepting the privilege the electricity department had offered. About a year after I became an MLA the Minimum Guarantee proposal worked out, and all the families received an electricity connection. I still remember the day we switched on the light in our home for the first time.

I was particularly lucky that my novice term as an MLA happened to be during the late Comrade E.K. Nayanar's term as chief minister. I admired him greatly for his humanist principles and for his deftness as a politician who could maintain relationships with people across political lines. He was a man blessed with a great sense of humour, which helped him deflect controversies and deal with the Opposition's attacks with an enviable lightness. Nothing could shake his sense of balance. I was close to his wife, Sarada Teacher, and both of them were fond of me. For anyone interested in politics, listening to and watching Nayanar's repartee with the Opposition in the Assembly makes for an invaluable theatre of learning.

I wasn't asked to contest the Assembly elections in 2001. Many of the projects I'd worked towards when I was an MLA were just getting off the ground, and while I would have loved to have been there to see them through, I wasn't a candidate and that was that. I had taken leave from school during my first stint as an MLA. Now I went back to being a schoolteacher and continued with local Party work. By that time I had also become a District Committee member. Teaching proved much more difficult now because a new education programme had been put in place while I was away. It was activity and assignment based. I wasn't trained for this type of teaching. I am from an earlier era where teaching was unidirectional, from teacher to student. Now it was more interactive and project oriented. I am grateful to my colleagues at the time; they jumped in to help me understand the nuances of this new approach and I was able to pick things up. The best part of this interval from the legislature was that I could return to my earlier routine and focus more on my family.

In 2004, the Party asked me to become a full-time Party worker, for which I'd have to take voluntary retirement from teaching. I faced a dilemma. As a public school teacher, I could retire at fifty-five years of age, so I still had nine years of service left. Without completing at least twenty years of service I would not be eligible to take voluntary retirement. While I had completed twenty-three years of service, I'd taught for only eighteen years, as I was on leave for five years when I was an MLA.

The only way to become eligible for voluntary retirement was through a special order from the government. The UDF alliance, which included the Congress party and the Muslim League, was in power at the time. I went to meet Chief Minister A.K. Antony to ask his permission for a special order that would consider my years as an MLA in the final count of my teaching career. He joked about it: 'Usually you only leave school after 4 p.m. to attack my party, now you want to do it from 10 a.m. every day?' But he was also very kind. He understood that I needed the consideration. He said, 'Social work is the best thing for you, I will make this happen.' He asked me to send in an application and meet Finance Minister Shankaranarayan. We didn't know each other, but when I went to see him, he'd already been briefed by the chief minister. 'Let the application come, I'll pass it,' he said. So even though our political rival was the government at that time, they gave me a special order so I could take voluntary retirement.

Two years later, at the time of the 2006 Assembly elections, the Party nominated me to stand for election from the Peravoor constituency. This area was a different ball game from Kuthuparamba. For one thing, it was a UDF stronghold. Though the constituency covered both my birthplace Madathil and Pazhassi where I lived, the hilly neighbourhoods of these parts were all strongly pro-Congress. I knew the campaign would be very difficult and unlike what I'd experienced earlier. This was definitely not going to be a shoo-in. But we worked hard; we all wanted to win this for the Left Democratic Front (LDF), the union of the Left and its supportive parties in Kerala. I was barely sleeping; I was out all day and largely cut off from my family as the campaign machine sped faster towards the election. Bhaskarettan was also in charge of some of the election work, and he was exceptionally helpful. The Party cadre's efforts realized a long-held dream: we won this Congress bastion by a margin of almost 10,000 votes. Perhaps our family history there had helped. Perhaps people just decided to give us a chance. I was especially grateful that the LDF also came back to power that year. I have in fact never sat in the Opposition. Every election that I won was also a winning year for my Party and the LDF.

One of the areas in my new constituency was a mountainous village called Uruppumkutti. It literally sat on top of a hill. It was settled by kudiyettam people who'd come from down south, when land was available. It was hard to imagine how people thought of making their homes there. The way up was via a bumpy, unpaved road that was only traversable in a four-wheel drive.

One day a jeep arrived in front of my house, carrying a young Catholic priest called Father Pious who'd come with my Party's branch secretary, Comrade Thomas. Historically, the church and people of the area were anti-communist, but here was Father Pious with a complaint and a request. He said there were several families up there on that hill living without electricity. This was in the year 2007. These people, a mix of Christian and Hindu families living in that remote place, weren't part of any grid and still lived by the light of kerosene lamps and candles after sunset. The church was the mainstay of the area's life, and this enthusiastic achen (priest), Father Pious, had decided to fix the problem. And he believed I could be the agent of change, as it were. 'Teacher, you must get us electricity. There is no line there. We have called a church meeting and we want the MLA to come.' Listening to him and seeing his confidence in my ability made me nervous. I said, 'I'll come but getting electricity up there on a mountain is going to be very expensive. I don't know if there's funding, or if there's a scheme for it. But I'll come.'

The achen called for a public meeting. When I got up there, every single person who lived there was in that church hall waiting for me. They gave a welcome speech and said, 'This is the first time an MLA has come to see us up on this hill. We're very happy.' Then Father Pious gave a speech. 'Teacher will bring electricity.' He was emphatic. When it was my turn, I thanked them and said I would try. If we all tried together, maybe it would work. Someone shouted, 'No, if you try it will happen.' And with the weight of those people's expectations, I came down the hill.

At the time Comrade A.K. Balan was the electricity minister. I went to see him. Minister Balan called the Kerala State Electricity Board (KSEB) engineers to check what could be done. According to them, to get electricity up there we needed more than about forty poles, and there was no scheme or provision to cover the expense associated with such a huge project that would benefit such a small number of people. Then, I had an idea. The Scheduled Caste (SC) and Scheduled Tribe (ST) communities receive priority for access to electricity and drinking water. And the Scheduled Caste and Scheduled Tribes Development Department usually had a budget to spend on upliftment-related activities. Since the village had some SC/ST families there, we could secure money via that route.

So we knew we would have funds to pull an electricity line up to a point near this area. Minister Balan said, 'We'll help you do the rest. Register a Minimum Guarantee proposal immediately.' We registered the Minimum Guarantee proposal and the work order was passed for the project on out-of-turn priority basis. Even though the money allotted wasn't sufficient to cover all the expenses, we were able to get it done because the poor people of the area contributed their labour and made up for the shortfall. Father Pious was ecstatic. But there was lots more left to be done before electric lights came on in Uruppumkutti.

The electricity line was pulled to the colony but cement posts had to be taken there to assemble the wires. The nearest pole-casting unit was in Pinarayi in Kannur. There, they only manufacture a few posts, which are immediately claimed. Neither does that factory usually have excess poles, or even a lorry strong enough to go up a hill hauling cement poles. The KSEB functionaries then said, 'If you get the lorry, we can give you whatever poles we can set aside.' I told Father Pious and Comrade Thomas, 'We have to get the lorry.'

And so, at every turn, there was a new problem, but here was a really cooperative community with a leader who wouldn't give up without getting light to his flock. It was inspiring to watch that man's fervour. And we all got swept up in the project and became determined to make it happen.

The achen and Comrade Thomas together arranged for money and a lorry to carry the poles up that hill. Then they needed metal wires to mount the posts and extend the connection throughout the area. In fact, to cover such a great distance, we would need a whole roll of wire. I went to meet the executive engineer in Kannur and told him we needed a roll. After a lot of back and forth he said, 'If you come right away you can have what's here before the next claimant comes.' And of course Father Pious and Thomas were there promptly. Finally, with money from the KSEB, and contributions from people, we got an electricity line up to Uruppumkutti. To get a connection to each house, we managed to get the funding from another project and I allocated some money from my MLA fund, which is a kitty of Rs 25 lakh per year that is given to every MLA to execute projects of their choice.

Finally, when the big day dawned, there was a festival-like atmosphere in Uruppumkutti. I went for the inauguration, as it were. When it was time to turn on the electricity, everyone ran off so they could see the lights come on in their own homes. To look over that hill and see lights twinkling across was one of my most special moments as an MLA. The whole process had taken one whole year.

For those five years, during my second turn as an MLA, I worked like a tornado. I knew from my earlier stint that the time I got in one term would never be enough to see projects to fruition, so I was always running against the clock to get things done. In 2011, the next legislative election came around. Several constituencies in our district were bifurcated, and in that bifurcation process, parts of my old constituencies, Peravoor and Kuthuparamba, were spliced together to make a new one called Mattanur. One municipality and three panchayats from the old Peravoor constituency, where the CPI(M) had sway, were now part of the new Mattanur constituency. And three UDF stronghold panchayats were added to Peravoor, making it more difficult to win.

The Party decided I should stand again in Peravoor. In the older parts of the constituency, people knew me quite well and they were familiar with my work. But in the newer parts, I was a completely new entity. I thought I could talk about everything we'd managed to do in the previous term and things would turn out fine. It seemed like things were going well, till they didn't.

Around ten days before polling, in one of the new panchayats of Peravoor, a young Adivasi man died under suspicious circumstances. People in the area knew he had been mentally disturbed but he wasn't troublesome, except if he drank. Under the influence of alcohol he was known to become violent. When he got like that, his family would restrain him in his room, letting him out when he'd cooled off. Anyway, one evening, he got into a scuffle with some LDF party workers who were putting up election posters in the neighbourhood. Even though he was from a family of LDF supporters, this young man was friends with several Congress workers and it seems someone egged him on. When he became violent, he was restrained and people called the police. Once the police arrived this man was sent off home to rest. And no one thought much of it. His family said they'd checked on him during the night and he was fine. However, the next morning, they found he'd committed suicide by hanging himself inside his room. Several LDF workers including the CPI(M) local secretary were charged with murder.

The incident, coming so close to the election, caused a lot of anger among the voters against the Left. Consequentially, the UDF candidate Sunny Joseph won by just 3,400 votes, a far smaller majority than the 20,000 vote margin they were expecting. Even though we knew the seat would be difficult for various reasons, the circumstances of the failure, the fact that a young person was dead … it all left me far more bewildered than if it had just been about a lost election. And it certainly was a failure, my first public failure at that. The police never solved the case to satisfaction, and the Party workers who were arrested were let off. But some people suspected it was a murder committed to influence the election. That year, the UDF won by a margin of four seats against the LDF.

My next election was in 2016 from the Kuthuparamba constituency. I won, and the LDF came back to power. I had become a CPI(M) Central Committee member by then. When the cabinet was being decided, I was asked to join. And for the first time, I became a cabinet member, taking charge as the minister for Health and Family Welfare and Social Justice (later split into Health and Family Welfare, Women and Child Development, and Social Justice). As an MLA, your role is always on behalf of the people, but as a minister, you have more direct power to make things happen. It is heady and chaotic, because everyone else knows that as well. Coming to grips with the seat's power to make decisions was the first thing I did. It requires quite a bit of mental strength to maintain your ideas, exercise restraint and focus.

About a year after I joined Chief Minister Pinarayi Vijayan's cabinet, my mother Shantha died, and two months later, my aunt Damayanthi also passed away. They'd been my well-wishers all my life. My mother had lived her whole life for me. Even when her husband abandoned her, as a single parent, she'd continued to push me to do well, to rise in society. Both women lavished so much of their attention on me, and I was happy they'd lived long enough to see me do well. My grandmother, mother and aunt had all lived with us, as I've mentioned, a retirement for a trio of women who'd worked their whole lives looking out for others. Our home in their final years was bursting with love and the joy you get from being able to give back to the people who'd taken care of you. Bhaskarettan loved having them all at our home and so we were able to spend the last of their years in happy togetherness.

So by the time I got going as a minister, the women who were most instrumental in getting me there had passed. Perhaps it was time. Bhaskarettan and my sons would prove to be the pillars of support I needed to get through the next five years. With a new state-level role I was essentially living in Thiruvananthapuram, while Bhaskarettan lived in Kannur. My boys were both married and settled in Dubai and Kannur. Though he was home alone most of the time, Bhaskarettan never complained about it, never questioned the situation; if anything, he made vast adjustments to accommodate my schedule. When he knew I'd be coming to Kannur, he'd have all my favourite foods prepared and waiting for me. Or sometimes he'd come to Thiruvananthapuram so I didn't have to travel. Unwavering support and pure understanding – my career has been built on the emotional infrastructure he set up.

The spiritual guidance, so to speak, for my work, and indeed my life, has been provided by communist ideology. It has helped me work through doubt and indecision repeatedly during more than thirty years of public service. Having a philosophy or a belief that is larger than us helps us deal with the minute disappointments that pepper our lives.

In 2018, on my very first trip to London, I was asked what I wanted to see. The answer was simple: Karl Marx's cemetery in Highgate Park. It had been a long-held dream, and the experience was perfect. It was autumn, the ground was covered by yellow-orange oak leaves. His simple tomb was inscribed with the phrase 'Workers of All Lands Unite'. It was quiet, with a bit of a chill in the air, as I sat thinking of this person whose work had impacted me so deeply. I remember

I was very hungry when we left the cemetery; we ended up going to the only nearby restaurant, a burger joint, and so I had a burger for the very first time in my life. The memory of one brings up the other in my mind.

8

A New Chapter Begins

On 25 May 2016 I took charge as minister for Health and Family Welfare and Social Justice. Even though I had already served twice as MLA, this new mandate, which brought with it the tremendous responsibility of decision-making, was completely unfamiliar. If there was ever a time when I couldn't afford to fail, it was this. The LDF came to power with the intention of creating a 'New Kerala', with goal-oriented, focused governance. As a minister in such a visionary government, I felt it was essential that I perform at the highest level. And key to achieving that would be a strong action plan, having the right officers in the ministry, and efficient people in my office. In the early days of accepting my new role, I didn't yet know who they were all going to be. The one reassuringly familiar face was that of Pramod P., who had been my faithful personal assistant since my first innings as MLA. He'd decided to stay on in my service and come to the capital.

In any government, it is the bureaucracy that really runs things. Up to that point, my own experience with the bureaucracy had been that of an outsider and then a semi-outsider. As a layperson I'd viewed it as being an omnipresent entity that could even be an impediment. Communism was also circumspect about the bureaucracy, a system that had feudal and imperialist roots. I remembered what Karl Marx had said about the bureaucracy. He believed it to be the bearer of private interests and the reinforcer of a private spirit in society. To communists, the bureaucracy is not simply a mode of public administration but also an instrument of exploitation of the working class. But even Marx himself had pointed out that it could also be an efficient instrument of administration. One could also consider Vladimir Lenin's opinion of it. After the Russian Revolution Lenin did not want to destroy the bureaucratic system of the bourgeoisie administration entirely. He sought to retain it and mould it for the use and benefit of proletarian rule.

Everyone knows that conflicts between ministers and bureaucrats are common in government. They are after all two entities with similar goals but completely different trajectories. A minister is a politician who holds a position for a short period of time. On the other hand, a bureaucrat is a permanent fixture in government, and comes to their job with the comfort of continuity. The nuance in the minister–bureaucrat relationship arises from the fact that a minister, while not always as experienced in administration, is – as an elected representative of the people – accountable to the electorate and the legislature. And that accountability empowers ministers to take important decisions regarding general administration and policymaking. In the final assessment, a minister is the higher authority. At the same time, a minister must recognize that the topmost officer of their department has passed through several stages of testing and possesses wide experience in public administration and knowledge of the system. So, to be truly effective, a minister must consult with a senior secretary to make actionable decisions.

It is in this mutual dependence and understanding that governance can move forward effectively. As I waited to learn the identity of the officers who would be in my ministry, all these thoughts passed through my mind.

The Health portfolio consisted of two separate departments: one was Health and Family Welfare; the other was Ayush, which represented indigenous medicine. I also had the Social Justice portfolio, representing women and children, people of older ages, the transgender community and the disabled. I must clarify here that, during my time as minister, I was equally attentive to all three departments, but as the health department would go on to be at the centre of multiple crises, it is the focus of most of the anecdotes in this book.

Soon it was announced that Rajeev Sadanandan, the additional chief secretary, would be in charge of the health department, while the social justice department would be headed by Principal Secretary Mini Antony; the National Health Mission state officer was to be Kesavendra Kumar – a cadre of talented officers, backed by a network of secretaries, directors and others with specific responsibilities in different departments. Rajeev came to see me soon after his appointment to the health department. As additional chief secretary, he was the seniormost bureaucrat in my department, and therefore represented the most critical working relationship for me. It was vital that we have a good understanding of each other and, most importantly, build trust. He'd been in service for more than two decades by then, serving in many different departments of government, with as many as thirteen years of experience in the health sector. I already knew Rajeev from his stint at the KSEB. He was a very efficient officer, very bold. But people always complained that he did not listen – that he had his own opinions and would not entertain a counterpoint.

Some even suggested he should be removed because he would block me at every turn. That wasn't something that concerned me. I fully believed I would be able to implement the policies that needed to be implemented.

When we met, I had all of this in mind, and of course I told him straight out: 'I know you're a very capable officer, that health is your passion and you are a good health secretary, but the complaint is you don't listen. That you are stubborn.' He laughed and said, 'During our Indian Administrative Services (IAS) training, we are taught that we should be familiar with everybody but friendly with no one.' Accepting his explanation, I said, 'When I don't think something is right, I will tell you and we will need to take the right decision.' I think he was happy we were starting off with a clear understanding of one another. When I have an opinion of someone, I prefer to put it out there, so that there is no ambiguity. And when it's a vital professional relationship, it is prudent to test the waters at the beginning so you know how to take it from there. Over the years that Rajeev and I worked together, I would come to realize that much of what I'd heard about him wasn't true at all. He's a bit rough around the edges, but he's passionate about what he does, incorruptible, meticulous and, in my experience, he never acted unilaterally; we discussed every decision the department took. If I had an idea about something, he was always interested in exploring the best way to get it done. As a minister, I found him very helpful and cooperative, and we couldn't have met the challenges we faced if he had been a different kind of a person.

The chief minister had already announced the Nava Kerala Mission, declaring the new government's goal to pull Kerala into the new century, and address problems in key areas so as to make a positive impact in the lives of the most marginalized. My portfolios, Health and Family Welfare and Social Justice, addressed issues related to the most vulnerable sections of society. There are seemingly infinite problems in each of these segments. What is effectively possible depends on a vast number of probabilities that one has little control of. So you can either be snowed under by the magnitude of the issues and remain static, or slow-crawl your way through multiple issues, one step at a time. I was going to try the second approach.

Kerala has always had a much lauded healthcare system, but of course those accolades are relative. People are rightly impressed that our infrastructure and healthcare access are in a better condition than our financial position would seem to allow. And relative to many other states, Kerala has been a leader in social development indices. The Communist Party's push since 1957 for an egalitarian approach to education and health – the fundamentals – had proved to be the right path. Every subsequent government that came to power added and improved the system in different measures, but there was still much to be done. Over the last three decades, infrastructure and the quality of healthcare delivery to the poorest sections of society had not kept pace with population growth, technological advancement and newer demands.

I knew that an empathetic, effective healthcare system isn't born in five years; its promises cannot be fulfilled in one term of a government. It starts with the right intentions, which helps allocate limited resources; then you build, bit by bit, sometimes over decades. Of course, when a state has more principles than money in the exchequer, you really must pull at the ends of those fiscal rubber bands and tie things together, hoping nothing snaps. What would be my term's contribution to Kerala's health story? That was what I was trying to think through. As a physics teacher, science and data are my default positions. When you draw conclusions based on these factors, you're most likely to have an impartial, logical outcome.

When I studied the health sector, I realized only 33 per cent of our people were going to medical institutions in the public sector. Though comparatively better than in other states, our system had many weaknesses, especially in rural areas, at the primary level of healthcare. The second time he came to see me, Rajeev asked me, 'Minister, what do you want to do in the health sector? What is your idea? What are your dreams and priorities for this department? As a minister you will have a political will, interests, projects in mind. If you tell me, I will use my understanding of the sector and give you solutions, and we can make a difference.'

For me to arrive at a plan, I did what I always do: I studied. When there is so much leeway and the parameters are vague, you can get lost if there's no direction. We spoke to experts and I looked at international precedents and the language around healthcare in order to understand where the impact would be greatest. There was the landmark Alma-Ata declaration of 1978, which identified 'primary healthcare as the key to attainment of the goal of Health for All'. Then there was the Astana declaration in 2018, which stated that strengthening primary healthcare systems was an essential step towards achieving universal health coverage. Half of the world's population lacks access to essential health services, including care for non-communicable and communicable diseases, maternal and child health, and mental health. And the only way forward, it emphasized, was to build sustainable primary healthcare. When the UN announced its 17 SDGs, or Sustainable Development Goals, the third goal focused on healthcare and emphasized that 'good health and well-being' for all could be achieved only through improvements in the primary healthcare system.

These ideas would shape my vision for the next five years of the health ministry. Make vast improvements to the primary healthcare sector in the state, so that people could avail of good-quality basic diagnosis and treatment at their nearest government clinic even in the remotest of areas. Focus on preventive care, because Kerala is the capital of lifestyle diseases and prevention is the only safety net against a lifetime of curative effort. Update public health facilities, making them more comfortable and accessible. The last, semi-formed idea in my mind, was that the state's medical colleges needed to be more research oriented and modern, which was also an intention stated in the LDF government's election manifesto. If Kerala's healthcare system was to remain of a higher calibre, this was an opportunity to make significant improvements, and our government would be continuing the state's modern-day legacy of people-centric policymaking.

It is hard to pinpoint what exactly shapes the mindset of a people: probably layers of changes in attitudes and outlook, occurring over a vast period of time. Kerala has always been an internationalist multicultural region, going back to ancient times when the erstwhile Muziris seaport traded with the Phoenicians, Arabs, Romans and Greeks. Later, with the arrival and influence of colonial powers – first the Portuguese, then Dutch and finally the English – many different mentalities became enmeshed in the collective psyche of our people. In this trade between cultures, of course many diseases were also imported and exported.

Each of the three regions that make up the modern state of Kerala – the erstwhile Travancore kingdom, Cochin and Malabar – had very different temperaments, history and healthcare records. Beginning from Maharani Ayilyam Thirunal Gowri Lakshmi Bai – she was the maharani from 1810 till 1813 and Regent from 1813 till 1815 – there was considerable focus on sanitation, eradication of disease, tracking of health statistics, and adoption of modern medicine in the old kingdom of Travancore. In 1865 when Karthika Thirunal Maharaja set up the General Hospital in Travancore, it was another symbol of the forward-thinking, scientific nature of that kingdom, which had an evolved public healthcare system in pre-Independence times. In 1879, by royal proclamation, a public vaccination programme against smallpox was started, though of course it was only by the 1950s that the disease was completely eradicated from our state. When the vaccine was first introduced and their subjects were hesitant about being vaccinated, the royal family made a public show of taking the injection themselves to reassure the population.[1]

The British-controlled Malabar region, which was under the Madras Presidency, did not see the same level of focus on public health by the colonial administration, but these regions had highly evolved Ayurvedic systems and plant-based treatment knowledge inherited through generations of healers. The most famous of them, the Kottakkal family, founded the Arya Vaidya Sala hospital in 1902. It was set up by Vaidyarathnam P.S. Warrier in North Malabar district of Malappuram. In Thrissur there was the Ashthavaidya family's Vaidyamadam founded by E.T. Narayanan Mooss. In my district of Kannur, broken bones, burns and small injuries were all treated by the local vaidyan, or herbal doctor. He was called a kalarigurukkal because he was an expert at massage and the use of poultices with local herbs and plants. When I was in college, I was diagnosed with jaundice. There were two popular courses of treatment: a one-shot ottamooli medicine made from a combination of medicinal herbs, or nasyam, in which drops of the medicine were put into the nostrils. A few minutes later, a trickle of yellow liquid would dribble out of the nasal passages. I was sent off with a strict diet that forbade oily, spicy, salty food, and that was it. Even today, many people infected with jaundice will go to a naatuvaidyan, or traditional doctor.

Such healers existed across the Kerala countryside. These people had a thorough understanding of curative herbs and plants for common ailments. These vaidyans were of various backgrounds; they could be Hindu, Muslim or Christian – all people who'd picked up the art of healing. They knew herbs and native plants and the potency of different recipes. And it wasn't just Ayurveda. Kerala also inherited an intricate network of homoeopathic, naturopathic, Siddha and Unani practitioners spread through the state.

Christian missionaries who set up educational institutions during the British era also played an important role in the healthcare sector. Their institutions took the caste factor out of education at a time when lower castes were denied access to schools and untouchability was rampant. The spread of school and college education greatly improved the choices that people had for their lives, even though for the poorest of the poor in the population these facilities were still inaccessible. The missionaries also set up mission hospitals across the state, taking healthcare to remote areas. With this, many young women, particularly from the Christian community, began to see nursing as an honourable and promising career. Those ideas have strengthened over time across the state's population, and today whichever part of the world you live in, you're likely to have encountered a Malayali nurse, doctor or teacher.

I'll offer up the example of the father–daughter Malayali doctors Dr T.E. Poonen, who was the superintendent of the Travancore General Hospital, and his daughter Dr Mary Poonen Lookose. She was schooled at the Holy Angel's Convent High School in Travancore and became the first woman graduate of Madras University. Upon completing her medical degree at London University, Dr Mary became the first Malayali woman doctor. This pioneering gynaecologist and obstetrician returned to Kerala in 1916 after many years of practice in the UK. In 1924, the progressive royal family of Travancore state appointed Dr Mary as the state's Surgeon General, thereby making its healthcare system the first in the world to be run by a female doctor. So great examples were set early in the life of this state and became reasons why social development is an indelible hallmark of Kerala.

After the first communist government under Comrade E.M.S. Namboodiripad was formed in 1957, and again came to power in 1967, land reform also catalysed dramatic social changes. The transfer of ownership from large landowners to their tenants reshaped Kerala at a cellular level. Big family homesteads broke up, an agrarian society began transforming into a professional one, and the tenant farmer became the master of his own destiny. The notion that every village must have some form of public health facility began in the 1950s and 1960s. The government announced at the time that if anyone donated an acre of land, it would set up a Primary Health Centre (PHC) there, usually with just a graduate doctor and nurse. Dr A.R. Menon, the first health minister, oversaw the setting up of such healthcare centres. Simultaneously, as more and more people graduated as doctors and nurses, small private clinics run by a single doctor, or a doctor couple, became a common occurrence in the small towns dotting Kerala. Medical education was seen as a viable productive career; it allowed people to establish small clinics wherever they wanted and become respectable members of society. And though every village in the state was not yet covered, great strides were made in that direction.

At the time of the formation of the state, the government's budget allocation for education and healthcare was considerable. In *Kerala's Economic Development: Emerging Issues and Challenges*, the authors present some interesting data about the beginnings and development of Kerala's health sector.[2] From 1961 to 1986, the number of state medical institutions and beds surged. The total number of beds in government hospitals in Kerala – in the modern medical sector – rose from around 13,000 in 1960–61 to 20,000 in 1970–71, and 29,000 in 1980–81. By 2015 the number was above 40,000. Thus the major expansion phase of facilities in the government sector was before the 1990s, after which the infrastructure couldn't keep up with the growth of the population or its varied concerns. At the same time, the public healthcare system's focus changed from primary healthcare to speciality facilities. I should also note here that over time, the central government's budgetary provisions for healthcare also reduced, sometimes dropping below 2 per cent of GDP.

In Kerala, we have three levels in the public healthcare system. Let's start from the primary sector where there are PHCs; below them there are family welfare subcentres to attend to smaller communities of at least 5,000 people. Five or six panchayats together form a community development block, which is served by a Community Health Centre (CHC). At the secondary level of the public healthcare system, there are taluk and district hospitals with minor speciality departments like orthopaedics, gynaecology, ENT and paediatrics. Then, at the highest and tertiary level, there are medical college hospitals, with major specialities such as cardiology, neurology, nephrology, etc. Poor or middle-class patients from rural areas with neurological or cardiological problems would have to travel a great distance for treatment at a medical college, or go to an expensive private hospital.

After the slowdown in public healthcare investment in the 1980s, private hospitals bridged the gap. Many expat Malayalis still get medical check-ups done when they are home on vacation in Kerala, because of the relatively low cost and good quality of private healthcare. At the same time there are also complaints about some private institutions becoming exploitative and prohibitively expensive for ordinary people. The state also harbours a robust medical tourism sector, with patients coming from Africa, Male and the Gulf regions for treatment, especially for Ayurvedic therapy. The Trivandrum Medical College and the Ernakulam Medical College both have tailor-made treatment packages for foreign medical tourists, and countries like the Maldives have direct agreements with these hospitals. But those are options for people from wealthy income groups.

In 2016, when we examined the staff patterns in the public healthcare sector, we realized those hadn't changed since 1961; the doctor–patient ratio had not kept pace with the increase in population. So, overall, we needed to pull Kerala's public healthcare system into the twenty-first century, and level the quality of care for the entire population.

Chief Minister Pinarayi Vijayan's Nava Kerala Mission was an initiative to address issues in the state's key social sectors: health, education, agriculture and housing. Of these four Mission projects, the health-related one, Aardram, was to be conducted by the health department. The chief minister gave us a brief about the Mission, but it was up to us to figure out the details of how we wanted to pursue it.

We looked at various international examples in our research. We examined the National Health Service (NHS) in the UK and the much lauded Cuban medical system, which relies heavily on a chain of family doctors at the grassroots level. But then Cuba's ratio of doctors to general population is very high. Kerala has one of the highest doctor–patient ratios in the country, standing at 1:500. This is far better than the World Health Organization (WHO) recommendation of 1:1,000 and India's national ratio of 1:1,500. But perhaps we could work on improving that. Could we aim for, say, one doctor per a hundred people? In his brief, the chief minister had also included patient-friendly hospitals as a goal of the Aardram Mission.

Keeping all of this in mind, I told the health secretary and his team that we must bring about an impactful change in Kerala's entire health sector. We needed to completely revamp public hospitals and modernize them to become up-to-date, patient-friendly places.

If my intentions sounded vaguely grandiose, Rajeev was the right person with whom to discuss lofty ambitions. He was particularly interested in healthcare, and he'd told me earlier of a primary healthcare development plan he'd created according to the central government's directive. He'd presented the draft to the previous Kerala government but failed to get any support for it. He now suggested that we base our new proposal on that old primary healthcare draft. I agreed that was a good place to start and we'd include the other two levels of the public healthcare system as well.

In the early days of a government, bureaucrats are very busy acclimatizing and creating the groundwork for another five years. But despite being in the thick of so much activity, the team consulted various experts to set precise goals, and created a comprehensive project report. Our focus within Aardram was the primary, secondary and tertiary sectors of the public healthcare system. We presented this project report to the cabinet and got it approved. The chief minister launched the Aardram Mission in February 2017. Our goal was to increase the public's use of public healthcare institutions by enhancing the quality of care at each level of the system.

There are 846 PHCs in Kerala. PHCs serve the public in the most rural and far-flung parts of the state; these are the first-line public institutions that patients visit for treatment. But many of these clinics had a doctor available only till lunchtime and were unable to handle most of the minor issues that patients showed up with. According to our multi-tiered plan, the PHCs would be upgraded to Family Health Centres (FHCs) with at least three doctors functioning from

9 a.m. to 6 p.m., and with staff trained to catch early signs of Kerala's most rampant lifestyle diseases, such as cholesterol, diabetes and hypertension. Where there was one staff nurse, we planned to increase the number to four, and to institute the positions of a pharmacist and a lab technician. The plan also proposed setting up of rudimentary pathology labs in every clinic that didn't have one, so that it could do basic blood and urine sample testing – essential in identifying lifestyle diseases at the outset. So, the human resource requirement would increase. Then there was the matter of infrastructure: we had to get a fix on how to scale it up to create space and capacity for all these new changes.

As ambitious as our plan was, we knew we didn't have ready cash for it. So we had to figure what we needed to do, exactly how much money would be required, and where to find the funds. Even as we began planning in earnest, we were sure five years was not enough to fix the system. But we could set the dream in motion, make a good start. It could take up to three years just to develop the concept and raise the money. But it was 2017, so we felt we'd have the time and mind space in the coming years to make at least some of this happen. Little did we know the scale of the distractions looming in the not-so-distant future.

We formed an expert group at the State Health Systems Resource Centre (SHSRC). This is a government organization created to provide technical advice and capacity-building assistance for the public healthcare system, and is particularly equipped for strategy development, programme planning and other key infrastructural help. At the inaugural discussion on the subject, we managed to create an outline for what each clinic might need. The intention was to change the atmosphere of these primary hospitals, starting from the outside, which meant ensuring cleanliness and greenery. Moving inwards, there had to be a streamlined reception with adequate low-maintenance seating for patients and bystanders. Doctors' rooms had to be spacious, with proper furniture, clean sheets, sterilizer, handwash and other basics. We believed the improved infrastructure would allow for more clinical, diagnostic and treatment capabilities.

By the time we met again, the group had created a draft proposal that was added to the wish list, along with a lot more detail and colour. The team was a set of really smart and engaged individuals who seemed enthused at the prospect of making significant changes in the existing system. They were idealistic and passionate. The proposal read like a dream. They'd fleshed out ideas for an observation room, child-friendly immunization rooms, yoga room, even mini gyms; it was like a vision for a five-star health resort! But there was no concrete plan that could be applied to Kerala's real-life clinics. They needed to do a gap analysis before an actionable strategy could be devised. I believed in order to analyse the gaps in the existing system we needed to first understand what could be even defined as a gap, when each of these 846 clinics were shaped and outfitted so differently from each other.

As per the Panchayati Raj Act of 1992, Kerala's PHCs come under panchayat administration. Some of these clinics are big, some small, some function out of rented spaces, some are just simple concrete structures, while others have a basic aesthetic sensibility. We needed to standardize these places and create a pattern. We couldn't tear down and build everything anew because some of these clinics had recently been renovated, so they could only be modified and improved. As insurmountable as it all seemed, it was also exciting. That's what a government is for. Reimagining the present for a better future and working towards it.

I was lucky enough to have with me a group of spirited bureaucrats who took up the challenge with a mixture of obstinacy and enthusiasm.

Within weeks, they came back with a description of the qualities of an ideal FHC. We then created teams at the district level, which went to each panchayat. In the presence of the panchayat president, who is the head of the local administration, they analysed the gap between our paper dreams and the ground reality of each PHC. With that gap analysis we had a better picture of what needed to be done. We understood we'd have to spend between Rs 50 lakh to Rs 2.5 crore/ Rs 3 crore on each clinic. An existing clinic with a good building would require only about Rs 50 lakh, but for clinics that weren't as well equipped we'd need up to Rs 3 crore to turn them into a well equipped, adequately staffed FHC. Now we had to find the money.

When Finance Minister Thomas Isaac presented the budget in March 2017, he announced an allocation for the Aardram Mission. While doing so, he alluded to M.T. Vasudevan Nair's short story 'Bheeru', in which an NRI Malayali couple visit a government hospital when the wife has a fever. She ends up feeling worse when she comes out of the place than when she went in. In a feverish state she lashes out at the hospital, its walls painted with drying paan stains, its dirty sheets and grimy floors. They wonder how such a place could be called a hospital. That story about the dismal nature of our hospitals stuck in my mind. Perhaps I was even embarrassed by it. While the condition of our public health institutions wasn't attributable to me, it was now my responsibility to do something about it. Having the collective engagement of the whole government made it feel doable.

The finance minister said we could finance major projects through the Kerala Infrastructure Investment Fund Board (KIIFB). This is a government-supported board that mobilizes funds for infrastructure development through loans from international agencies. It divvies up its funds to provide different government departments with capital expenditure if the project proposal fits its guidelines. The KIIFB declared its willingness to provide up to Rs 3,000 crore to the health department, since our proposal involved improving public health infrastructure. While that sounds like a lot, it wasn't going to be enough to cover all the public health institutions in the state.

So, we decided on a two-pronged plan. We'd use money from the KIIFB to improve hospitals at the secondary and tertiary levels, including all the large hospitals and medical colleges across the state. At the primary level, to action our plan to refashion PHCs into FHCs, we'd activate local self-governments and canvass for people's participation in strategizing, funding and execution. Our idea was based on the fact that Kerala had long practised the art of decentralized planning and execution. And I believed that people would not be averse to contributing to such a project that would ultimately help them. Of course, that was easier believed than done.

Around this time, someone told me, 'You should go see the state of one of the general hospitals.' When you take on a role like state minister, a lot of suggestions and stray comments come your way. Somewhere, sometimes, some things they say, and the way they say them, can be useful. I could tell from the way the suggestion had been made that such a visit was going to be more adventure – or shock – than pleasant surprise.

According to our estimates at the time, 67 per cent of Kerala's population sought medical care from the vast number of private hospitals in the state, even though many of these hospitals are expensive. The people who go to the public hospitals are often the poorest of the poor. And while there are many public hospitals in bad condition, there are also an equal number of them with attentive superintendents and staff that take good care of their institutions, offering people quality treatment.

I decided to pay an unannounced visit to the hospital that

individual had referred to. We went without warning so that we could see the tableau any ordinary citizen would, instead of the cleaned-up sanitized drama that is usually part of a ministerial visit. Dr Saritha R.L., director of health services (DHS), was also with me. She was excellent at prying open situations and learning what's underneath. We got there early on a May morning, at a time when dengue cases were flaring up through the state in the summer heat. The hospital, constructed before Independence, was in the colonial-Kerala style, with gabled roofs, wooden ceilings, segmental archways, wrapped verandas and open passageways connecting different buildings. Once an exceptional example of local–colonial fusion architecture, some of the buildings of the institution had fallen into disrepair over the decades.

You didn't have to enter the hospital's main building to understand there were problems. A car shed, with a bunch of parked motorcycles, was littered with old clothes, bottles and waste. As we made our way into the building, we came upon an old refrigerator standing in an open corridor, as if waiting to greet someone. On top of the decrepit fridge was a pile of waste: files, cups, paper, etc. When I opened its creaking door, another collection of random bottles awaited us. It turned out that a patient's family had donated this refrigerator to the hospital in memory of their father who was treated here years ago. Broken down and unused now, it was standing around because no one had bothered to throw it out. Like many government institutions, everything was all over the place. Doctors were treating patients while seated at one large table, even though there was plenty of space in the building. In fact, there was both space and adequate staff. The only thing missing was intent.

A wastebasket was overflowing with food waste; it seemed that people had thrown their rubbish at the basket rather than in it. And there must have been a few days' worth of waste. It was only around 10 a.m. – far too early for the stench that was emanating from that bin. On expeditions like these, toilets are always the best barometer of the problem. But the sight of that waste bin was enough to imagine the condition the toilets would be in.

The building was fully staffed and patients were milling about the place. When I asked one of the unsuspecting nurses who'd walked into our cordon why the place was in such a condition, she said, 'Patients don't listen.' The subtext of the statement being that the poor people who used this hospital didn't have civic sense. In India, that is the worst kind of classist falsehood. The same set of people using public facilities versus private facilities will treat each differently. Why? I often find myself lecturing people and I'm sure they are annoyed by it. And in this case it was unavoidable. I said to the group that had assembled by then, 'Public institutions like hospitals are where people learn public civilities. The respect an institution gets from people depends on how it treats itself.' I am very uncomfortable putting people in an awkward position, but I understand that sometimes anger is a very useful tool for communication. Having said that, there in that situation, my annoyance was as reflexive as my repulsion at the sight of the dustbin. Somewhere in the chaos, a staff member parroted another common government-run-institution excuse: 'We don't have enough staff.'

In fact, our team had already looked at the staff strength of that hospital and knew there was adequate staff to clean the place and, if needed, to stand in every corner instructing patients not to throw food around. 'Do you need money to fix this?' I asked loudly. One doctor piped up with the truth: 'Madam, we have money.' In fact, they had almost Rs 1 crore in the Hospital Development Committee Fund. In Kerala's government hospitals, people from households below certain income levels are entitled to free service, while others are charged a nominal fee, much lower than what a private hospital would cost. This income feeds a government hospital's development fund, which it can use for repairs, engaging temporary workers, purchasing equipment and for sundry maintenance activities. Every government hospital has this kind of a development fund. Fixing those toilets wouldn't have cost more than Rs 10 lakh/Rs 15 lakh. The structure of the building was fine, the insides needed to be put right. This hospital always had the cash but never the interest to use it. I asked them how long they'd take to sort out the place. They said one week, I said take two. The very next day they appointed people and began fixing things that had been broken for a long time.

During my visit there, someone recorded a video of everything that happened and published it online. The Malayalam media called it the minister's 'lightning visit'. I was embarrassed it had become such a talking point, and I felt bad for the staff that had been caught in this awkward public admonishment. It was never my intention, and I certainly understood it wasn't one or two individuals' fault; it was systemic laziness. Few people in our country care about government property. Most of us don't think twice about spoiling public property, when in fact we should be paying extra attention to maintaining it because the infrastructure of these institutions costs crores of rupees of public money, essentially our taxes. However, there was one happy fallout of the publicity that visit received. I got a call from the Police Officers' Association with an offer: what if our people help clean up the hospital? We'd be more than happy to have the help, I said.

Kerala has two police associations: the Police Officers' Association for senior officers, while the other is simply the Police Association, comprising the constabulary. Members of both associations were offering to lend a hand in cleaning that public hospital. It was a very generous but, in Kerala, not unusual, offer. There have been many instances where groups such as youth organizations, women's units, NGOs and others come together to perform acts of public service. I told the police associations they'd need loads of cleaning equipment. They said they'd be happy to do it if I inaugurated the clean-up drive. The next day, when the DHS and I went there, groups of people were hard at work inside and outside the campus. Even the doctors, nurses and other staff were at it. Work at this scale had probably never been done in the hospital since it had been built. By the end of that day, the whole place was cleaned up. I appreciated the effort of the entire team that had worked to make it happen.

That visit was a turning point for me. I understood that we were not lacking in facilities but in intent. There are plenty of examples of well-managed public health institutions and, equally, there are mismanaged ones. I understood our goal more clearly: we needed to professionalize the whole system to eliminate the bad outliers.

9

Reviving the Healthcare System

When we began planning to kick-start the Aardram Mission, my intention was to overhaul the public healthcare system from the bottom up. We did not need to have such an ambitious plan. We could have left the system untouched and just polished it up, because there was the danger that I wouldn't be able to complete the job in the time I had at my disposal. There was also the risk of the work of fixing all the hospitals and clinics within our system not being carried on by successive governments; in that case, everything we did do would amount to nothing. But we had to try to at least make some basic changes that could not be reversed.

With Aardram, our first target was the 846 PHCs in Kerala. We decided that in the first phase we would renovate 170 of them and transform each into what we called the FHC, as I've detailed before. These new FHCs would have doctors available to see patients from morning till evening, plus a host of other early intervention and diagnosis capabilities to address the health challenges of the current era.

When a ministry makes a decision, it is essential to get the buy-in of everyone in the system, especially the local administrators, or panchayat presidents, because the success or failure of projects really depends on how well each of them runs it. The panchayat is divided into wards, constituting 350 to 600 families in an area, and represented by elected ward members. So, from a single household in a rural area all the way to the ministry in the capital, there is a chain of communication. Anything decided at one echelon is conveyed to the next, and this way we're able to access direct information right from the grassroots of the state. This top-to-bottom linkage would serve Kerala very well in the challenges we were about to face very soon.

We got in touch with the panchayats where the first lot of 170 PHCs were located. Panchayat presidents and medical officers from twenty panchayats were called at a time to the capital, and we held round-the-clock meetings. Those first meetings were extremely entertaining as well as frustrating – for them as much as for me.

We explained to each of these groups that depending on the condition of the PHCs in their panchayats, anywhere between Rs 50 lakh and Rs 2 crore would be required for the proposed FHCs. Where would this money come from? My answer wasn't what they had in mind. I told them they would have to put up at least half of the budget required for each of their clinics. When they heard this at the first meeting, the faces of those people, which had been alive with enthusiasm, just fell. They were completely aghast. Here they'd come all the way to Thiruvananthapuram expecting money to be doled out to them to create something new; instead, they were being asked to canvass resources from the countryside. 'Madam, we don't have money to do all this,' they said. I told them, 'There is a scarcity of money in the state government also. The central government spends only about 1 per cent of the overall GDP on health, so this can only be done with people's participation. Don't be overwhelmed by the full picture. Consider it part by part.' I wanted them to understand this was a challenge they needed to take up in order to improve their own health facilities. We were asking them to fix what belonged to their people, not someone else. And we offered a simple breakdown of the money that would be required: the health ministry could give half, the MLAs and MPs of these areas could give up to Rs 50 lakh, and the shortfall could be raised from their public as funds or even as material and labour.

Some said they'd do it, some said they'd try. You have to understand that as humans differ from each other, so there are also differences in how various units of government function; this holds true from the lowest branch of government to the highest. In some places the panchayat president and the medical officer of the panchayat just don't get along. The doctor may have a poor opinion of the president, or the president – who is an elected representative – thinks they have the backing of people so they don't need to confer with an unelected government employee like a public health doctor. When you're speaking to a group in this way, you can sense the tensions in these relationships. And yet this couldn't be done without the cooperation of both entities, so I wanted them to understand this wasn't about individual differences of opinion. It was a mission and they would have to helm it, working together – however uncomfortably.

Perhaps the biggest lesson I'd learned in my public work was that you cannot get anything done on your own. And whether I agreed with each of these people or not, it was important to rally them to work with me and with one another. Some panchayat presidents got very excited. When they went back to their constituencies and convened meetings to discuss this, I attended some of them.

And in this way, we met all the panchayats, day in and day out. We sent many ideas down the chain of administration. In some places the strategy worked quickly, MLAs took a lot of initiative and gave significant amounts, and there were panchayats which secured good sponsorships from various entities. For instance, in Malappuram district, VPS Healthcare constructed an FHC for Rs 8 crore as part of their Corporate Social Responsibility (CSR) scheme. In Calicut, the Chennai-based Apollo Hospital built one. In fact, many local businesses and individuals put in far more than we'd expected. And wherever there was a concerted team effort to get people to contribute, the plan clicked.

The first FHC took shape in Thiruvananthapuram, in a place called Chemmaruthi. People were so thrilled and thought this was such a landmark moment that the chief minister came to inaugurate the building. The hospital was transformed. There were laboratories, defibrillators, a nurses' station, depression clinic, dental unit and, perhaps most importantly, three doctors to tend to patients in that small rural clinic. At the beginning, as new FHCs began popping up, it created a sense of competition amongst everyone. Following our basic guidelines and suggestions, some got sponsorships for televisions in the reception areas, others created a play area for children, breastfeeding rooms for mothers, a yoga centre, walking paths for older patients; many doctors applied their aesthetic sensibilities to improve their hospitals as best as they could.

In my constituency in Kuthuparamba, one of the panchayat presidents was a smart young woman called Shabna. She was undeterred by the task at hand. I was able to donate Rs 80 lakh from the MLA's Special Development Fund; then she secured funding from an urban scheme, and to fill the rest of the requirement, she went to the people and asked them to contribute what they could to refashion their local PHC. Some people agreed immediately, while some were of the opinion that if the government couldn't fund it, they shouldn't bother doing it. One gentleman was asked to donate Rs 5,000 for landscaping work. He refused. Shabna got the money from another sponsor and started off. The old clinic building was demolished and construction began for a new one. One day the man who had refused to give Rs 5,000 happened to pass by and, seeing the hive of activity, he went to take a look. Later, he called Shabna and told her, 'I didn't realize you were serious. Usually, people take money and do a cursory job but you're overhauling everything. That's what we need. You asked for Rs 5,000. I'll give you Rs 45,000 more than you asked, and make it a round figure of Rs 50,000.' To hear these stories of people participating in a cause greater than themselves was inspiring for everyone involved in this work. When that FHC was done, it was a two-storey spacious building. It had undergone an ugly-duckling-to-swan transformation from a small clinic with broken chairs to a seemingly urban private hospital.

When we started, we'd aimed to complete 170 within the first year; instead, in the first year itself we were able to create 230 FHCs across Kerala. When people saw the first few succeed, it was no longer tough to convince the others to follow.

But there were plenty of other problems to deal with. The doctors' association was livid when we announced there would be three doctors working from 9 a.m. to 6 p.m. in an FHC. They opposed extending outpatient hours unless we created positions for five doctors. I didn't agree, because we were not asking them to work longer; we were adding more staff to attend to the longer working hours. And there was no need for five doctors in a small clinic. Moreover, the finance ministry had agreed to fund five new positions at the FHCs, for one doctor, two staff nurses, one lab technician and one pharmacist, creating some extra 830 new posts in all. There were fewer pharmacists than ideal, but we were happy with what we'd got.

We asked the panchayat minister at the time for help. He offered to use the panchayat fund to source one more doctor and another staff member. So, now we could tell people we'd kept our promise. The FHCs would have five more permanent staff on call. It was a massive upgrade.

But some of the public healthcare system's doctors didn't think so. There were huge protests. Someone announced, 'We will bring the minister to her knees.' We asked them to come for a meeting and tried to explain what we were trying to do, to convince them to withdraw. It wasn't my personal plan; it was a mission declared by the government to propel the state's healthcare system into the twenty-first century. They weren't convinced. While many doctors were supportive, some government doctors went on a flash strike to oppose the move. But the health department refused to back down; the chief minister advised me to continue with the reforms. The government also decided to terminate doctors who were striking while on probation and transferred others. This was an essential services department, and there was no unfairness in the new changes that could justify these doctors taking off from work. The chief minister called the strike 'anti-people' and 'anti-government'. Eventually the doctors themselves called off the strike. I didn't see it as a failure or a win. These doctors are part of the government, the very healthcare system we were trying to improve. It was too bad that we couldn't secure their cooperation right at the beginning. Eventually, these very people were responsible for the success of the Aardram Mission; later, they became heroes during the many crises that followed.

In the second year, we declared 500 more PHCs would be converted to FHCs, and we created 1,200 new posts for staff. By then there was a lot more enthusiasm and people knew what to expect. Some improvements far outpaced my expectations. There were fountains and play areas and all sorts of improvements – a far cry from the hospital in M.T. Vasudevan Nair's story. As we write this, nearly 600 FHCs have been created in Kerala and the rest will also hopefully be transformed soon. This has come to be even though we've had to deal with several public health crises in the midst of this transformation. But it is also because of the major improvements we instituted at the primary level that we were able to get a grip on COVID-19 when it hit us in 2020. Without looking at the changes achieved just before the pandemic, it would be difficult to comprehend how a healthcare system in a financially deficit state was able to withstand such a huge public health crisis. When you think of all the challenges the healthcare system has faced in these years, being able to have met our goals at this pace is hugely commendable. At the same time, if there aren't continued efforts to maintain the quality at this level and constant vigilance over its functioning, things will stagnate and fall apart.

Once we'd worked out the plan for the primary healthcare system, we turned our attention to the larger taluk hospitals in each district. A district is divided into three to five taluks. In order to create a realistic master plan, the health secretary Sadanandan and I met with all the superintendents of all the taluk hospitals. We asked them, 'What do you need? What specialities do you already have?' Some said they needed better operation theatres, laboratories and inpatient wards. Many needed better imaging systems. Most of these hospitals – which fall between grassroots-level clinics and better-equipped medical colleges – were working out of old, rundown buildings. When they have some funds, they carry out ad hoc fixes, so most taluk hospitals' front yards were a patchwork of makeshift buildings.

We created a team to conduct a gap analysis of all the taluk-level hospitals. The story the team came back with was like a classic Malayali avial. There were eighty-six hospitals of this grade, each different from the other; some had between sixteen and twenty-five doctors while some had as few as nine doctors. In one revenue taluk, sometimes four different hospitals were called taluk hospitals, but only in name and without the right facilities. A taluk hospital is supposed to meet certain specifications; it isn't just a tag bestowed at random. We thought we should bring at least a few of the hospitals up to scratch. These hospitals serve a larger population, so they need to have minor speciality departments such as orthopaedics, gynaecology and dental, and adequate infrastructure to run them. In an ideal, well-funded world, we would standardize all of them and bring them up to a similar quality at the same time. But we couldn't take up all of them together. So, we decided that in each revenue taluk, one taluk hospital would be modernized; the MLAs and people's representatives of the area could decide which one they wanted revamped. The team would create a master plan for the redevelopment of the chosen taluk hospitals. The hospitals would then have to submit project proposals to the KIIFB to get the money.

Can a government hospital ever truly become an aspirational, even welcoming, space? Even if we renovated the spaces and bought the equipment, would the improvements be sustained? I had these questions in my mind all through this process because looking for great examples in the government health sector is a hunt for unicorns. Then I visited the Punalur Taluk Hospital. Punalur is a small town in Kollam district in southern Kerala. It is a commercial, buzzy township by the Kallada river, its hillsides dotted with old estates from colonial times.

For ten years the taluk hospital has been headed by Dr Shahirsha R., the superintendent. And through the decade of his leadership, his team has put the money in the Hospital Development Committee Fund to better use than any other hospital I'd seen. Over the years, as the hospital began to serve more and more patients, they'd created a series of well-maintained buildings and, unusually, it was all managed efficiently; there was a synchronized system in place. When I first visited the hospital, I was taken aback. The team at the Punalur hospital had invested in proper signage and communication devices like LED boards, the hospital beds were up to date, and for such a busy hospital treating nearly 1,000 patients a day, the place was immaculate. It was definitely not driven by the mentality that leaves a broken fridge in the corridor!

Dr Shahirsha told me they'd been able to accomplish a lot with the help of the local Plantation Corporation. It helped them set up a waste management system, and I went to inaugurate it. Even back then, before the pandemic, they already had an oxygen manufacturing plant at the hospital. He said setting up the oxygen plant had cost them just Rs 15 lakh. At that time there was no major need for oxygen, but the hospital ensured whatever oxygen was used there was self-produced. I understood from the Punalur example that a government establishment that has people who care and understand their responsibility can become an exemplary place, even if there aren't enough resources.

As someone attuned to the government system, Dr Shahirsha and his team reached out to us before anyone else, promptly submitting the first plan for the redevelopment of this hospital. And with the Punalur hospital, as we had proof they would make the best use of the money, giving to them was a relatively easy decision. They came up with a master plan for an up-to-date nine-storey building, with well-equipped OTs and all sorts of facilities. They also wanted a helipad in order to evacuate people during the monsoonal floods, but we said no to that. The Punalur hospital's redevelopment plan was sanctioned for Rs 112 crore. The building was inaugurated in 2021, and I'm happy to report that it has soared past our expectations. They even have service staff in uniform to greet people in the waiting area. It feels very much like a place that cares about serving its patients. But I need to add a footnote to this success story: unless the government continues to support the hospital with resource management, these types of public institutions can easily fall into ruin.

We decided to redevelop seventy-eight out of the eighty-six taluk hospitals in the state, and allotted funds and equipment to those institutions. All of them did not receive the same amount of money, and there were priority lists in terms of facilities requiring improvement. For instance, the outpatient areas in hospitals are usually crowded, dingy places, so there was a transformation plan for those. In hospitals where the outpatient areas were too small, rooms were demolished and refashioned to expand the space. For the Aardram Mission, the chief minister had highlighted this change in particular: making the reception areas of hospitals patient friendly.

We also prioritized the casualty departments. I know the emergency areas of a government hospital are absolute chaos. I remember, from my days in grassroots politics, visiting colleagues who were injured in a demonstration at a government hospital, and you can't tell the difference between a bystander and the victim. Everyone and everything will have blood splatters, and confusion reigns over the place. It's worse when there's a road accident or a mass casualty of some kind. Victims are often brought to hospitals by large groups of people and it's hard to tell what is going on. If a patient's head is injured and the blood has flowed down to the leg, a doctor may start checking the leg first. It is a place of drama, heartache and pain, when it ought to be calm and organized, governed by a systematic flow of functions, because time is of the essence there. A confused doctor can mean a dead patient. We decided to overhaul the whole set-up and introduce a contemporary triage system and other facilities to manage both trauma and casualty cases. Another problem that's taken over the Kerala countryside is kidney disease. In a private hospital, dialysis is an extremely expensive treatment, so we set up dialysis units in each and every taluk hospital.

It has now been about five years since the master plan was first created. During this time, some of the hospitals have already finished their revamp work, some are in the process of getting things done, while some are still at the stage of issuing a tender. The outcome, when it's entirely finished, will be revolutionary. As with primary health sector improvements, I think we pushed things forward for the taluk hospitals at an amazing speed, given the circumstances.

Our next focus was the district hospitals in the fourteen districts which serve a larger population. The intention was to bring lifesaving specialized care within a reasonable distance and budget of every single person, across the varied terrains and corners of the state. So we decided to bring superspeciality facilities, like cardiology, neurology and nephrology, to the district hospitals. Since then, we've constituted stroke units called Stroke Identification Rehabilitation Awareness and Stabilisation, or SIRAS, at the district level, so patients can get faster treatment and the aftermath of a stroke is managed such that patients don't suffer paralysis. (In Malayalam, the word siras means head; I remember it was a master coinage by a senior health department officer called Dr Vipin Gopal and his team.) These centres are also equipped with facilities for thrombolysis treatment, including the distribution of very expensive medicines to treat the condition. The first stroke unit was set up in Pathanamthitta district which has a high quotient of older residents, and it has saved a great number of lives. Similarly, for cardiology care we decided to establish catheterization labs in all district hospitals; seven are already functional while others are under way.

When you live in remote areas, there are many basics of life you learn to live without – I've seen this in my own world over the years – and yet it shouldn't be that way. Our rural areas are the heart of Kerala, but over the years many of these places have been left behind. If a patient is able to go to a nearby hospital, get stabilized, do an angiogram or angioplasty right there, then there's diagnosis and care at a much earlier phase of their ailment, which aids faster recovery.

We also focused on natal care, making vast improvements to labour rooms (for this we utilized some funds from the central government's Laqshya scheme), OTs, neonatal intensive care units (NICUs), equipping these spaces with the equipment and capacity to reduce infant and maternal mortality rates. In 2016 the Infant Mortality Rate (IMR) was 12 deaths per 1,000 live births; we managed to reduce that to 5.5 deaths per 1,000. The maternal mortality rate dropped from 67 in 2016 to 43 in 2019, and the central government gave us an award. At the time our declared goal was '30 by 20 and 20 by 30' but in fact we were able to bring the mortality rate down further and faster, such that it was down to 20 by 2020 itself. All in all, a lot got done, though of course a lot remains to be done.

The third segment of the public healthcare system we looked at was the medical colleges. In Kerala's health hierarchy these teaching colleges are the highest level of medical care, and within the government system, these have the best resources. When I took charge of the health portfolio in 2016 there were five established government medical colleges and five newly created ones. The Kerala government was waiting for approval from the Centre to start four more medical colleges in the state. To complete the infrastructure development for these new hospitals, we prepared the master plan and secured funding through the KIIFB. I'm very happy that in 2022 two new medical colleges, one in Pathanamthitta district and one in Idukki district, received permission from the central government to accept a hundred medical students each. Wayanad and Kasargod are still awaiting approval.

Through Aardram, we were able to improve and better equip these superspeciality medical colleges. For instance, at the Thrissur Medical College, there was one cobalt machine in the radiology section. A cobalt machine is used for radiation, as part of cancer treatment. This cobalt machine used to break down every time the radioactive source was depleted, and since the source was imported from other countries, they'd have to wait several months with a broken-down machine that required replacement. So radiation treatment there would stop entirely, and when that happened, people had to go to another medical college or, more likely, a private hospital. When such things occur, there are conspiracy theories that the government hospital is in cahoots with the private health sector and deliberately causing the machine to break down in order to push patients into the private health sector. To deal with the problem once and for all, we procured a Linear Accelerator, or LINAC, which is a newer technology for radiation treatments. Now all major medical colleges in the state are equipped with new LINAC machines.

The proliferation of new technology and equipment made a world of difference. As doctors and superintendents realized we were funding new purchases and improvements, there were plenty of requests and results. For instance, in the middle of the COVID lockdown in April 2020, the Kottayam Medical College was preparing its infrastructure and staff to perform a liver transplant. As a result in 2021, the Kottayam Medical College was able to carry out the first such successful surgery in Kerala's government sector. Other medical colleges were similarly getting equipped for these types of complicated surgeries. We were able to achieve all of this through the KIIFB. The process of creating better infrastructure and modernizing these hospitals is continuing, and I foresee a revolutionary facelift in this tertiary sector of government healthcare in the near future.

One particular aspect I'm especially proud of is the focus we brought to trauma care. In reality, more people die in road accidents every year than they do of communicable diseases. When we organized discussions on these topics, the experts said, 'People can make it out alive only if they're treated correctly in the golden hour'; they were referring to the first hour after an accident. There is a gap in the emergency care response, with ambulances not being outfitted with basic life support systems nor manned by emergency medical technicians. When we understood this gap we decided to create the Total Trauma Care project for the state and roped in two young doctors, Dr Mohammed Asheel and Dr Srikanth under the leadership of a senior doctor called Dr. Vishwanath, to head it. They created a project report within two months.

To explore how we could implement it, we visited the All India Institute of Medical Sciences (AIIMS) in New Delhi, which has one of the best trauma care departments in the country. It was the little things that stuck with me. In Kerala, when a patient is in the operation theatre, well-wishers throng outside to learn how the patient inside is doing. When a nurse comes out of the door, you can always see a crowd desperate for answers. Sometimes the nurses will stop to speak to the relatives, sometimes they're too busy and leave a trail of confused, worried people behind. At AIIMS, there are LED boards to declare the condition of the patients. They display the names of the patients in different zones. People in critical condition are in the red zone; when a patient is moved to a yellow zone the news is updated, along with their vitals. There is no need to ask, and nurses don't have to convey messages; chaos is minimized.

Dr Sanjeev Kumar Bhoi, the head of trauma care at AIIMS, told us we could replicate the AIIMS facility at the Trivandrum Medical College. I asked him to come help us set it up. And he did. Dr Bhoi along with Dr Tej Prakash came to Kerala and met with Dr Vishwanathan and the Trivandrum Medical College superintendent Dr Sharmad and together they formulated a plan to establish this centre. I must make a special mention here that Dr Bhoi and Dr Tej Prakash did all of this completely gratis and I must thank them for their service.

We didn't have space in the existing casualty building to install this facility, so the first task was finding land to build it on. Thankfully, we were able to identify some space right by the hospital's entrance, and built a trauma centre there for about Rs 9 crore. Just as it started functioning in 2020, COVID landed in the state. Since this centre was a separate building, it was suitable for conversion into a temporary COVID care area. Now that COVID numbers have reduced, this facility functions as a trauma care centre again. We instituted the same trauma systems in all the medical colleges in the state, and beefed up the emergency medical care system by adding a fleet of 315 basic life support (BLS) ambulances to the arsenal; this ensures there is an ambulance available every 30 kilometres along major highways in the state.

There are some instances which make me believe author Paulo Coelho's assertion that if one really wants something, the universe will conspire to make it happen. The creation of the Apex Trauma and Emergency Learning Centre in Thiruvananthapuram was such an instance. It came to be thanks to a serendipitous meeting with an iconic figure in the UK.

In 2018, my team and I were invited to the University of Warwick for a seminar by Vinod Menon, a professor at Warwick. Learning of my presence there, Professor Lord Sushanta Kumar Bhattacharyya, founder of the Warwick Manufacturing Group at the University of Warwick, invited me to dinner on my first evening there. A British citizen but Bengali by birth, Lord Bhattacharyya was something of a legend in the UK's industry circles, lauded for his role in the takeover of Jaguar–Land Rover by the Tata Group, and hugely respected by polity and citizenry for creating thousands of jobs in the UK. Over dinner, Lord Bhattacharyya quizzed me on the modernization programme of Kerala's healthcare system we had embarked on. Towards the end of the evening, he asked, 'Minister, is there anything I can help you with?' As a close friend of Ratan Tata's and with his association with the Tata Trusts, he could help push through a CSR proposal, we realized. Once we came back to Kerala, we put together a proposal for the Apex Trauma and Emergency Learning Centre. Before this chance meeting, the centre was a dream whose fruition I was sceptical about. It needed resources of course, and technical and training assistance as well. We had assumed it would take a hard slog to find the funds. But within two weeks of submitting our application, a team from the Tata Trusts met us and the project was approved. We found a suitable location near the Trivandrum General Hospital. In 2020, we inaugurated the emergency learning centre. This centre now has all the facilities required to simulate and train for emergencies. We're extremely grateful to Lord Bhattacharyya for the way he stretched out his hand and asked if he could help. Sadly, he passed away in March 2019, aged 79. It would have meant a great deal to us if he'd been around to see this centre materialize in Kerala.

While we worked on improving the infrastructure of healthcare in the state, we also wanted to impact people's health more directly.

Right at the beginning, when we first set out the goals for the health department, we were very concerned about focusing on preventive healthcare in the areas of communicable and non-communicable diseases, both of which are exceptionally relevant to our state.

In Kerala, non-communicable lifestyle diseases are an abstract enemy, even in rural areas. For instance, Kerala is known as the capital of diabetes in the country. Having a lifestyle disease like cholesterol or high blood pressure is almost considered a rite of passage into middle age. With the changes to our diet and lifestyle in these fast food and fast-paced times, such diseases and attendant problems affect almost every family. As health officials we decided it would be worth our while to battle these ailments, particularly cancer, thyroid malfunction, diabetes and hypertension. I saw these efforts as a way to increase awareness within our population about things they needed to think about in relation to their health.

So, we formed twenty-two expert groups under the SDG programme, one set focusing on noncommunicable disease control (NCD) and one set on infectious disease control (IDC). Under IDC, one of the key targets was elimination of tuberculosis and leprosy, through work at the grassroots level. Under NCD, we had a project called Amrutham Arogyam, or Sweet Health, focused on screening people for non-communicable lifestyle ailments like hypertension and diabetes, and giving them both information and treatment as required. It was executed using the evolved down-up and up-down administrative communication link that exists in our state, through accredited social health activist (ASHA) workers and public health nurses who visited houses, identified patients with particular complaints, and even distributed medicines. In situations where residents were too old or could not procure diabetes medication and so on, medical health staff delivered the drugs to them.

We also created an app called the State Health Application for Intensified Lifestyle Intervention (SHAILI), which could help create a registry of diabetic and hypertension sufferers in the state. We also extended that focus to children suffering from Type-1 diabetes. Caring for Type-1 diabetes is a lifelong effort, and for poor families the cost of treatment and support can be overwhelming. We created the MITTAYI initiative to provide comprehensive care to children and adolescents with this condition. It also supported their families by giving the insulin pumps and lifelong medicine supply that are critical to Type 1 diabetes treatment.

Even though the state's IMR is low in comparison to other states, we knew that congenital heart disease (CHD) was the largest preventable cause of death among infants. Many babies born with heart-related ailments die within weeks of their birth if the families are not able to get them adequate care at the right time; this could be because of financial constraints or because the child was delivered in a hospital where this sensitive paediatric surgery was unavailable. The health department launched the Hridyam scheme to address this issue. Overseen by Dr Sreehari, who was the nodal officer, Hridyam was constructed as a web-based solution focused on the management of the care of children with CHD. Hospitals across the state were informed of the scheme so that whenever a child was born with CHD and needed assistance the birth could be registered on the Hridyam website, alerting the system. There were public and/or private hospitals empanelled in every district to conduct the corrective surgeries for this condition. Once a case was registered, a Hridyam ambulance would take the little one to the nearest empanelled institution, and oversee the arrangements for the operation till the child was ready to go home. It was a people-centric scheme specifically focused on ensuring that all children, irrespective of their family's situation, stood a good chance of survival. The scheme has managed up to 5,000 operations till date.

Similarly, we embarked on a war against cancer. Every year more than 50,000 new cases of cancer are reported in the state. We created the country's first Cancer Strategic Action Plan set out by a team of experts. As part of that we constituted Cancer Control Boards and mandated the state's three Regional Cancer Centres (RCCs) to oversee a population-based cancer registry. Through the FHCs, we were able to screen potential patients early. At least with the three types of cancers that can be detected from the beginning – breast, cervical and oral – even an FHC could be instrumental in saving lives. The district hospitals were provided mammogram machines and facilities to conduct chemotherapy and cancer care. The medical colleges would then become tertiary cancer centres in addition to the RCCs.

At the same time, we felt we also had to focus on supplementary health-related issues, such as the issue of antimicrobial resistance (AMR), which is caused by the misuse of antibiotics. AMR occurs when pathogens like bacteria, virus and fungi mutate to become resistant to the medicine, making infections harder to treat and therefore increasing the risk of disease spread and mortality. It is a social, political and economic issue that affects people all over the world and can result in significant loss of productivity and, by extension, stall development. Getting medical doctors to economize on the use of antibiotics wouldn't be enough. These drugs can enter the food system through meat and dairy that's commercially produced, jeopardizing our health. Which means this topic needs the cooperation of the health, agricultural, fisheries and animal husbandry departments. In 2018 we organized a workshop on the topic and then drew up an AMR strategy called the Kerala Antimicrobial Resistance and Stewardship Action Plan (KARSAP) with inputs from all the concerned departments in the state. As part of that we started the antibiotics stewardship programme and increased AMR surveillance in Kerala. With the support of the WHO we were able to work out a public communication plan to make Kerala an antibiotics-literate state, and institute processes to ensure that expired and unused antibiotics were removed from the system and disposed of properly. By now tonnes of such medicines have been collected and dispatched to Bengaluru, which has a centre that destroys this kind of medicine effectively.

Mainly because of this kind of concerted effort, in 2020 Kerala's health ministry became one of just seven from around the world to be awarded by the United Nations for its 'Outstanding Contribution' to the non-communicable diseases-related SDG. And between 2018 and 2020, Kerala's healthcare system became one of the most awarded healthcare systems in the country. By December 2020, despite the onslaught of COVID, nearly 200 government health institutions in the state had received the National Quality Assurance Standards (NQAS) certification by the National Health Mission. This included several FHCs, urban PHCs, taluk hospitals and district hospitals. The NQAS certification is based on a checklist of factors, including patient service, functionality and equipment, and on inspections by national-level inspectors. Two young doctors, Dr Amjathkutty and Dr Latheesh led the effort, travelling to hospitals all over the state encouraging them to spruce up their operations in such a way that they would earn the NQAS certificate.

Modernizing a system means digitizing it, in today's parlance. If you see a crowd of people standing at the reception of a public healthcare facility clutching bags of papers and medical files, the impression conveyed is of inefficiency or unreliability. Digitizing patient care is an obvious part of improving the overall healthcare system, but it had never been attempted in the state before. In 2013, Kerala was granted Rs 92 crore for an e-Health project by the central government but it was never utilized. No one did anything with it. We however believed this was a vital aspect of the state's health rejuvenation plan. If the system was electronic, it would ease up patient management and pharmaceutical drug management. Reordering medicines, having patients' history on file – all of this would become so much easier; a patient's electronic health card would have all the information on the individual.

When I took over the ministry in 2016, I learned from the health secretary that the amount of Rs 92 crore from the Centre would lapse if we didn't implement the e-Health project immediately. After discussing with the chief minister we wrote to the central government asking for an extension, and once we had that, the project kicked off in 2017.

There are some stipulations you should understand about central government funding. One, it never comes in a single tranche. It is always provided in a phased manner. In this case the Kerala government had received a portion of the promised amount of Rs 92 crore. With that partial payment the Centre expected us to complete digitization activity in seven districts, but we realized that amount wouldn't cover even two districts. The concept of digitization may sound simple but the exercise requires an enormous amount of hardware, software and time to incorporate a massive amount of data existing on paper for several institutions and functions. And to complicate things further, there was the problem of state versus central bureaucrats and the way the two sides saw the project. In 2019, about two years after the project was launched, a team of bureaucrats from the Centre arrived in Thiruvananthapuram to evaluate the status of the programme, secure a project report, and get what is called in official language the Utility Certificate, which could be used to release the next tranche of payment.

I was in the middle of something else when I got a call saying there was an argument between bureaucrats of the two sides. I rushed to the venue of the meeting, the Mascot Hotel in Thiruvananthapuram. There was irritation in the air, and an assembly of sullen faces in a vast conference hall at the hotel. Neither group looked like it was interested in listening to the other. The central team lead said, 'The time is over, and we have to report back to our department.' I said, 'With the money you gave, we won't be able to do seven districts and connect all the hospitals. Just give us the initial funding, we will figure out the rest from somewhere else. You don't mind if we fund the rest ourselves, do you?' I asked. They were astounded. 'No problem,' they said immediately. I told them ours was a decentralized plan, where we would delegate some of the fundraising requirements to the local self-government bodies; all the central government had to do was hand over the initial funding due to us. 'We can't do a perfect job in seven districts, though; we can do one,' I said. They countered with, 'We will have problems with reporting if you only do one. Can you try two districts?' I agreed. The central team was happy with that; it meant they would get a project report and a Utility Certificate for a portion of the project.

After that everyone calmed down and the air cleared. The central team lead officer even declared that Kerala was the only state that could get this done. After they left, I told off our officers for the initial impasse and tone of the meeting. If state-level officials treat central officials with apprehension or hostility as soon they land from Delhi, projects are jeopardized. We had risked losing Rs 42 crore of investment in that meeting.

When we started working on collecting the rest of the funding needed for that project, it was again a combination of sources that came through. Money came from MLA funds in some cases; in Ernakulam city, all the work was sponsored by the Indian Oil Corporation, which has refineries there. And like that, one by one, we managed to cobble together the money for the project. The funding from the central government – the Rs 42 crore advance – came in 2021. It had taken two years since that meeting. That is how government funding works. Being promised funds doesn't mean they will arrive when you expect them. It is just a budgetary allocation; the actual money will wind its way through the system over a long period of time. If you can anticipate that problem and work on other sources simultaneously, things can move forward. Today in Kerala, nearly 600 hospitals have been inducted into the e-Health framework. The work to include the others is ongoing. Once this project gets completed, it will stand out in the world as an exemplary system.

One thing I came to realize in my years in government is that money is not the only problem. Having the will and the motivation to do something is even more rare than money. Financing has always been a problem in Kerala; we just don't have enough. But we have an empowered decentralized system of self-government, a socially minded community of business and individuals. And perhaps this comes from my experience as a teacher, but I always feel a bit of competition helps to get people motivated, even when there's no money at the end of the rainbow. In our battle against dengue, we decided to give an award to a panchayat from where no dengue cases were reported. We were looking to make local self-governments more alert, and reward them for their leadership. With the Aardram Mission Award, instituted with the cooperation of the panchayat department, since 2018, panchayats have competed among themselves to do away with such diseases. I must acknowledge the cooperation and help of the local self-government ministers at the time, K.T. Jaleel and A.C. Moideen. What we were all able to do together is a great example of people participating in making the environment better for themselves, instead of waiting for someone else to hand them everything on a platter.

Putting pieces together like a puzzle, we were able to forge ahead with a number of projects in Kerala between 2016 and 2021. But five years is not enough. It takes up to three years to develop a concept and raise money. Then, the tender has to be raised, land has to be procured, and by the time we reached year four of the government, we were almost entirely distracted by disasters: Cyclone Ockhi, floods, Nipah and COVID-19. But we didn't let anything fall by the wayside; I can proudly say that in all districts of the state we made sure there was money kept aside for the modernization drive to continue.

10

A Flood of Disasters

When we started on the modernization plan for Kerala's healthcare, we were making a road map for our collective future. There was no indication when we began that our ideas would be tested for proficiency in our own time. We also certainly never imagined there'd be so many fires to put out, one after another. But nature had plans for us. Over the five years that the first LDF government headed by Pinarayi Vijayan was in power, we dealt with repeated shocks, in quick succession, till the COVID breakout of 2020.

The first of these was the Very Severe Cyclonic Storm Ockhi in December 2017. Ockhi was the strongest tropical cyclone in the Arabian Sea in many years. And it ravaged our fishing community in Kerala, particularly in Thiruvananthapuram. The cyclone killed almost a hundred people; close to 150 people are still missing from our community due to that storm.

The government acted swiftly; all departments were immediately activated to search, rescue and treat people who had faced the wrath of the angry sea. When you're in government, you receive the first phone call about a disaster. Realization of the ramifications settles in pretty quickly, though I've never got completely used to a call with bad news. People were looking at us for help, and there are times when there is nothing we can do. When someone has lost a child or a spouse, anything we could say was just useless balm on a wound that was never going to heal. The only people we could help were the ones that were rescued. I remember some of these men had been floating on the open sea for days, clinging to pieces of wood, when the rescue boats saved them. Their fingers had frozen from the tight grip with which they'd hung on for their lives; they wouldn't unfurl, wouldn't unclench. When they were brought to the Trivandrum General Hospital, the first thing we had to ensure was that they were warm. The staff realized they didn't have enough blankets, so we spoke to the district collector, who sourced adequate blankets for everyone.

The fishing community is tenacious; their livelihoods depend on it. They believed their relationship with the sea is based on faith and trust. And for these people at that moment, having been through the shock of losing their friends, watching the sea turn against them, and holding on for dear life with little hope that they would make it, the trauma was unbearable. They were incoherent and in a manic state. Crying out, trying to run out of the hospital, their minds were replaying their ordeal. I remember one man telling me the waves looked as tall as a multi-storey building to him, and they were at the bottom, looking up at the sea closing in on them. They were stuck in that situation, unable to let go. We understood that and organized groups of mental health volunteer workers to counsel the survivors and their families to help them recover from their trauma. But it would probably be years before they really could.

The rescue operation was manned by the chief minister himself and every department was involved. Once they were rescued the survivors became the responsibility of the health department, and all involved took on that role with a lot of compassion. It was the first time, under my watch at least, that I was seeing our system and its people in an emergency. Doctors and nurses did all-nighters taking care of the survivors, coaxing them over and over again through their trauma. The hospital staff tried to ensure the rescued fisherfolk had whatever they needed or liked, to ease their pain as much as possible. Many of the survivors and their families were not used to eating vegetarian food, so we made adjustments to ensure the meals included meat. I learned from observing the fallout of that huge storm that no matter what you do at a policy level, everything comes down to the people who are at the front lines and how they take on the challenges of a situation. I cannot commend our people enough for how they dealt with the survivors of Ockhi, and with every grave situation that came after that.

Even before we'd completely dealt with the aftermath of Ockhi, Kerala was overwhelmed by the floods of August 2018. Torrential rain isn't new to our parts, but all fourteen districts of Kerala were affected by severe monsoonal rainfall that year. While they were impacted to different extents, there was severe loss of property throughout the state. Declared a Level 3 Calamity – which means a calamity of a severe nature – it was the worst flood the state had seen since what is called the Great Flood of 1924.

In Malayalam the strongest period of the monsoon is called perumazhakkalam, or the season of relentless rain. In 2018, for days on end, the skies just poured down water. The lowland areas began to get flooded, landslides affected the hillsides, the dams filled up, and large parts of the population were at risk. The floodwaters rose very rapidly and enveloped everything seemingly overnight; lakes and rivers breached their banks so completely that villages and towns went under water. People were forced to seek refuge on their roof terraces or leave their homes on boats that plied through erstwhile roadways. The entire government was called into action by the chief minister. One department cannot ensure the functioning of so many areas of public life when there is a disaster of this magnitude. In fact, even the government isn't enough. With a seemingly impossible task at hand, one of the first things the chief minister did was ask the fishing community for help in rescuing people from flooded areas. Their work was so crucial and effective that he declared them Kerala's own army. From housewives to college students and everyone in between, people from parts of the state that weren't affected as badly reacted spontaneously, helping one another, rescuing, gathering resources and ensuring everyone had basic necessities and food.

Though the rain abated, the waters remained, stagnating in many parts of the state, and there were fears of a torrent of communicable diseases. Dead carcasses, and pools of water could become breeding grounds for mosquitoes, which could spread dengue, H1N1, etc. In places with dirty, stagnating water, diseases like leptospirosis and cholera were almost guaranteed. The doctors had a suggestion: administer doxycycline prophylaxis, wherein high-risk populations take doxycycline every day for a period of time to prevent infections. Did we have enough of the medicine to distribute to almost 1 crore people? It had to be given to everyone living in areas under water and those who had waded through water for long periods. All the volunteers at the camps, all camp residents – people whose homes had been submerged – and everyone who was part of the government's health squad, needed the dose. So, we began collecting doxycycline tablets and distributed them at the relief camps.

Despite these efforts, a few people died of leptospirosis. When we checked we realized they had not taken the medicine as directed. We understood that some people were just ignoring the advice, and since they weren't sick it wasn't easy for them to understand the importance of taking the medication. So we organized a squad of healthcare workers, armed with packets of biscuits, bottles of water and doxycycline tablets. They would give people the biscuits and the pill together with a bottle of water, and make sure they swallowed the tablet. It was a mission. And because it was conducted with that level of seriousness, there were no acute outbreaks of disease. When a disease doesn't happen it's just a footnote, but what if it had spread and added to the body count? We lost almost 500 people in the floods, and if there had been a disease outbreak, the outcome would have been even worse. People would have cursed us.

I visited the camps throughout Kerala during those weeks. I often feel very uneasy and disturbed just sitting in my office in the capital city, getting information on the phone, during such times. I need to go see for myself whether things are moving according to plan. So, I went to as many places as I could.

The flood caused more than Rs 40,000 crore worth of damages, destroying roads, homes, hospitals, schools and public infrastructure. The rebuilding of the state after this disaster was extremely difficult. In the absence of adequate assistance from the central government, the chief minister put out a call for donations to the Chief Minister's Distress Relief Fund (CMDRF), and people from across the country and the world responded to help the state.

On the ground, with all the different departments of government working together, the health department started a programme of chlorination and spraying to eliminate mosquitoes across the state as soon as the waters began to recede. Many waterbodies had been contaminated by sewage or other kinds of impurities brought in by the water and silt, so cleaning water sources was a key activity. The entire system worked in tandem, and I think that is the only reason we were able to come out of that nightmare fairly swiftly. When the Union Health Minister J.P. Nadda came to visit after the flood, at a media briefing he commended us for a job well done – for anticipating disease outbreaks and preventing a health crisis. This was despite the political ramifications of applauding a rival political party's good work. When you hear praise from unexpected quarters it is even more heartening.

I also understood from these experiences that we are stronger than we give ourselves credit for. Sometimes when the worst thing you can imagine happens, your instinct to fight and to work out solutions kicks in – and you survive.

11

Taming Nipah

It was the week of 17 May 2018. The LDF government had just completed two years in office, and there were several big functions planned to commemorate the anniversary. In between, on 19 May, the CPI(M) had organized the inauguration of the Nayanar Academy, an institution to honour the late former chief minister of Kerala, Comrade E.K. Nayanar. It was such an important moment that CPI(M) General Secretary Sitaram Yechury was to be present for the occasion in Kannur, as was the chief minister and many others. Another milestone coming up then, especially in the history of Kerala's health sector, was on 20 May. The Cochin Cancer Research Centre was a long-held collective dream that we'd finally managed to kick-start by getting Rs 350 crore sanctioned through the KIIFB. Dr Moni Kuriakose, a renowned cancer expert, was confirmed to join as its managing director, the tender had been issued for this mega project, and the chief minister was going to lay the foundation stone of the hospital. As minister for health, I was meant to preside over this important event.

But by late evening on 19 May, I was far too anxious to look forward to any of these things. I had received a call from the minister for labour and excise, T.P. Ramakrishnan. Three members of one family residing in his constituency, Perambra, in Kozhikode appeared to be suffering from some unusual illness. A young man named Salih, his father Moosa and another family member, Mariyam, had been admitted to Kozhikode's Baby Memorial Hospital, a private hospital, exhibiting similar symptoms of high fever, headache and encephalitis; they were in a serious condition. Even more worryingly, my colleague told me that just two weeks before, Salih's elder brother Sabith had passed away of the same series of symptoms while admitted at the Kozhikode Medical College. Minister Ramakrishnan was of the opinion that as their illness seemed atypical, we should take immediate steps to understand the situation. I got hold of the district medical officer (DMO), Dr V Jayashree, and soon we knew something grave was underfoot.

Kerala has always been haunted by tropical diseases. Even though we've made great strides in dealing with many ailments, communicable tropical diseases like chikungunya, H1N1, dengue, malaria and various types of fevers are a constant threat. In 2017–18 we'd dealt with a dengue outbreak that also affected many of our neighbouring states. We fared well, the number of deaths in the state was relatively low, but we knew we had to be more vigilant, preventive and better prepared. From the moment we came to power in 2016, dealing with this problem had become an important goal for my ministry.

In January 2018, the health department began a year-long programme called Arogya Jagratha, or Health Vigilance, which sought to sensitize and educate the public, and to increase vigilance in the medical community. We put together a road map of activities, data and ways for different government departments that would have to strategically work together to combat these menaces. The docket of information tabulated twenty key communicable diseases

Kerala grapples with, a breakdown of the most vulnerable areas in every district, and a calendar of preventive activities. It also included a list of responsibilities and focus areas for the various departments that needed to exercise vigilance and implement clean-up measures – from animal welfare, education, local self-government to railways and fisheries – because we realized all government departments had to work together on this effort. So, we were already alert, but no matter what you draw up on paper, the success of an effort ultimately depends on individuals. Timing is the other vital factor in minimizing the fallout of an infection.

At Baby Memorial Hospital in Kozhikode, Salih's doctors were Dr Anoop and Dr Jayakrishnan. These young doctors were at the front line of the vital work of diagnosis. With infectious diseases, spotting something out of the ordinary is critical, but it is more difficult than it sounds. The peculiar series of symptoms, knowing that another son of the family had died recently with the same set of symptoms, and the rest of the family presenting the same way alerted the doctors. They suspected there was an unusual virus at play and acted immediately, setting in motion a set of events that possibly saved many families from terrible losses. The doctors sent the samples of their patients for further examination to the Manipal Institute of Virology (MIV), informing the DHS, Dr Saritha and the DMO Dr Jayashree about the situation. If there had been the slightest delay, this might have been a completely different story.

By the time the results came, Salih had passed away. The health department was now on high alert. I asked the health secretary Sadanandan to send Dr Saritha immediately to Kozhikode, and together with the labour minister, T.P. Ramakrishnan, they set up a rapid response team. On 19 May, at the event for Comrade Nayanar, I was extremely troubled. We were still awaiting test results from MIV, and my mind was furiously at work on the what-ifs. On the dais, I quietly updated the chief minister, and we both agreed it was best that I get to Kozhikode immediately.

Kozhikode is about 90 kilometres south of Kannur. It was past 5 p.m. when I set out. I asked Dr Saritha to convene a crisis meeting that evening, if possible after 8 p.m. when I was likely to get there, with all the heads of hospitals in Kozhikode, senior officials from the district medical college, the collector, police chief and other necessary officials. A strong defence in this kind of situation really depends on the advice you get from the right people; the more field experts we could get, the better off we were. En route I spoke to Dr Arun, the head of MIV who'd run the preliminary investigation on the virus. He said he'd found a virus that closely resembled the Nipah virus. 'There is something peculiar in the sample,' he said. Dr Arun was already headed to Kozhikode as well, about half an hour away from where I was. He rang me again a little later. 'It is confirmed. It is the Nipah virus,' he said sombrely. To corroborate the finding, the health department had instructed that the samples be sent to Pune's National Institute of Virology (NIV). Dr Arun said we shouldn't make an announcement till NIV also confirmed the findings of the Manipal institute.

To have my fears realized was a huge jolt; for a second, I felt I couldn't breathe. Once I had a moment to accept this fact, I knew there was nothing for it: we had to start working on this post-haste. My first call was to the chief minister to give him an update; then I rang Rajeev. At this point, I didn't know much about this virus or what to expect. That two healthy young men should have died from it in such quick succession told me what lay ahead if things got out of hand. A Google search showed the virus came up seasonally in various parts of the world, and it was very infectious.

By the time I reached the government guest house in Kozhikode, Dr Saritha and Dr Jayashree were ready to begin the crisis meeting.

I should note that we still didn't have confirmation from NIV that the virus was indeed Nipah. But given the evidence that it was infectious and deadly, we decided that all hospitals in the district must immediately adopt the necessary measures to identify and combat the illness. Segregation was key: people coming with fever were to be directed to a separate queue at hospitals; anyone with tricky symptoms had to be isolated. The Kozhikode Medical College would immediately prepare to treat patients exhibiting the most severe symptoms, with small hospitals sending their complicated cases to the medical college hospital. With Drs Arun and Gafoor, a microbiologist from Chennai Apollo Hospital, who understood the behaviour of these kinds of infections, and under the guidance of the health secretary, Dr Saritha and her team created a scientifically sound road map. It was past 9.30 p.m. when we finished our deliberations. A throng of media had gathered outside the guest house by then.

In that instant I didn't think it was right to hide the truth from people. I told the press an unusual virus had surfaced in Kozhikode's Chengarothu village, and we were taking strict preventive measures to control the infection. One person asked which virus it was. 'We can't say for sure till the NIV confirms the nature of the virus,' was my response. 'But we're not waiting to know,' I stressed. Our key messages were: the health department is on alert; report the seriousness of the situation but please don't scare the public.

It had been a long day, begun early in one district and ending in another. The next morning, on 20 May, the chief minister was going to lay the foundation of the Cochin Cancer Research Centre. I had to be there, but I had to be in Kozhikode too. I decided to head to Kochi immediately, preside over the event, and hurry back as soon as it was done. The Pune lab would likely give us a confirmation or negate our worries by then. I remember that late-night car ride particularly well, because it was my first as minister in that sort of a state: of uncertainty combined with deep worry. At that time, this type of a panic situation was new to me. 'If it's Nipah, what will we do?' I kept thinking. The state was used to chikungunya, dengue and such, but a virus that affects the brain within a few hours and kills even healthy young people was terrifying. Could Kerala's health sector really deal with something so virulent? My mind kept racing but I was exhausted, and I fell asleep somewhere in between. By the time we got to the government guest house in Kochi, it was past 2.30 a.m. I didn't know then that there would be many more difficult, long and worrying nights ahead in the near and long term.

I was completely distracted through the event at the Cochin Cancer Research Centre. I must have called Dr Saritha more than ten times asking for an update. In my mind, I had decided it was Nipah, but till we had the results we couldn't move forward with confidence. By lunchtime we knew. NIV confirmed Salih's samples showed he'd been infected by the Nipah virus.

At this point, the main job for our team was to try to identify the experience of Nipah in other countries. Bangladesh, Malaysia, Singapore and Siliguri in India had gone through traumatic Nipah infections. It was categorized as an emerging zoonotic disease. The World Organisation for Animal Health defines an emerging disease as 'a new infection resulting from the evolution or change of an existing pathogen or parasite resulting in a change of host range, vector, pathogenicity or strain; or the occurrence of a previously unrecognised infection or disease'.[1] Reading the literature about the discovery of the virus gave my team a pretty accurate picture of how bad it could get if left undetected. In that moment, when people are dying of a mysterious, painful illness, without clear causes, without preventive measures or cure, fear rules over everything. The movie *Contagion* was inspired by the first manifestation of this virus in Malaysia in 1998. Kerala's Nipah crisis was also captured later on film in the movie *Virus* by Malayali director Aashiq Abu. Both convey perfectly the creeping fear that is created in such situations.

In 1998, in three provinces of Malaysia, more than 200 people manifested symptoms that authorities initially believed to be Japanese encephalitis. That is a mosquito-borne infection and the health authorities took measures to control the mosquito population. But, of course, those efforts proved futile and people kept falling ill and dying. In early 1999, months after the first infections were reported, a Malaysian virologist named Dr Chua Kaw Beng identified a new RNA virus, part of the Henipavirus genus. He later recalled that when he realized what he was seeing glimmering under the microscope lens was a new highly infectious strain, he felt the blood drain from his face. Once the virus had been identified and symptoms mapped, experts realized that this disease, which is as deadly as the Ebola virus, attacks the brain system, causing the onset of encephalitis and therefore has a 70–100 per cent mortality rate. This infection could bring down even healthy young people like a ton of bricks. The new virus was named Nipah, as a reference to the Nipah River Village, or Kampung Sungai Nipah, in Malaysia, where the first infection occurred.

Nipah usually manifests in fruit bats and jumps species from bats to pigs and possibly other domesticated animals. But it can go from animals to human beings, from person to person, and from animal to animal. Anyone interacting with an infected person is very likely to quickly get infected themselves. Consuming fruits that had been bitten into by infected fruit bats, or coming in contact with secretions of any infected creature can infect an individual. But the incubation period is between five and 14 days, so it takes a while for an infected person to manifest the range of symptoms. Fever, headaches, dizziness, severe cough and delirium are common symptoms. At the same time, stomach pain, nausea, fatigue and sight problems can also show up. There were cases where victims ended up in a coma within two days of showing symptoms. And there were patients who were diagnosed with encephalitis, which affected the brain and proved fatal.

During the Malaysian outbreak, once the nature of the virus had been identified, they traced the route of the infection from bats to pigs and from there to humans, so the authorities culled the area's pig population. Abattoirs were virus-producing factories, the newspapers declared. But by then more than a hundred people had died. The infection showed up in Singapore around the same time; there, some families were wiped out entirely. In 2000 Bangladesh lost hundreds of citizens to a Nipah surge. Bangladesh had one more wave of deadly Nipah infections in 2004. It took months for them to identify fruit bats as the source of the infection.

In 2020, the results of a six-year study of the Nipah virus were published in the *Proceedings of the National Academy of Sciences of the United States of America (PNAS)*:

> Our data and previous experiments show that henipaviruses can be shed orally, urogenitally, in feces, and in birthing fluids. This suggests that multiple mechanisms for transmission are possible, including mutual grooming, fighting, mating, exposure to excreta or birthing fluids, and ingestion of food contaminated by saliva. Roost size also increases seasonally during mating and birthing periods, which the fitted models suggest would increase transmission.[2]

In every country, the route of infection, and how the virus jumped species, differed. In Malaysia, the infection was first detected in pigs and probably spread to other animals and humans through fruits contaminated with bat excreta. In Bangladesh, areas with large date palm cultivation were found to have sap contaminated with the virus, and because of the association with agriculture, there is almost an annual outbreak of Nipah infections there in areas that have come to be called the 'Nipah belt'. In India, Siliguri in West Bengal first reported a case of Nipah infection, which killed many people.

The strain of the virus detected in Kerala was the same as the one in Bangladesh. So we were dealing with a virus that didn't have a cure yet, and carried a terrifying mortality rate. Our only sign of hope and optimism: Kerala had detected the infection in its earliest stages.

At the time, Nipah was the biggest challenge I'd faced as Kerala's health minister. Sitting in my car, on the way back to Kozhikode, the weight of what the result meant, the responsibility I had, settled like a stone in my head. But the thing about bad news is that once you have it, you are forced to confront the situation, and in taking action, there's some solace. The potential death rate meant only one thing: we couldn't afford to fail.

I rang the chief minister. We agreed that I needed to be in Kozhikode for as long as required. I spoke to the health secretary as well. He'd already considered the next steps. We both agreed that the most efficient and appropriate protocol we could follow was that drawn up by the WHO for Ebola. By the time I reached Kozhikode, a response team led by Dr Saritha, the principal of the district medical college Dr Rajendran, Dr Naveen of the National Health Mission, and others had already created a combat road map; they were waiting to take me through it. Having that team of dedicated doctors, experts who backed their ideas with science and understanding of the infection, was reassuring. We turned the government guest house into a permanent control room, with a call centre to man incoming information and address people's concerns. A room right next to the control room would become my home for the next 40 days till the Nipah crisis abated.

The Indian Council of Medical Research (ICMR) had also dispatched a team to assist. Together, we built a more comprehensive road map that included a clinical management protocol, containment, prevention and a methodology to safely take samples from potential Nipah patients. We drew up a chain of command, with Dr Saritha as the nodal officer in charge of issuing directions. Kozhikode District Collector U.V. Jose and the entire health set-up of the district – from the medical college down to district and taluk hospitals, PHCs and private hospitals – were an integral part of the road map. Other public departments – forest, police and revenue – were called as well, so everyone understood their department's specific responsibility. We set about organizing 24/7 call centres and recruited teams of young people and trained them with information so they could man it.

What stays with me from that period is the sense of urgency we all felt. Having entered politics because I believed that would give me opportunities to make a difference, this was the first time responsibility was mingled with fear and anxiety. Yet, when I looked around that war room I strongly felt we were doing our absolute best – and I held on to that feeling. It was manned by efficient officers and an army of experienced doctors – including the National Centre for Disease Control (NCDC) team led by Dr S.K. Singh, Kozhikode Medical College Principal Dr Rajendran, Superintendent Dr Sajith, microbiologist Dr Chandini Sajeevan, and epidemiologist Dr Indu from the Trivandrum Medical College – leading a vast number of young doctors and volunteers. District Collector U.V. Jose was on call 24/7 coordinating work between departments, and answering every worried phone call he received.

Not everyone thought we were doing a perfect job, of course. I was asked why we weren't able to identify the source virus when it claimed its first victim, Sabith; that marked a major failure on the part of the health department, some people declared. In fact, identifying the virus when it had claimed two lives was the most important factor in our overall success in beating this infection. No other affected region, in India or outside, had managed to get such an early start.

When the crisis began, the focus was on one district, and ground zero was the little picturesque village of Chengarothu. Against the advice of my team, I decided to go there and meet the villagers. We knew that many of the residents wanted to leave the place, and I thought it was important to go there and speak to them directly.

Kerala is the most densely populated state in India. We have 860 people per one square kilometre (the national average is 430). Most parts of the state are semi-urban areas. Even a village is not a completely rural outpost. They are usually places with urban facilities and some of nature's best offerings, set together in such a way that life just slows down. And where there are trees, there are bound to be other inhabitants as well: fruit bats, civet cats, mongoose, snakes, fireflies, cicadas, monitor lizards; the ecosystem is always teeming with variety.

Chengarothu is a place like that. And that summer, the jackfruit trees were already fruiting, mangoes were blossoming, the air was hot and sweet and sticky. As anyone who's plucked a fruit off a tree knows, bats, ants, civet cats and squirrels know when fruits are ripe for the picking. Part of the reason why Nipah is seasonal is that it occurs during the time of year when trees are laden with fruits. It was difficult to imagine that such bountiful nature could harbour any sort of danger. When Minister T.P. Ramakrishnan, the MLA from that constituency, and I got to Chengarothu, you could tell there was something amiss because the roads were almost deserted. A village has its own sounds – cycle bells, the occasional bike, public bus, calls of tradespeople, roosters, crows; despite the heat at all times, and especially in summer, there's always activity. In Chengarothu, it was as though the people had retreated; a disconcerting silence had settled over the place. Losing two members of its little community, another three people from the same family critically ill in hospital, the residents of this small place were understandably nervous.

On the other hand, the village's panchayat office was thronging with people when we arrived. They had many questions, fears; most wanted to leave the place. We understood by then that there were measures people could adopt, and I believed seeing two government ministers there would reassure them that the air itself wasn't contaminated. We wanted to help them understand that taking precautions, without succumbing to fear, was key to getting through this. Our team consisted of central and state experts. They explained our findings thus far: that only fruit bats, at a certain time of year, carry the virus and spread it; that the infection passes on to people if someone consumes a fruit bitten by these animals since it spreads through spit and other fluids. That person-to-person infection only occurs through close contact so if people kept a distance of 2 metres from anyone suspected of an infection, they'd be safe. We admitted there was no cure yet. But if a cure or treatment was identified, we would get it to Kerala. We met the local public health nurses, health inspectors, ASHA and Anganwadi workers to instruct them on how to keep track of information in their wards and protect themselves in case anyone was suspected of infection. It was extremely important to me that the people of the village knew we were on full alert, that the health ministry wasn't just a vague, notional entity far away in Thiruvananthapuram but a team of public servants working on their behalf.

At a broader level the only strategy was prevention and containment. The crisis management team understood from the beginning that it was important to track the contacts of people who had been infected. Where did they come into contact with the virus? Who did they meet and where did those people go then? We had to investigate the network of relationships between individuals who were not necessarily related to one another. For instance, Sabith was the index case, so the contact-tracing team set about creating a list of the people he'd come in touch with. These included the people who: (a) took him to the hospital; (b) the staff that took care of him; (c) any other patients who were in the outpatient section while he was there; and (d) the staff and any patients who were at the CT scan department where Sabith was tested. With this list of primary contacts, we knew the identities of people who could potentially be carriers of the disease and therefore they were all quarantined. From this list of primary contacts, the team derived the secondary contact list, and these people were put under surveillance.

One of the snags in contact tracing is that not everyone is upfront about information when they're asked. So the medical team had to personally go to people's houses and even places of work to speak with them directly. The process often required a lot of cajoling and convincing. The team doing that work was not made up of investigators; they were medical experts hunting for clues in a social haystack, but some of them truly rose to the occasion. There was a young woman called Seethu Ponnuthampi, a postgraduate student of community medicine at the Kozhikode Medical College, who quickly acquired the nickname 'CID' (Crime Investigation Department) for her ability to pry details out of people through questioning.

Through geomapping the contact list, we knew the places where infections had occurred and then mapped how many were connected with positive cases in those areas. Every day, we checked the list for people who were at the end of their incubation period; if they were clear, a new list was formulated. Consistent daily reporting was crucial. It told us how many people had moved to isolation wards, the number of ambulances and ventilators available, the number of drivers on duty, and whether ambulances had all the requisite emergency apparatus.

And of course daily reports covered the number of tests, positivity rate, sample collection numbers, and assessment of the transportation and collection of samples.

Meanwhile, other guidelines and the structure to handle the situation were being laid. The Kozhikode Medical College, as the district's paramount public health institution, was to be the main treatment centre. It had the room and necessary facilities to create isolation wards. The institution's principal, Dr Rajendran, felt it was important we communicate with the staff directly and allay their fears. So we called a meeting with everyone. The doctors, nurses and housekeeping staff filed into the conference hall, their faces reflecting their trepidation. There was a feeling there that as the community of people set to care for these patients, they were likely courting death. After all, they were people with their own families and responsibilities. One young doctor spoke of his pregnant wife and how he might have to send her away to keep her safe. We reassured them saying we'd make all efforts to ensure they were all safe. Their workspace was about to turn into a crisis centre so it was a completely understandable worry. However, it was a responsibility only that team and such an institution could take on. I was relieved when the nursing superintendent, Sheena, piped up and said they'd already started their training to receive high-risk patients.

The medical college staff were at high risk of infection from their patients, so it was absolutely critical that we train them to protect themselves, their families and others. We started mock drills and training for everyone, from doctors to cleaning staff, involving relearning of safety protocols, the process of donning and doffing personal protective equipment (PPE), and how to deal with patients and their families. The model we created here in Kozhikode would come to be repeated a short time later when this infection reared its head in the nearby district of Malappuram.

Nipah was a society-wide problem, but the solution wasn't in the hands of everyone. In that crisis, our most competent defence lay with the medical community: doctors, nurses, attendants, hospital housekeeping staff, etc. Their awareness, alertness, care and safety constituted our most effective armour. It was crucial that they remain confident and calm. In every meeting I had with medical teams, I spent much of my time reassuring and canvassing people, because no matter what policy decisions we made, the execution and care came down to the staff. So the thought of losing even one of our own to that infection was unconscionable. But that fear was realized when Lini Sajeesh, a young nurse at the Perambra Hospital, died of Nipah.

When Sabith, the index patient, was brought to the Perambra taluk hospital, Lini was on duty. So, as a primary contact, she was placed in quarantine. The incubation period of the virus is about two weeks, and in most cases symptoms develop within five to eight days after the infection. While she was still in quarantine, a few days after Sabith's death, Lini got a fever. This extraordinary young woman, who found herself in a crisis she'd never prepared for, acted swiftly, focusing singularly on the well-being of her family and her co-workers. Lini's husband was working in Dubai at the time and she had small children at home. In the ambulance on the way to the isolation ward at the medical college, she made a video call to tell her husband she wasn't well, but didn't mention how serious it was. Her father had passed away some years ago, and she refused to allow her mother and two sisters to see her in the ICU. She wouldn't allow any of the hospital staff near her either. As her temperature rose, this medical professional knew things were getting serious.

Feeling that her life was slipping away, she wrote a letter to her husband Sajeesh. I add the translated version here because it speaks to the enormous burden that hospital staff always carry. Risks that are tremendously personal and potentially devastating. 'Sajeeshetta,

I'm almost on the way,' she wrote. 'I don't think I will be able to see you. Sorry. Please take good care of our children. Please take Lavan and Kunju to the Gulf with you. They shouldn't end up alone like our father did. With lots of love. Kiss.' She passed away shortly after writing that letter. Though Sajeesh was in Kerala at the time of her passing, the two did not get to see each other one last time. One of the most difficult phone calls I've had to make in my life is the one I made to that young man to tell him his wife had died. In addition to giving him this devastating news, I had to also convey to him one of the cruellest aspects of the situation: that he wouldn't even be able to see his wife's body because the cremation had to be done in isolation as per protocol. Sajeesh accepted all that pain calmly. I remember I didn't sleep at all that night. It felt as though I'd lost someone close to me.

Lini was only twenty-eight years old. Hers is the story of hundreds of thousands of young Malayali women who work in India and elsewhere in the nursing profession. It is also the tale of a young couple who lived in two different countries, but were both working towards making a better life for their family. While Sajeesh was in Dubai, Lini and her two little boys lived with her family in Kozhikode. At the time she got sick, Lini had worked at the taluk hospital for six years.

Losing this dedicated young woman was a turning point for me. What we were asking of our staff, the danger they were putting themselves in – all this felt like a tremendous weight. Despite all the reassurances we gave, what could I really guarantee when these people went to their jobs every morning? I had no answer. The only thing we thought we could do was ensure that Lini's story didn't fade into a statistic. The health department instituted the 'Sister Lini Memorial' award to reward an outstanding healthcare worker. We hoped her family could take some solace from knowing how thankful we were for her, and that her colleagues and the nursing fraternity all over the state would know that we understood the enormity of the task confronting them.

Even after seeing what had happened to Lini, her nursing colleagues, doctors, cleaning staff all went back into those isolation wards to take care of their patients. Many of them were doing this work after only a few days of training, because this was an epochal crisis that we hadn't seen for generations. The slightest error while using a PPE could result in an infection. That is a fact, but you have to understand what that means in the day-to-day. We're talking about a crisis born during Kerala's tropical summer heat when temperatures can rise up to 35 ℃. When a person has donned a PPE kit, which is a polyester-woven material, the temperature inside the kit goes up. If that kit is on for, say, an hour or two, an individual sweats so much that the water flows down their forehead and even gets into the eyes. Once the kit is on, a doctor or nurse cannot have a drink, use the bathroom or even breathe easily for several hours, especially in critical care and isolation units. We'd heard the story of a nurse who was tending to patients during the Ebola crisis in Africa: she put a finger through her mask to wipe her eyes, later caught the infection and died. Was it because of that small infraction? We'll never know. But it is entirely reasonable that a person would feel compelled to try to alleviate their discomfort while trapped in a PPE.

A single individual who worked in close proximity with a Nipah patient had to change their kit up to three times a day. In the early days, before we completely understood the route of infection, even staff members who weren't in direct contact with Nipah patients were instructed to wear safety kits. That of course meant that as the crisis escalated, we were at risk of running out of protective gear. Kerala Medical Services Corporation Limited (KMSCL) is a government-owned company that was set up in 2007 to serve as a central procurement agency for all essential drugs and equipment required by public healthcare institutions under the state's health department. KMSCL's managing director Navjot Ghosa and general manager Dr Dileep Kumar were quick to pull supplies of N95 masks and kits from wherever possible. I believe that a significant reason why we have been able to manage our health crises without desperation is that we are self-reliant in many aspects of our product and service delivery.

Wherever there were gaps, or when we thought stocks may dwindle, we reached out to the vast network of Malayalis in the healthcare segment worldwide and they helped generously. VPS Healthcare chief Dr Shamseer Vayalil dispatched materials worth almost Rs 2 crore on a special chartered aircraft from the United Arab Emirates. Similarly, we received help from Dr Azad Moopen of Aster DM Healthcare and several others. Over the weeks, we were able to refine the processes we'd implemented at the beginning. We recruited more people so that the staff in the isolation wards could get enough rest in between their shifts, patients with fever coming into the OP were segregated, and those with symptoms were quickly moved to the ICU. I really cannot imagine how this crisis would have panned out if our medical community hadn't shown the consistent courage that was essential to deal with it.

Just as things in Kozhikode were getting under control, new cases showed up in Malappuram, about 50 kilometres north. The realization that the virus had crossed districts meant that the state was at a high risk of this infection getting out of hand. Remember, it was still at a 70–100 per cent mortality rate. Three patients who were brought to Kozhikode for treatment from Malappuram died of the disease. We had no information on the contacts of people who'd met some of these patients and then travelled out to other places. It was clear that we had to open another war front in Malappuram.

Between District Collector Amit Meena and DMO Dr Sakeena, they were able to quickly round up MLAs, chief medical officers of the main hospitals, the medical college's community medicine head, and everyone we needed to create and institute a plan of action. Together, it was decided that suspected Nipah patients would be taken to the Kozhikode Medical College, which already had a functioning isolation wing.

What we discovered was that the infections in Malappuram were also related to the index patient, Sabith. At the time he was at the Kozhikode Medical College for a CT scan, these people from Malappuram happened to be at that same location. They then developed symptoms later. When we realized that the source of the infection was the same, there was tremendous relief. On the other hand, we now had to consider a whole new network of contacts.

We made arrangements for more ventilators and took over another building in the Kozhikode Medical College to make room for additional isolation wards and special care units. The plan of action to combat the spread of the virus really boiled down to good management of resources to ensure the safety of patients and the medical staff. Of course there were staff members who backed out of having to do anything with these Nipah care units, but at the same time an army of humanitarians worked overnight to create almost fifty isolation wards, and emergency care units came up like magic.

The phones in the call centres were constantly ringing. Some had our personal numbers and rang on those. People called with fears, suspicions, worries, questions. There were times when someone would ring from another district to say that an individual with Nipah-like symptoms was being brought to the Kozhikode Medical College. In every single instance, no matter what hour of the night, Dr Rajendran, Dr Sajith, Dr Kuriakose, Dr Sreejayan, Dr Ranjini and their team would be at the hospital to receive the patient. With each case would come the waiting. It felt endless. Waiting to get the results of tests, waiting to assess the contact lists, waiting to see if someone got better.

I worried constantly about my team, starting from volunteers to Dr Saritha, Dr Jayashree, Dr Arun, Dr Asha, Dr Naveen and everyone else involved in managing the crisis.

On 4 June the chief minister called for the first all-party meeting to discuss the situation. The health department provided an update; of course there were opinions and counter-opinions, but we had assurances of cooperation from across the political landscape. Everyone agreed that families with Nipah patients should be given assistance; in addition, 2,400 families in Kozhikode and 150 families in Malappuram would be given free rations. Opposition leader Ramesh Chennithala praised the efforts of the health ministry and assured us of the support of the Opposition in fighting the crisis. In the coming days we would call upon a number of our legislative and political colleagues for support on a broad spectrum of things – from combating misinformation, allaying public fear, to working with community leaders on the fallout of Nipah deaths. The central government and the health ministry under J.P. Nadda, too, were extremely attentive, offering all help necessary. Central Health Secretary Preeti Sudhan often checked in and we were able to use the help of experts from ICMR, NIV, NCDC and the National Institute of Epidemiology (NIE).

By mid-June, nine people who were in quarantine showed symptoms and ten people had died of the disease in both districts. For families, the most difficult aspect of dealing with the death of their loved ones was not being able to say a final goodbye. Every single body, including that of Sister Lini, was cremated at the city corporation's gas crematorium, with extreme caution. When it came to Salih's, Moosa's and Mariyam's bodies, cremation went against their beliefs, so an alternative had to be found. We found that the WHO recommends a procedure called 'deep burial', where the body is buried at more than six feet and within a short distance of the place of death. We identified a burial ground attached to a mosque near the Kozhikode Medical College. The WHO recommends that in such cases, each body is double-bagged: first covered in a thick polythene bag secured so tightly that no air escapes, then secured in a second bag treated with bleaching powder to kill off any possible microbes. Local leaders across the political spectrum spoke to the family and community leaders, and helped secure everyone's cooperation and agreement with our plan. As a concession, we allowed a few people – less than ten – to stand a considerable distance away and pray as each burial took place.

The people transporting the bodies had to be very cautious. Each of them had to wear a body bag-like suit made of polypropylene plastic, a special face mask and goggles. Afterwards, these clothing items were immersed in sodium hypochlorite solution to bleach any potential microbes out and then burned. The city's health officer Dr R.S. Gopakumar, who was part of the Nipah task force, took charge of this arduous task – from directly taking the bodies from the morgue till each one was respectfully laid to rest. With him, there was Seema, a scientist at NIV, and two temporary workers, Shashidharan and Rajesh. Despite all these precautions, when people heard bodies were being shifted out of the hospital for burial, there was a little gathering of protestors outside the cemetery. District Collector U.V. Jose had to get involved to placate them.

All the victims' final belongings, every piece of clothing, even the bed linen they used, were first put in an autoclave to sterilize them and then burned. There was an image on the front page of *Mathrubhumi* newspaper one morning, showing Shashidharan and Rajesh, clad in their PPE kits, walking through the monsoon rain as they carried the victims' personal belongings on a stretcher. It is a picture of the human condition in all its frailty and helplessness, but also of the tremendous courage and empathy that people are capable of.

While we managed the infection rate, there was a simultaneous hunt for medication. Our search first brought us to a tablet called Ribavirin. It hadn't been proven as a complete cure but we administered it to all the Nipah patients and it offered some respite from the symptoms. At the same time we heard about a human monoclonal antibody (m102.4) medication under consideration in Australia. We understood that this treatment hadn't been patented and its effectiveness for human beings had not been established yet. In Australia they'd successfully used it to treat a Henipavirus infection in horses; there were also anecdotes that fourteen people with Henipavirus infection there were given the treatment and all survived. We believed that in case there was a surge in the caseload then this medication might become useful. Rajeev Sadanandan reached out to Manoj Mohan, a friend of his based in America; he had some connection with the Australian scientist Robert Forder who discovered this antibody. We found out that the state government of Queensland had stocks of the medicine. But in order to get it to Kerala, the request had to be made through the central government. We then rushed to the chief minister to explain the situation and ask if we could find a way to expedite the process of getting it here. He was extremely supportive and immediately dispatched a letter to the Centre for approval. With the help of Union Health Minister J.P. Nadda, the central drug controller issued a no-objection certificate for importing the drug within a day. That is a process that usually takes up to four months. The medicine was then brought to Kochi by air immediately.

By the time we had this medicine in our hands, there were only two surviving patients and both were on Ribavirin: Ajanya, a nineteen-year-old nursing student, and Ubeesh, a Malappuram resident. Ajanya had caught the infection while treating a patient. Ubeesh's wife Shijitha was infected first, and she later died of the virus; we think he was infected via his wife. When the medical board met to discuss whether these two patients should be treated with the human monoclonal antibody (m102.4), the final decision was that since they were improving with Ribavirin, we shouldn't try a new drug on them. We can't be precisely sure of the factors that made the Ribavirin treatment protocol effective in these two people; perhaps the explanation is just their own immunity.

Overall, there were eighteen positive Nipah cases. Out of those, sixteen people died and two recovered. Sabith died before he was tested but because of the infections that resulted from him, we include that index case in the body count. Of the fourteen cases from Kozhikode, only Ajanya survived. In Malappuram, four people tested positive, with Ubeesh surviving the infection. A few months after the crisis had abated, the health secretary Sadanandan and a doctor published an article in *Lancet* magazine, and that article became a point of controversy. In it, they quoted a different set of numbers. They wrote that twenty-three people were infected with Nipah and twenty-one died. Kerala's 9 p.m. debate club on cable television had a field day when this piece was published. The government is lying, hiding the truth; the list of accusations was long and complicated. Actually, the explanation is very simple: since they were writing a research paper, the authors had included probable Nipah deaths that took place at the hospital at the same time as Sabith's. Before Sabith died there were five other cases with some of the same symptoms at the medical college but these are only suspected; there is no proof those people had any direct contact with the index case, and they were never tested for the Nipah virus.

On 30 June, forty days after the crisis began, we knew we were in the clear. To have even two people survive the infection meant the world to us. However, we understood that there remained considerable trepidation among the public, and for these two survivors, assimilation back into their lives might prove difficult. At the second all-party meeting where we declared Kerala free of Nipah, I announced my intention of meeting Ajanya and Ubeesh in the presence of the media that evening. I wanted to show the public that there was nothing to fear from interacting with them, especially when they'd tested negative for the virus four different times. A throng of us, including members of the Nipah task force and Ajanya's and Ubeesh's families, met in the corridor outside the isolation ward, where the two former patients had spent several days. Though people advised me to wear a PPE kit, I thought that would be completely counterproductive when we were trying to reintroduce these young people back to society without trepidation. So we met as we were, without any protective gear. It was after a long while that these two young people were able to do something so simple, so ordinary, yet it had seemed impossible. Ajanya was full of confidence and joy. She was eager to get back to her nursing training. Later in interviews Ajanya would talk of how much that meeting meant to her. She said she felt relieved when I interacted with them so closely and patted her on the back, as though things would now go back to the way they were. On the other hand, Ubeesh had lost his wife to the disease, and I could see the toll the despair and illness had taken on him.

But the healthcare system had prevailed under massive pressure. Doctors, nurses, contract staff, administration officials and everyone in the effort had banded together and beaten this virus, and pulled two people back from the brink. It was a major breakthrough for us. Nipah had swooped down on us without warning; I believe what helped us overcome the crisis was the speed and agility with which we responded. The steps taken to combat the crisis were expert approved, scientific and unified. One department, one person or even one team of individuals cannot deal with a situation like this. For instance, working together with the animal welfare and forest departments helped us conclude that the spread in Kerala had occurred through fruit bats. Some fifty-five bats in the area where Sabith lived were tested and some of them tested positive for Nipah. While there was no way to establish with absolute certainty how he was infected, we were told by neighbours and friends that the young man was very outdoorsy, fond of animals and often took care of different creatures. One presumes that perhaps he picked up a little bat and thereby caught the infection. It is common for small bats in particular to fall off trees and it is humane to put them back. He couldn't have imagined that his love for nature would prove so catastrophic.

Particularly in tropical regions like Kerala, the balance between human beings and other elements of nature is extremely important. It isn't a new discovery, and public health departments have been aware of it for a long time. Over the last several years many governments have come to understand the importance of looking at public health policy through the lens of the One Health approach, which emphasizes that animal health, human health and environmental health are intertwined and interdependent. It recognizes that we cannot expect to live healthy lives if the health of other species or the environment is compromised.

Nipah was also viral in other ways: with social media and WhatsApp, misinformation and fear spread as fast. In one instance a fake document carrying the insignia of the health department circulated online with a false message that attributed the spread of the Nipah virus to eating chicken. When we investigated the matter, the chap who posted it online first said he was only trying to reduce the price of chicken. But misinformation, especially during a crisis, isn't funny, so we had no choice but to initiate his arrest. Then there was the fake doctor on Facebook who claimed there was no virus, that it was just fake news. To prove the point, he uploaded a video of himself eating fruits he claimed had been damaged by bats. When the police got involved, he apologized and withdrew his claim. I felt the right way to combat these social media viruses, as it were, was to be completely transparent with information. So the health ministry released information to the media daily and updated its platforms such as the Arogya Jagratha Facebook page and mobile app. And in order to ensure the source of information was absolutely reliable, we – often I myself – conducted press meetings every evening with updates for the public. Having a straightforward televised briefing gave people a clear understanding of what was being done. This strategy would prove to be pivotal for the larger crisis we would face soon: the pandemic.

Natural disasters and disease notwithstanding, we continued working on the legislative and structural changes required to modernize our public healthcare system. A key component of the overhaul was the enactment of the Kerala Clinical Establishment (Registration and Regulation) Act, 2018. The central government had passed a similar piece of legislation in 2013, and we wanted to modify it in the Kerala context. The intention was to standardize the quality of care provided in private and government health-related establishments. This would mean setting benchmarks for the entire system. Starting in 2017, for more than a year, a team of experts had worked to create a draft of the legislation that could be presented to the public. It was passed in 2018, and the rules were prepared in accordance with the Act. The significant parts of that legislation were that institutions could not operate without registration, and in order to get the registration they had to meet certain quality checks of pricing, standards, hygiene, etc.

By 2019 I had been in the ministry for three years, and during that time I'd worked on all kinds of important matters with the health secretary Sadanandan and his team. Now, he was getting ready to retire from service. With the floods, Nipah and the changes we'd implemented in the healthcare system, we'd been trialled by fire, and I knew I could trust him implicitly. Working with someone for three years, particularly through a crisis, you understand the fabric of the person's character. In three years we took on many things and pulled off some outstanding successes. The late IAS officer Babu Paul wrote a column for the *Mathrubhumi* newspaper remarking that our working partnership was what had made the difference in Kerala's health sector. The political willpower of a minister combined with the acumen of a bureaucrat who understood the health sector – the Shailaja–Rajeev team, he called us.

But the sense of a team went beyond just Rajeev; that feeling of banding together as a unit extended to others in the ministry as well, such as the officials of the health directorate, department heads of the medical colleges, DMOs, district programme managers (DPMs) of the National Health Mission, and so many others in the network. Even during the most difficult times, my stress was greatly reduced because of the kind of people they were. This may sound clichéd but over those years we became a family. Whenever a situation cropped up, we went into a huddle to solve it. We disagreed, argued, I told them off, but there was an intimacy and understanding in the team. I could be stern knowing they understood where I was coming from. It is rare, and a privilege, that one gets to work with such a perceptive team, especially in government.

It was Rajeev who suggested Dr Rajan N. Khobragade should be his replacement as principal secretary for health. I'd thought of Dr V. Venu, who was an officer in the revenue department, and a very sincere and passionate officer. At the time there weren't enough senior IAS officers of additional chief secretary rank to choose from. I'd heard of Rajan. He was in the tax-department at the time. Rajeev said, 'He's a very sincere officer, hard-working, and most importantly, completely trustworthy.'

Another of Rajan's distinctions is that he is a trained medical doctor, which would prove to be extremely beneficial for us. He was a very methodical officer, who documented everything we did. Even if we were in the middle of an urgent matter, he'd make sure the junior officers were keeping the documents in order; the paperwork had to be shipshape. He created files that contained comprehensive information, so things were very standardized and systematic when he was there. Rajeev's and Rajan's styles were very different!

I was extremely grateful that with all my worries about the change of guard, I'd again landed a good officer I could rely on. After all, the health department's biggest challenge was yet to come.

12

A Deadlier Virus Strikes

The first I heard of COVID was in the newspaper – like everyone else. It must have been the middle of January 2020. Reported first in Wuhan, it was spreading fast through China. We learned that it was caused by a virus of the coronavirus family, which includes strains like Severe Acute Respiratory Syndrome (SARS) and Middle East Respiratory Syndrome (MERS). The mortality rate was lower than for Nipah but the infectivity rate was extremely high, and the symptoms were very similar to those of other influenza viruses. This new strain was being called the novel coronavirus or SARS-CoV-2 (SARS coronavirus 2). Later, the WHO would name it Corona Virus Disease 2019 or COVID-19. Viruses are cohabiting entities that can cause diseases stretching all the way from the common flu to more serious infections like COVID. There is a plethora of viruses that we haven't even discovered yet, and most are not likely to be dangerous. But when something causes an imbalance in nature and a virus becomes infectious, the results can be deadly, as with the Spanish Flu of 1918 in which some 50 million died.

After the experience with Nipah, every time someone mentioned an infectious disease, my antenna would go up. But in this particular case there was another reason. Kerala had a Wuhan connection. A year before, I'd met some medical students who had applied for an internship with the government. They were students from a medical university in Wuhan. It stuck with me because it was a Chinese city, and I hadn't realized till then that there was a contingent of Malayali students over there. When I read about this new disease in the newspaper and remembered our students in Wuhan, I called the health secretary, Rajan Khobragade, immediately. Rajan said we should be worried. Vacation season was starting in Wuhan, and during their holiday, Malayali students would be coming home to Kerala. What should we do? We were already planning a Nipah mock drill at that time, and we decided to also use it as a dry run for dealing with a new virus.

On 24 January we formed a rapid response team and decided to open a control room in the office of the director of health services, making the DHS the nodal officer for the control room. In the control room we created eighteen expert groups, which looked at various tasks that are part of the larger strategy, such as logistics, quarantine, isolation, contact tracing, etc. Good officers were picked from each district and we gave them specific roles; training started in hospitals all over the state. If the coronavirus arrives on a flight, what should we do? That was the context of our groundwork. At the time many people made fun of us. A viral infection was spreading in Wuhan, a city in China that no one had heard of at that time; most people didn't think it would ever become anyone else's problem. 'Why are you overreacting?' they asked. 'Are you looking for attention? We can deal with it when it comes, stop creating hype.' We heard all sorts of things, from criticism to bad suggestions. But we just went ahead and did what we thought we needed to.

By 26 January 2020 the Kerala health department had issued a circular titled 'nCorona Guidelines' which analysed all the information available till then about this new virus and enunciated response procedures. This document covered everything from safety protocols for collecting samples, pre-hospital preparedness, surveillance and contact-tracing guidelines, and standard operating procedures (SOPs) for field surveillance of asymptomatic passengers under home isolation; it even stated the protocol for sending daily health status of passengers under observation. Depending on whether one saw the glass as half-full or half-empty, you could say we were either prophetic or fearful, but the fact is that we were the first in the country to create a novel coronavirus combat plan, even though we were not sure then if a plan was required. One of the key components of the nCorona Guidelines was the 'Algorithm to be followed in case of suspected coronavirus cases'. It set out the procedures to be followed for all passengers whose travel originated in China.

Even though Kerala is a small state, given the vast number of Malayalis who live abroad, it has four airports. And we had medical teams at each one so that people could voluntarily declare any symptoms. On 27 January, a passenger flight arrived in Kochi. We already knew that some people on that flight were medical students from Wuhan. Airports come under the jurisdiction of the Airports Authority of India, and since the central government still hadn't declared universal contact tracing, we couldn't get the details of the passengers at the airport. But once the passengers came outside, the medical teams checked them. And because we did that, we found three symptomatic students. All of them were quarantined and tested for the novel coronavirus.

On 30 January at 7 p.m., I was participating in a programme in Thiruvananthapuram called 'Night Walk'. It was an initiative of the women and child development department, which was a part of my ministerial portfolio. We had started a women's empowerment programme called 'Be brave and go ahead'. Even in Kerala, there is a notion that it is dangerous, or even inappropriate, for women to be out alone very late. The Night Walk was meant to persuade women that it is their right to be outside whenever they wish; the time of day shouldn't be chosen for them. We began the walk from Martyrs' Square in central Thiruvananthapuram, heading for Gandhi Square about 2 kilometres away. I was walking at the head of the group when my personal mobile phone began to ring. I had told my staff to contact me immediately when the results came. The call was from the Thrissur DMO, Dr Reena. 'Madam, the sample has been identified as coronavirus,' she said. I remember that I immediately stopped walking, and the person next to me stopped as well. Even as we had prepared for the worst, I had been hoping the results would turn out to be negative. It was not to be. Kerala had become the first state in India to record a novel coronavirus infection.

I left the walk right there, telling T.V. Anupama, director of the social justice department, to take my place and keep going with the rest of the group. After calling Chief Minister Pinarayi Vijayan to update him and ask his permission to leave for Thrissur immediately, I returned to my residential quarters and told my personal assistant, Pramod P., to arrange travel to Thrissur. In a crisis, Pramod is always a clear thinker and able to work out simple, effective solutions for me. And he pointed out that in a car it takes more than six hours to traverse the distance of more than 270 kilometres from Thiruvananthapuram to Thrissur. At the time it was already 8 pm. He suggested an alternative: there was a flight to Kochi at 9.30 pm; if we took that we could travel to Thrissur – about 85 kilometres away – by road, getting there by midnight. I felt I should also notify the ministers from Thrissur district. So, while Pramod hunted for tickets, I spoke to A.C. Moideen, Sunil Kumar and Raveendranath. Two of the ministers said they'd come with me, while Raveendranath, who was in Kozhikode at the time, said he would travel from there. The health secretary Rajan Khobragade also accompanied me.

We didn't even have time to eat; we left straight away to catch the flight to Kochi. Before we boarded, I rang up the Thrissur Medical College principal and the DMO Dr Reena, and asked them to set up a meeting with all the key stakeholders in the district. By the time we reached Thrissur it was almost 12.15 a.m.; they were ready and waiting. The media, which had got a hint of the situation, was there too. I told them we'd brief them in the morning, but they said they'd wait.

There were more than sixty people at that meeting. It was really late but I think it was the adrenaline, from fear and expectation, that kept me going. On the one hand, we'd already dealt successfully with Nipah, so there was some clarity on how to get going with a response, but at the same time, this virus was highly contagious. My team was definitely more confident about how to move forward than when faced with Nipah: the practice and process established in 2018 guided them now.

We established expert groups that would monitor key functions. In order to create the Nipah protocol we'd looked at the Ebola protocol as a guide. Now, with COVID, we referenced the Nipah protocol, making changes based on what we already understood about the disease. The incubation period for both was almost the same; however, it was believed that Nipah was only transmitted from symptomatic patients, while it was said that COVID spread through asymptomatic carriers as well. That made COVID far more infectious. So we based the protocol and the SOPs on these factors. We were already hypothesizing how we'd deal with a situation of vast numbers of patients and increased pressure on hospital capacity.

The young medical student who tested positive had been admitted to the General Hospital in the city. At the meeting, I asked that she be moved to the Thrissur Medical College, with the area being turned into an isolation ward. I was encouraged to see that everyone in that room was charged up, like firefighters who'd already practised on smaller fires. Or perhaps it was because at the time we genuinely believed that if we did everything right, scrupulously followed the protocol, this infection would turn out to be as short-lived as Nipah. We decided that the patient would be moved discreetly in the morning, before sunrise, so that no one would find out. I didn't want an image of that young woman on a stretcher being moved between hospitals to be on the front pages the next day.

It was almost 3 a.m. by the time the meeting got over. The media was waiting outside. We were transparent about what we knew till then. We informed them we'd received the results for one out of the three people tested and it was positive for the novel coronavirus. At the same time we had a plan prepared to meet the situation. So the message was simple: 'Not fear but vigilance'. It was of course the headlines the next morning. By 2 February the sample of another one of those three medical students tested positive. This individual was in Alappuzha district. Then, on 3 February, results for the last of the three samples came in, and it was positive as well. That patient was in Kasargod district. I spoke to all three over the phone and told them they shouldn't worry. Since they were medical students they understood what we were dealing with. There was no treatment protocol at that time, so prevention was really the only route of defence at our disposal. We decided to enforce a twenty-eight-day quarantine, following the same principle we had adopted during Nipah. While the incubation period was generally only fourteen days, there were a few rare cases in which the disease manifested after fourteen days. So, to be extra cautious, we decided on a long quarantine. Within two weeks, all three of Kerala's first COVID patients recovered and were discharged from hospital.

For two weeks after that, there were no cases. It was as though the spread had stopped, and we were relieved. But, given the news around the world, we didn't withdraw the team from the airport. I began getting a lot of annoyed calls from very important people. The insinuation, or rather accusation, was always the same: the health ministry was overreacting. I had one conversation with a gentleman who complained that the health department staff at the airport was standing watch over passengers, pointing 'a gun' at their heads. He was referring to the infrared thermometer used to get a reading on the forehead. It was the beginning of a profusion of public reactions to every decision we made. But our process remained in place. The staff at the airport continued to scan people as they came out of the exit.

When there's a crisis, all the many elements that shape your life suddenly converge on every decision you make. As a student of science my instinct is straightforward: go where the data leads you. All over the world at the time there was debate over the appropriate approach to the evolving situation. There hadn't been a health crisis of this magnitude since the Spanish Flu of 1918. In 2020, some governments adopted the mitigation method, believing that by allowing the virus to spread, the community would attain herd immunity. The opposing view was containment; protect the public from getting infected till a vaccine is found. In Kerala, we opted for the second approach. Why? Even though the state is ahead in many health indices, when it comes to infectious diseases, Kerala has several demographic and epidemiological vulnerabilities. Three particular factors characterizing

Kerala informed our decision: (a) the state has the largest density of population in the country; (b) we have a large old-age population, with almost 15 per cent of the 35 million people being over sixty years of age; (c) Kerala has a number of individuals suffering from lifestyle diseases, including diabetes mellitus, hypertension, renal diseases and cancer. These three factors meant that Kerala was the most vulnerable state in the country for potentially very high mortality due to COVID. So if we followed the mitigation method, large numbers of people with comorbidities would definitely catch the virus, and it would spread through our high-density state at a time when there was no vaccine. I believed strongly then that if we could protect our population for as long as it took for a vaccine to be found, it would save many lives. In the long run, I would be proven right.

The chief minister advised the formation of an advisory committee with experts from outside. Under the leadership of Dr B. Ekbal, a public health expert based in Kerala, we formed a thirteen-member group that would monitor developments around the world related to combating the virus and offer their expert view on decisions to be made by the health department.

There are Malayalis all over the world, and we knew that if cases were to pop up here it would be through contact with someone who'd travelled. Soon Europe became a hotspot. Since passengers heading to Kerala from Europe usually connect via stops in the Middle East, the only way for us to identify passengers who'd started their journey in Europe was if they identified themselves. So there were announcements on every flight asking passengers to present themselves to the health department help desk.

A mother and son landing in Kochi from Doha identified themselves at the help desk as travelling from Italy. The son had symptoms so both were sent to isolation and tested for the virus. The son would eventually test positive, but the mother didn't. On that same flight there was another family – a father, mother and their son – who'd also started their journey in Italy but they chose not to approach the airport help desk and reveal this information. There was still no mandate for universal checking of passengers, so we were entirely dependent on voluntary reporting. This family left the airport without revealing their original port of departure, and went home to Ranni, a small town in the central Kerala district of Pathanamthitta.

They didn't think it was very serious. The son in the family was between jobs and they'd come to Kerala just for a meet-and-greet with their extended family before he started his new employment. Not wishing to get caught up in a government-mandated quarantine at a time like that, they had sneaked off. There were announcements being made all over the state at that point: precautions, warnings and appeals to contact the health department if someone had recently come from abroad. It would have been pretty much impossible not to hear any of those. These people, though, chose to ignore these warnings and visited all their relatives, moving around the central districts, Kottayam and Pathanamthitta, and Kollam in the south. If you pinned their destinations with a thread on a board you'd have ended up in criss-crossed knots. Then one day a couple went to the General Hospital in Pathanamthitta with a fever. The hospital staff had been trained to identify and screen cases with symptoms of fever, cold or cough. So the doctor asked this couple a series of questions. Have you travelled outside Kerala? 'No.' Did anyone who has been abroad come to your house? 'Yes,' they said. 'Our relatives have just come from Italy.' This couple was put in quarantine, and they tested positive.

The health department officials immediately went to the house of the people who'd arrived from Italy. When the family saw the department vehicle, they got into a frenzy, arguing vociferously that only one of them had some fever, they weren't sick, there was no need to go to a hospital. Once they were informed there could be police action taken against them, they agreed to go to the hospital in their own car. They were brought in, isolated and samples were taken, even as they continued to voice objections at the steps being taken. The hospital arranged for counsellors to meet with them and talk, but to no avail. The trio, and later the grandparents – eighty-eight-year-old Joseph and eighty-two-year-old Mariam – all eventually tested positive for COVID.

It now became essential to find every single person they'd come in contact with and test those individuals. But the family wouldn't cooperate. The Pathanamthitta district collector at the time was a smart young man called P.B. Nooh. Since he had taken charge in 2018, his district in particular had faced crisis after crisis, from severe flooding to the Sabarimala temple entry controversy, and now this. Each time, he took action decisively and fast: nothing is more important in an emergency. When he realized how uncooperative these patients were, he decided to forge ahead without wasting his time asking them. He opened a control room to deal with the situation, and together with the health department and police, they tracked the patients' cell phone usage, tracing tower locations of all the places they'd been to, marking them on Google Maps, and doing a sweep of each location with an army of field staff. In less than a week, they tracked down nearly 4,000 contacts, which included secondary contacts, and everyone was quarantined. Several tested positive, and the spread had moved to other districts. At the time, this was the largest number of infections in the country.

Once this information got out, we had to deal with the social media backlash against this family. There were WhatsApp forwards and jokes on television. In the beginning, when I realized they'd slipped out from the airport I was furious, but I was equally unhappy about the public vilification campaign against them. I sent out a WhatsApp message saying I didn't hold these people responsible for anything. They were scared and they didn't know the ramifications of what they were doing. Everyone imagines that bad things happen to other people.

Treating the grandparents, Joseph and Mariam, proved especially nerve-racking. Going by what was happening in other parts of the world, we were convinced we'd lose them. I'd asked for them to be admitted to the Kottayam Medical College immediately. They'd never spent a day in a hospital in their lives and were extremely uncomfortable and angry. They refused to rest or to eat, and insisted on going back home. I got a call from Dr Jayakumar, the superintendent of the hospital. He said there was a more comfortable ICU in the neurology department and we could admit them there, moving the one patient currently housed there to another ICU. The head of the neurology department was against the idea but his patient was stable so finally we managed the switch.

Looking out of open windows with some fresh air in their faces, the old couple finally settled down. They still hated the food, but we put them under the care of two very good nurses, who spent a great deal of time cajoling the two to cooperate. They looked after them like they were their own, taking them to the bathroom, feeding them, spending as much time as they could with them. And despite all the precautions the nurses took, one of them, Reshma, got infected. That really shook me. We'd lost one nurse, Lini Sajeesh, during Nipah, and I was petrified we were about to go through the same thing. When I spoke to Reshma on the phone, she was very positive, telling me she would be going back to the COVID isolation ward and continuing her work once she was better. Reshma recovered shortly, and to our own surprise, so did the old couple. It was unbelievable at the time, given their age. When they all got better I spoke to the family, and they were grateful they were in Kerala because the situation in Italy at the time was much worse.

I realize now that perhaps we were naive, the way we were seeking to fend off this virus, to prevent it from ransacking the state. We were working on available know-how and were fuelled by hope and the experience of outrunning another infection a year ago. Our team at the health department and the chief minister were certain of one thing: we didn't want the virus caseload to go up. When we realized COVID was becoming a pandemic, the chief minister called a meeting with the heads of all the government departments and assigned responsibilities to each department. By this stage COVID had ballooned from a health-related problem into a larger social issue, so it required concerted effort. At the same time, the chief minister took on the responsibility of relaying daily COVID updates to the public.

At the time, we knew every patient by name, every case's situation and circumstance. One day I was told that a group of seventeen British tourists had disappeared in Idukki. The leader of the group was a man called Bryan, whom the locals referred to as 'Brayansayyppu'. His friends and he had begun feeling feverish at the hotel, and were asked to give samples. Three out of the group tested positive, but by the time the ambulance reached to take them to isolation they'd vanished into thin air! It seems they managed to get airline tickets through some middlemen and had left for the airport.

When the police and the health staff reached the airport they learned the group had already boarded the flight, so they got the airport authorities involved to disembark them. The group was furious, arguing loudly inside the aircraft in front of the rest of the passengers. And given the confusion and fear around the virus, everyone was upset. Someone called to ask me if they should be allowed to leave. I said, 'They can't go to the UK under any circumstances.' We had no idea how many places they'd been to in Kerala and without them here we'd never be able to find out. Once they left, they wouldn't even answer our phone calls, I was sure. We had to treat them and get them better before they could be allowed to leave. We asked the chief minister for his opinion, and once he agreed, they were taken off the flight.

The group was admitted to two government institutions in Kochi, the Ernakulam Medical College and the General Hospital. Bryan had plenty of comorbidities; he was diabetic and had high blood pressure, so his treatment protocols were complex. Then there was a call from the UK embassy to the Chief Minister's Office, asking after their citizens. As per the embassy's request the chief minister thought we could offer them rooms at a private hospital if that would make them feel more comfortable and give them more privacy. At the time, the government was paying for all COVID treatment, whether in a private or public institution. I called the medical college principal, Dr Thomas Mathew, and the superintendent, Dr Ganesh, who had video calls with these patients every day since they were in isolation. They asked Bryan if he wanted to go to a private hospital. He said he was very comfortable and opted to stay on at the medical college. Finally, after three weeks of treatment and quarantine, the group was ready to go back to the UK. When they were leaving, they gave an interview to the media about their experience. They said they were grateful they'd been pulled off that flight, and truly believed that their lives were saved because they were in Kerala at the time. They thanked the chief minister and myself for looking after them.

There is another incident I remember involving an NRI Malayali, who was visiting Alappuzha from the UK. Since he'd arrived from abroad, we asked him to self-isolate and then get tested. He roundly refused and left his home to go visit the local market. According to our mandate at the time, he was meant to be in self-quarantine for twenty-eight days. When the health department team went to speak with him, they got yelled at. After a lot of back and forth, including observations that the system in Kerala wasn't good enough to deal with this situation and other impressions of the NRI kind, he was forced to follow the quarantine mandate. He got tested first after seven days, then after two weeks. The second test came back positive. So we had all sorts of people, some angry, some desperate to leave, some very cooperative, and others just looking to lash out at someone.

By 11 March there were less than twenty people who were COVID positive in the state, but the Kerala government declared a health emergency. Some weeks later, on 24 March, the national government declared a nationwide lockdown. Monitoring became easy then, because people couldn't go anywhere. Kerala declared an aid package of Rs 20,000 crore to make sure the poor got foodgrains, to take care of the needs of workers from other states, and for COVID care facilities. The state government also set up community kitchens to prepare food for people who couldn't cook for themselves. More than 150,000 migrant labour, or 'guest workers' as we call them, were stuck here during the national lockdown. We knew that with the loss of daily work most of these people would be in trouble. The government ensured they were given food kits or cooked meals so there was no desperation to leave. The non-communicable diseases control group from the health department made sure people with lifestyle diseases were provided for; medicines for diabetes, high blood pressure, etc. were all delivered home so people didn't go without them.

The whole effort was hugely expensive, and the government was essentially running people's lives in small and big ways. The government pulled in resources from all over, including the Chief Minister's Distress Relief Fund. Every single panchayat raised funds from its own population for foodgrains and other items; they recruited volunteers to cook and make deliveries, distributing food through the community kitchen and often supplying food to homes. Hunger Watch India conducted a study across ten economically strong states and found that there was a 21 per cent increase in the number of families who went below the poverty line in 2020. At the same time, because of the Kerala government's timely intervention, people in our state never faced a hunger crisis of any form.

Everything we talk in theory about a socialist-minded state came into play during that time. The government put people at the centre of their policy. Empathy was the guiding principle. Every single life was worth fighting for. And the citizenry also came through in ways we didn't expect. I've heard of auto drivers who took on volunteer work delivering food, housewives who worked in the community kitchens to make food, community groups that helped people who were too ill to buy essentials for themselves, and a vast army of young people who set forth to help in every way they could.

By then infections began showing up in Tamil Nadu, Delhi and other places. Some of these states reached out to us for our SOPs, since we'd been the first to deal with the crisis. There was no sense of politicization of the crisis then, and we were happy to share our learnings with whoever asked. At one point the chief minister asked why we were continuing to enforce a twenty-eight-day quarantine period. Why couldn't we do fourteen days? I admitted we were being over-cautious. We were looking at double the incubation period of the virus in order to be extra safe. That way we could be sure that a negative test was really negative. People didn't complain then, because there was a lot of fear in the air and they were willing to sit indoors if that meant they'd be safe.

The lockdown was an opportunity for the health department to ramp up our efforts. Our main intention was to control the spread such that our hospital system would not be overwhelmed at any point. We had evolved a three-pronged strategy to deal with the situation. Part one was 'Trace, quarantine, test, isolate, treat'. The second was 'Break the chain' and the third was 'Reverse quarantine'.

To address the first element of the strategy, we boosted the existing bed capacity in hospitals. In addition to that, Covid Care Centres (CCCs) were established around the state, while Covid First Line Treatment Centres (CFLTCs) and Covid Second Line Treatment Centres (CSLTCs) were set up in schools, hotels and auditoriums. Some of them were sponsored by private individuals and organizations. For example, M.A. Yusuff Ali, the chairman of the Lulu Group, equipped the company's auditorium in Thrissur at a cost of Rs 2 crore and gave it over for use as a CSLTC. While all the centres had the necessary medical equipment, some of them also had television sets and other amenities. The CCCs were for people who came from abroad and didn't have the capacity to separate themselves in their own homes for two weeks. At the end of two weeks, depending on whether they showed signs of the disease, they got tested or were sent home. Patients were divided into three categories: A, B and C. Asymptomatic, positive, stable patients were 'A', positive patients with comorbidities but stable were in the 'B' category. Patients with severe symptoms and requiring ventilators were part of the 'C' group. Category A patients were admitted to CFLTCs, Category B patients were treated at CSLTCs, while Category C patients were sent to medical colleges. All CFLTCs and CSLTCs were manned by trained doctors, nurses and volunteers. Through this network of free treatment centres we were able to prevent a patient surge in our hospitals.

At the time, the WHO was saying, 'Test, test, test.' But with our 'Trace, quarantine, test, isolate, treat' strategy, we were taking a slightly different path, based on our local experience. Some people objected to our way of dealing with the situation, and of course to the long quarantine, especially because the mortality rate didn't seem high at the time. In the Kerala Legislative Assembly, the Opposition leader said the US was using the mitigation method, while in Kerala the health department was scaring people; it was just a flu. It hadn't been declared a pandemic yet. My response to the Opposition leader in the Assembly was, 'We are not doing this to frighten people. If we are not overprepared, we will be more at risk. It is highly infectious. The mortality rate is low but if the infection rate increases, the death toll will increase.' I explained the difference between the mitigation/herd immunity and containment methods, pointing out, 'Many people are dying in America.' Kerala has a high number of senior citizens, as I have already mentioned, and the idea that we allow them to bear the consequences of spreading immunity to the younger population was simply untenable. So we continued to trace everyone, quarantine them, then test those with symptoms. But the agitation and disapproval continued.

Some IAS officers were annoyed that while other states had increased their testing numbers, we were not doing the same thing. When the health department decided against antigen tests, it proved controversial. Our decision was based on the fact that all the cases at that time were imports from other countries. The antigen test is a useful tool to measure the infection rate if the infection has spread through the community, which had not happened as yet. It can tell you if the body has developed antibodies because of exposure to the virus, but there is a high chance of false-positive and false-negative results, so we didn't believe it was an effective tool for the stage of the infection we were in at that time. The golden test then and now is the RT-PCR, the Reverse Transcription Polymerase Chain Reaction Test. With the RT-PCR test, the presence of the COVID RNA is directly identified and proven. So that was enough, we thought. But the criticism continued: 'Kerala is not testing enough.'

In terms of tests per million we were well ahead, but when it came to total testing, Maharashtra was far ahead of us in numbers. But that comparison was with a much larger state. Kerala's entire population is 35 million; just Mumbai has more than 20 million people. Besides, test kits were limited in number, so we reserved them for testing symptomatic individuals, close contacts of patients, and people in high-risk groups such as health workers, police and volunteers. Then the chief minister opined that the criticism was warranted, that we were not testing enough; so finally we increased the total testing numbers and began antigen testing.

The ICMR, the country's main body for biomedical research, gave us a batch of RT-PCR test kits. At the time everything was done through the central government so we had to use what ICMR gave us. We distributed the kits and started testing the medical staff first. At the Kozhikode Medical College, all the tests turned positive – every single sample. Then in Kannur District Hospital, six healthcare workers underwent random testing for a seroprevalence study. All six samples came back positive. The health workers maintained they'd never had any symptoms, nor any contact with anyone travelling from abroad. Today it's impossible to know if there'd been contact with outsiders but back then it wasn't that difficult to prove. Since it was still an imported infection, some form of contact with an outside entity was essential for a person to catch it. There was no community spread yet.

The doctors felt there was something amiss. And I was very worried: those days every positive result was a huge blow. Because the doctors were sceptical about the results of the tests, I called Dr Beena at the Kozhikode Medical College lab to double-check that the tests had been done correctly. She insisted they were, and that all the RT-PCR tests were positive. I asked the DMOs in Kannur to send samples to the NIV in Alappuzha – which had a different batch of test kits – for a second opinion. After conducting the tests the institute's head, Dr Sugunan, called me: none of the samples were positive. I spoke to the Kannur DMO and DPM, asking them to keep the staff members under observation. When they showed no symptoms whatsoever, we knew they were COVID negative. I told Rajan that the second tests were all negative, so either the first testing was faulty or the kits themselves were defective. The lab that had done the first testing was quite annoyed with me for asking for assurance over and over again! After that, wherever samples were tested with these kits, all got the same results. Shortly after that, we received a notice from ICMR asking us to stop using these RT-PCR kits immediately; they withdrew the whole batch.

When the demands of the health crisis got too much, we entrusted the public communication and campaign strategy to officers like Dr Mohammed Asheel, Biju Prabhakar and T.V. Anupama from the social justice department, which was also part of my portfolio. Snappy communication may seem like a secondary concern, but when we looked at historic examples of public health crises we found that effective communication saves lives. In 1969–70 there was a worldwide campaign to beat cholera, and a popular line then was 'One glass of water, a spoon of sugar and a pinch of salt', a recipe for oral rehydration solution (ORS). It is believed that the campaign's message saved 2.8 crore children by preventing dehydration.

Dr Asheel and his team took great pride in designing effective communication that would become catchphrases with the Kerala public. On 15 March 2020 we started the 'Break the chain' campaign, which was a really important message: the second prong of the overall COVID combat strategy. Infections were still entering Kerala via people from other places, so following quarantine strictly, isolation and ensuring that no one at home got infected was really up to individuals. The team came up with another simple way to reinforce their message: SMS, or 'Soap/Sanitizer, Mask and Social distance'. During that period, we estimated that there was some 30 per cent transmission among the population, significantly lower than in other states.

The third aspect of our strategy was reverse quarantine. Many of Kerala's large percentage of older population live alone, with children based outside. The over-sixty population is at very high risk for COVID, and we wanted to make sure there was no increase in fatalities among that segment. We asked that people above sixty not stir out of home at all. We counted about 2.5 lakh people who were in the extremely vulnerable category, and these people were continuously monitored. People coming from outside the country were told not to visit anyone over sixty or have any kind of contact with them. In homes where we knew someone had tested positive, the rules of conduct were printed out and pasted inside the house to reduce chances of the social stigma of being marked out. We organized 315 mobile ambulance units that could be sent to help older residents with any type of difficulty. All houses in panchayat wards were regularly checked by ASHA and Anganwadi workers. There was a battalion of counsellors working under the state mental health wing who called every passenger newly arrived in Kerala and in quarantine, checking in on them and asking after their emotional and mental well-being. They did this up to three times a day because sitting by themselves for weeks in quarantine was having a terrible effect on a lot of people. Throughout that period, there was vigorous continuous activity, on a war footing.

On 3 May 2020 the national lockdown was lifted. By then, because of the strictures that had been in place for weeks before the lockdown, Kerala had made unbelievable progress. Only 499 people in this state were COVID positive when the lockdown lifted. Three people died, but the mortality rate was below 0.4 per cent in Kerala. While many other states were seeing a spike in cases, there was no community spread here. That was the high point of our fight against the pandemic. The same month, *The Guardian* published a profile of me by Laura Spinney, the British science journalist and author of the award-winning book *Pale Rider*, an account of the 1918 influenza pandemic. The headline was 'The corona virus slayer! How Kerala's rockstar health minister helped save it from COVID-19'.[1] While there were problems all over the world, Kerala seemed to have beaten the virus, so it made sense that the international media would look at what we were doing. In that interview, I said we had been able to stave off a disaster because of the strict curbs on movement, but once the lockdown was removed, there was likely to be an influx of Malayalis into Kerala from various places. So despite our success thus far we had worked out Plan A, Plan B and Plan C: three strategies for three possible scenarios.

Our Plan A scenario looked at the possibility of 5,000 cases per day, and how and where those could be treated. Plan B considered a situation in which there were more than 5,000 and up to 25,000 cases a day. And Plan C was a strategy to tackle the possibility of endless cases. In the first situation, we could manage well. Beds had already been set aside at the government medical colleges and district hospitals. The staff were trained to allocate beds such that no hospital in one district would be full at any time. Every single evening, we had briefings. The government was also fielding a lot of calls from Malayalis desperate to come back home. When interstate travel began, droves of people began arriving at our borders. At the check-posts, people with symptoms were sent to hospital. We had staff posted for checking at airports, roadway checkpoints, train stations and seaports, covering multiple exit and entry points. But of course, we still had cases: the population is too large and everything is leaky; there is really no absolute way to ensure people don't sneak past.

Kerala is a consumer rather than producer state; a lot of our produce and provisions come from other neighbouring states on trucks. Out-of-state drivers coming in from Tamil Nadu and Karnataka, which were hotspots, arrived at Kerala markets bringing infections. With all that going on, clusters of infections began popping up around such areas, and we were worried. The first wave had begun in Kerala.

The health secretary, DHS Dr Saritha, and the team created a cluster management strategy. We were the first state to do this. We applied this strategy first at a place called Poonthura, a suburb of Thiruvananthapuram, in July 2020. This area has some 38,000 people, mostly fishermen and their families. Most people live in dense groups here, and their livelihood depends on working in close proximity with one another, so it made sense that the infection would spread through the community.

When we began testing there, for every hundred people, almost half had the infection, so we knew there was likely to be more than 15,000 cases and the death rate would rise. The most critical element of the cluster management strategy was to contain the infection in one cluster. So we shut down the place, and healthcare workers concentrated all their energy on that area. The residents there got very angry when it was closed off. There were rumours flying that they'd starve. When health officials visited the place, they were harassed. The government had also appointed IAS, police and revenue officers at each cluster to manage social issues. In Poonthura these government officers kept explaining to the population that these strictures were all for their own good, promised them no one was going to starve, and underscored that all these measures were essential because this was an emergency. Eventually, things calmed down. And because of the strict enforcement, there were only some 600 cases there. At the time there were under forty deaths in the state, mostly among the older population and those with serious comorbidities. We believed we were effective with containment.

When Mumbai's Dharavi, considered Asia's largest slum, had a wave of COVID infections, Maharashtra's then health minister, Rajesh Tope, called me. He wanted to understand our strategy when the infection spreads to high-density places like slums. We don't have any areas with the scale and population density of Dharavi, but we have thickly populated colonies that are home to the state's poorest urban population, particularly in Thiruvananthapuram and Ernakulam. Our strategy, I told him, was to enforce a total shutdown of the areas that became clusters. Completely close off the area: no one in, no one out. Otherwise it doesn't work. At the same time, ensure citizens are not starved of essentials like food and medicines, and that the death rate does not increase from secondary factors. In the end, the Maharashtra government employed a strategy that suited their population and did an outstanding job. Iqbal Singh Chahal, the IAS officer who was Commissioner of the Brihanmumbai Municipal

Corporation (BMC), evolved a model of crisis management for his city that was exemplary for large urban areas.

Before the BMC shut down Dharavi, many Malayalis living there came back to Kerala, and we had a bit of a spillover of infection from that situation as well. As clusters popped up, the numbers continued to go up in some places. Then there was the Onam festival season, in September 2020. At the time, according to projections by the Indian Institute of Technology, Kanpur, cases in Kerala were expected to surge to 20,000–40,000 per day. But in reality the spike from the Onam festival wasn't as bad as forecast. There were about 11,000 cases per day at the peak; it was a far cry from the daily caseload of 30,000 we'd prepared for. And we were able to bring it down soon. So the first wave was flattened very effectively.

After the first wave, ICMR conducted a sero-surveillance study and found that in Kerala only 10.6 per cent of the population had been affected by COVID. So from 35 million people, 90 per cent people had never been infected. In other states, this rate was around 50 per cent. There was another interesting finding of this ICMR study: that in India if twenty-one people caught COVID, only one out of the twenty-one would get reported, while in Kerala it was one out of three cases. That showed the robust reporting in the state.

Once community transmission began, our focus was to flatten the curve and delay the peak of infection. Those were our clarion slogans back then. And we accomplished that. COVID-19 came to Kerala before anywhere else in the country but our peak occurred after other places had theirs. Ours was a long-drawn-out pandemic. But, because we were able to stave off the peak, we had time to continue to develop and build up the healthcare system. That process, which we had begun in 2016, had been continuing all this while, even as we made adjustments according to the realities of the crisis engulfing us.

The team was learning all the time, both from our own experience and from the experience of health sectors around the world. We were fixing things and preparing for potentially worse eventualities.

The worst-case scenario we were plotting at this time was a situation where cases increased to 50,000 a day. That was where Plans B and C had to be activated. Kerala has good public health institutions at every level of administration and we involved all of these rungs for meeting a potential crisis. The bed strength at all public hospitals, both in general wards and in ICUs, was continually increased. We chased sponsorships from private companies and individuals to secure funding for more ventilators and other equipment. In every panchayat, we set up a Domicile Care Centre to care for positive cases.

Anticipating a rush at this time, we advised the population that asymptomatic COVID-positive people could be treated at home, maintaining complete isolation, which meant they had to have exclusive use of a separate bathroom and toilet. We wrote all these things up in a notice and distributed copies everywhere. A healthy person could give the patient food, but separate utensils had to be used. Patients had to clean their own spaces and dishes, because no one else could enter the room where a patient was isolating. After ten days, if they tested negative, they could come out. While many people scrupulously followed all these rules, there were plenty of cases where that didn't happen. I know of doting mothers who couldn't fathom their sons having to clean up after themselves, so they went into the rooms where they were quarantining to clean the bathroom and such. Well, they got sick. In some cases entire families became ill one after the other.

Despite our best efforts to control the wild imaginations of people, there were rumours and fears about the virus, how it spreads, and what causes infections; just about any internet theory was taken as fact. Sometimes there were problems we didn't expect, from quarters we didn't anticipate trouble from. As I have noted, the government had requisitioned several hotels, hostels and conference halls as CCCs. A well-known Opposition politician called me one day complaining that he could see one of these centres from his house. I told him no one is likely to get infected if they look in the direction of a CCC! But he was worried because a man was standing outside the hotel that was being used as a centre. I asked him what the distance was between that hotel and the nearest house. He said, 'There's quite a bit of distance but you can see it.' I told him as long as he was more than 2 metres away from the centre and any human being in it, nothing would happen to him. Viruses just couldn't fly that far. He said, 'You're joking, like a doctor, but the rest of us are scared.' He wanted me to move the CCC to another location. That got me irritated. 'What should we do with these people?' I asked. 'Should we dump them in the Arabian Sea? It is a thickly populated state, there are no isolated places here. If they come out and walk around, you tell me. Or if they're jumping over the wall, we'll catch them. If not, relax.' That was the end of our conversation.

From November to December 2020, the numbers continued to fall and the mortality rate was 0.5 per cent – always below 1 per cent. A spike occurred after the panchayat elections in December 2020, but that too gradually died away and we ended 2020 with a little over 5,000 cases per day.

To understand the behaviour of the virus and the causes behind the surge, a study was commissioned around September 2020 at the Kozhikode Medical College in collaboration with ICMR; the team found that variants were prevalent in Kerala. At the same time, international scientists announced that the virus had mutated into the more virulent Delta and similar variants, and this was also causing a surge in infection rates all over the world. This increased the threat of a second wave in Kerala.

From January 2021, Kerala began preparing for the upcoming state assembly election. In February, the Party declared its candidates' list and it included the chief minister and I. The elections were scheduled for April. During this period, our continued surveillance and enforcement slackened. It wasn't intentional, it was the nature of election operations. Once the dates of the election were declared, the police and revenue department officers shifted focus to election duty. Till then the police were heavily involved in ensuring people followed quarantine mandates and any area-wise restrictions. Now they couldn't do that any more. Previously, revenue officers were appointed as sectoral magistrates who coordinated quarantine efforts and enforced rules pertaining to public gatherings like weddings and funerals. This band of officers were now diverted to election-related work. Basically the entire state machinery shifted gear towards the election. And with that, people took things easy as well. The election gatherings, an essential part of the process, further aggravated community spread. We were all at risk at the time. Standing on stages, giving speeches, the microphone was both our friend and our enemy: an unsanitized microphone could certainly be a source of infection. And given the crowds at rallies a surge of infections was bound to happen. There were numerous closed-room meetings and other gatherings that were previously completely banned.

Occasionally we'd reassert the old strictness and involve the police and sectoral magistrates, but the reality is that once you lose day-to-day focus, it is difficult to regain that intensity and stitch the system back together tightly. After polling and till the new government took office, the state had a caretaker government in place. Immediately after the oath-taking ceremony in May 2021, once the LDF government came back to power, there was an effort to tighten up again, but it was certainly not easy. The lockdown fatigue among people, the pressure and difficulties in terms of livelihoods and businesses, meant that the strictures of the previous year were impossible. Also, psychologically, we'd all acclimatized to the presence of COVID; the peripheral fear was still in the air but not to the extent we felt when it was a new, completely unknown force.

In April and May 2021, as the country was suffering through the worst wave of COVID and people were dying from lack of medical facilities, Kerala also saw a surge in the number of cases. But we're lucky we did not face the levels of heartbreak many parts of the country faced back then. There was no desperation here because we had already allocated resources anticipating such a situation, and since we'd planned for it, we were able to go through that horrific summer without suffering as much devastation. The average mortality rate in the state remained around 0.5 per cent at that time.

In late 2020, the central government had announced two vaccines. Right away, we created a public campaign encouraging people to take either of them, and we prepared the healthcare system to start the distribution. But then we realized there was a shortage of vaccines because the central government had placed restrictions on vaccine numbers. We offered to buy it ourselves but they wouldn't allow that. Then, a large part of what was available went to other countries. The directive changed once more, and the Centre told the states to buy directly from the manufacturer. So we went to the Serum Institute in Pune and booked 1.15 crore vaccines. This was done before I left the ministry. We were then told by the central government that a single state can't buy such a large number of vaccines in bulk, that only 5 lakh vaccines could be bought at a time. Now, that is a big difference in numbers and we got hit very badly.

We had an alternative suggestion: if the central government shared their vaccine technology with us and supported us then Kerala State Drugs and Pharmaceutical Limited (KSDPL) in Alappuzha could make the vaccines. But we didn't get permission. I believe the Tamil Nadu government had made the same offer, so did Telangana. In fact, many regional centres could have made it and distributed it. There was no need to wait as long as we did for the vaccines. When the first vaccines rolled out, it was at the rate of 10,000 to 20,000 at a time. Kerala got permission to distribute it at 113 centres when we could have activated 2,000 centres to administer it. We have great staff and training, and it's not hard to administer the vaccine. We wrote to the central government, saying if they gave us the amount of vaccines we needed, we could finish the vaccination round in a month. I even called the Union health secretary. The answer I got was: Kerala can distribute it properly but some other states will waste the vaccine, and we cannot have a selective strategy for different states. My counterpoint to him was that because others are weak doesn't mean we should be punished. Anyway, it made no difference; we had to make do with what we got, when we got it.

When we finally got the vaccines, we managed to use them with zero wastage. A vial of the vaccine can be administered to anywhere between five to ten people. In many places around the country at the time, people weren't showing up to take the first dose when it was made available. Once you open the vial, if you don't use it all up, you simply have to discard the vial. That is a total criminal waste, especially when there weren't enough vaccines being distributed. In Kerala, a centre would only open a vial taking into account the number of people registered or lined up to take the vaccine. In many rural and small urban places, the FHC and PHC staff would personally call people, make sure they got there, and administer the vaccine to all. If there was excess, they'd call people who they knew were waiting for the vaccine and make sure they got it.

If you are focusing on the process with a great degree of intention and understanding of the population, it is possible to execute a vaccination programme quite well. Another cause of wastage is spillage while opening the vials. Our staff was well trained, and we never found that to be a problem. At one point, we were told by the Centre that because of our zero-wastage reputation, they would replenish our batch of vaccines faster. That never happened. Of course things eased up considerably after June 2021, but I wish we'd been able to administer the vaccines faster to a larger population right from the beginning.

It's worth noting here that as long as the vaccine remains out of reach for the vast majority of poorer countries in the world, no one is really safe. Vaccine socialism is essential if the world is really to be protected, and of course there are ways to achieve this. In June 2021 I participated in the Summit for Vaccine Internationalism, organized by Progressive International, which brought together healthcare workers, vaccine manufacturers and public health experts, alongside representatives from regional and national governments like Argentina, Mexico and Cuba. Speaking at the summit, I said, 'Options like compulsory licensing should be explored and public sector pharmaceutical companies which are capable of producing vaccines should be immediately mobilized into action.' National governments know what it would take; they just have to do it.

As the health minister (May 2016–May 2021), I oversaw the early phase of Kerala's COVID challenge. My responsibility was to create a solid foundation that would help our state cope if the infection became a crisis. I believe we did that. When I weigh our entire set of decisions and moves, I think the most important thing we did was also the simplest: the Kerala government took COVID seriously. We didn't wait for anyone to tell us it was a grave situation; we didn't look around for affirmation or listen to the critics. Taking this infection seriously even before it was a problem became our early-mover advantage. This allowed us to be prepared when we had the first infection in the country. The nCorona Guidelines released by the Kerala health ministry on 26 January 2020 was a prophetic piece of government literature. It pre-dated the arrival of COVID on our shores, so when the pandemic hit, we had a ready protocol to follow; we weren't scrambling around in utter panic. That set the tone for the rest of our COVID management system.

It bears reiteration that we face tremendous demographic and epidemiological disadvantages: India's old-age population is 9 per cent while Kerala is at 15 per cent; the density of population is 437 nationally, while in Kerala it is 856; our state is the diabetes capital of the country; and it is a semi-urban state, so infection spread between urban and rural populations is rapid. Yet, in Kerala the healthcare system has prevailed throughout, never crumbling as waves of infections came and went. The investment of time and energy in equipment and training, the disaster management planning: this is what helped a government save its people from needlessly dying. Looking back, I believe we did the best job we possibly could, and we laid the foundation for strengthening the system for another generation.

~

Postscript

Sometimes it seems like no one is more surprised by our successful health crisis management than our own people. And for those who are the most sceptical, there's a single explanation why the number of fatalities was so low: the health ministry must be hiding deaths. In October 2020, if I remember correctly, there was a report in *Malayala Manorama* newspaper asserting that the health department was covering up deaths – basically, under-reporting cases. We used to publish the name of every individual who died from COVID, so the newspaper listed the names of sixteen people they said had died of COVID but whose names were not declared by the government on its website.[2]

At the time there was a procedure we followed to ensure we were publishing the correct information. When there was a death in a district, and if the dead body was suspected to be COVID positive, it was disposed of following COVID protocols, and a sample was sent to the NIV, Kerala unit, in Alappuzha for confirmation. If the result was positive, we'd announce the name as a COVID case the next day and publish the name in the official list of COVID deaths. During that period, since there were fewer cases, we could take the time to be certain and scientifically sure. Every hospital has a medical board which sends the medical bulletin to the state board, which examines the data and announces the information. So sometimes, a death is announced a day or so later because of the procedures in between and the time those take. The announcement might come first at the district level but for it to make its way to the state's death toll takes a day or so. At the same time, as per rules established by the WHO at the time, deaths by suicide and those who died shortly after recovering from COVID, were not included in the official COVID stats.

So I wanted to get to the bottom of that newspaper story. I asked the State Medical Board to check the medical bulletins of death analysis from the districts to ascertain if some names had been omitted. They said the names would be included in the following day's official report. And indeed, they were. Out of sixteen, fourteen names were published and two were not, because one person was from Tamil Nadu: he'd died as soon as he got to the Trivandrum Medical College and his body was sent back to his state. The other person had died by suicide, and as I said before, that wouldn't be counted as a COVID case. The department handed over all this information to the newspaper, telling them they'd accused us of hiding facts and that untruth had since become viral fake news. The paper acknowledged the information and put out a clarification the next day – but with a big difference. The news article about the health department concealing numbers was front-page news; however, the clarification acknowledging the error in their reporting was in fine small print. Positively, a tiny bit of news!

Sometime later, columnist N.S. Madhavan wrote something that again made it sound like we were hiding deaths: he said of all the declared deaths, some 300 were not in the official record. The point he was trying to make was that there were actually at least 300 more deaths, but even if you take those into account, Kerala's mortality rate wouldn't go above the 0.6 per cent mark. I was quite annoyed by this backhanded compliment. The accusation about not counting or hiding deaths was a very serious one, but more than that, it was ridiculous.

There would have to be multi-department, multiparty collusion to hide the actual death numbers in Kerala. And it's impossible, especially in Kerala's activistic media and political climate, to corral entire departments into colluding with you. The health department and the levels of administration were not filled with my cronies; there were people from across the spectrum of Party affiliations. If anyone had found even the smallest shred of impropriety, they'd have excitedly announced it to the world. Even among the medical staff, there were plenty of people who would have done an exposé on any sort of cover-up. And we had never received a single complaint from the public that a COVID death was being covered up. In Kerala because of the vigilance of local self-governments, a death cannot go unregistered and unnoticed. Awareness among the population is very high, so at the very least a neighbour will inform someone that there has been a death. So, I took umbrage at Madhavan's point that while the rate would remain the same if all deaths were counted, we were hiding the true number of deaths.

Over the next three days the health secretary personally double-checked the lists of deaths from the districts. He found that only five to ten were not included as the results from NIV were inconclusive. The rest were all checked and had been included in the official tally. So, no one knew where this number – 300 – had come from. We informed the media of these facts, and I thought the conspiracy theories would end there. But I was wrong. This idea of hiding deaths has continued to hang in the air, to question everything we did in 2020 – it is a pipe dream of the naysayers.

In 2021 when there was a massive caseload it is possible there were high numbers of omissions, but in 2020, when it was a completely different scenario of lower numbers and strong tracking, it was just not possible. Also in 2021, the norms were changed by the central government, and it was decided that any COVID patient who died by suicide and death of anyone who'd recently recovered from COVID were also to be included in the official COVID death count.

In December 2020, we also did an analysis for excess deaths. If there were any discrepancies in the number of deaths, that would show up in the overall number of civil deaths in the state. The results for 2020 were surprising. There were 29,000 fewer deaths in 2020 than in 2019, that is, a drop of 11 per cent! Some people said that was because of the travel curbs during COVID, because of which fewer road accidents had taken place. Even if you deduct the total road accident deaths of 2019, the number is low: 24,000 deaths lower, which is nearly 8 per cent. That proves there was no hiding of deaths. Such numbers occurred only in a few places in the world. One was New Zealand. There was a 7 per cent drop there. Kerala has 100 per cent civil death registration. In many other states in India, the civil death registration is anyway low; even then overall deaths were higher.

Everyone loves a David and Goliath story, and Kerala's fight against COVID during that period must have seemed like that to many. No one had expected a fiscally deficit state like ours to become the best performer in a crisis. The period between 2018 and 2021 was perhaps the most feted period in the history of Kerala's health department. The United Nations awarded the Kerala government for its 'outstanding contribution' towards preventing and controlling non-communicable diseases; the UN also invited me to speak on Public Servants Day at the UN General Assembly. I received the Central European University's Open Society Prize, was listed as one of 'the world's top 50 thinkers for the COVID-19 age' by *Spectator* magazine, and became *Vogue India*'s 'Leader of the Year'.[3] Every award and honour has been a source of scrutiny and annoyance for many people. I think it particularly irks some when a woman is at the receiving end of such accolades. When a man proclaims his successes, he's stating facts. When it's a woman, she's showing off.

I take decisions quickly: that is my way; I don't wait around in doubt. In a crisis the most important thing is to make decisions. If we hesitate – should we, should we not – people die in that vacillation period. And I'm happy with the decisions I made. There was no false step on our part: the results of those years and the way the healthcare system has held up since then prove that we made the right calls. And I refuse to doubt myself for the convenience of others.

Of course, I am happy about the acknowledgements, who wouldn't be? But I am also aware that the hard work of a vast, dedicated and purposeful team – who relied on science and data – was what pulled us through it all.

13

The Kerala Model

For me, as a committed socialist, the success of Kerala's health department during the several crises between 2016 and 2021 is also a vindication of the communist dream. We were tested in ways that one cannot prepare for, and despite the challenges, I firmly believe the Kerala Model sustained us. What is the Kerala Model? The Kerala Model of development focuses on strengthening social indices related to literacy, accessible healthcare, life expectancy, mortality rate and birth rate. It lays stress on governmental practices and programmes that ensure a high quality of life and equal distribution of resources. To understand our model of development, you must understand the communist dream that underpins it. In 1946, EMS wrote a treatise called *Onnekalkodi Malayalikal* (1.15 crore Malayalis), in which he set out the communist dream of a new, united modern Kerala. This was a policy document that spelt out the priorities for a united Kerala: employment, ending religious divisions, equal opportunity, education and public health improvement.

Even though Kerala escaped the trauma of Independence-related violence, the population was mired in poverty, unemployment and extreme hunger at the time due to World War II and British policies in the Malabar. There were several public health crises: cholera in 1943, and then smallpox, which haunted the state till the 1960s and 1970s, killing more than one lakh people in Kerala. In the 1940s the life expectancy in the state was in the forties. In that bleak situation *Onnekalkodi Malayalikal* painted a picture of a hopeful new age for the state. EMS wrote about the need for people to access employment. He spoke of the need to attain food self-sustenance, generate electricity, develop various sectors such as shipping and fisheries, and connect agriculture and business by applying scientific methods to farming practices. EMS laid special emphasis on improvement of the social sector, on ensuring that all sections of society developed equally. Eliminating caste barriers was an essential part of his prescription for Kerala's healthy future. That spirit of development led EMS when he became the state's very first chief minister. With him and that first communist cabinet, the nature and spirit of how Kerala would develop was established.

Feudal culture is still strongly prevalent in many parts of our country. Most northern states haven't experienced what they really need: an anti-caste revolution. For generations politicians in those areas have not made the effort to disrupt the existing systems and effect real social change, where society looks beyond identities of caste and religion. But unless the upliftment of all becomes a primary objective, you can't get ahead. You can't go forward if your wheels are stuck in the mud. The Left ideology prioritizes egalitarian development above all else, and that is the fundamental reason why Kerala has shaped up differently in the years since Independence. The social revolution in Kerala was undoubtedly sparked off by the communists of that era. In fact, many early communist politicians gave up their caste-based symbols to shed the allegiance and entitlements attached to them.

It is extraordinary that our state democratically elected a communist party to form its very first government. And in that radical act, the foundations of forward-thinking, social development-oriented policymaking were set. Take the phrase 'Krishibhoomi karshakanu', for instance. That line translates to the stance 'Farmland for a farmworker'. The underpinning of that Leftist slogan is the principle that a farmer who works on the land must have the dignity of possessing some land of their own. It's only when restoring human dignity becomes government policy that real change can occur. Everyone becomes influenced by that thinking. And that is why I say that most Malayalis are socialists at heart and that is what makes Kerala exemplary. Socialism also made its way into our collective psyche through popular culture and literature. There was a play in the 1950s called *Ningalenne Communistaki* (You Made Me a Communist) by the famous theatre group Kerala People's Arts Club (KPAC) founded by Thoppil Basi. It tells the story of an upper-caste Hindu man's metamorphosis into a Communist. The play was staged as a protest against feudalism, amplifying the message that existing systems of oppression must be dismantled. It was later made into a popular film by the same name.

So, if you ask me how other states can emulate the Kerala Model of development, I would say you have to begin with overall social development. Everything is interconnected: people need the basics of food, income and access to education; then they can start thinking of the next aspect: their quality of life. The health sector, or any sector for that matter, cannot operate in a vacuum. In many states, ensuring food for all through the public distribution system and focus on education are not prioritized. What is the point of discussing healthcare for people who don't have adequate food to eat? Therefore, a macro approach and micro planning are vital.

In this regard, the southern states of the country have made considerable headway.

As a communist, I can't think of a scenario that doesn't begin with breaking the bonds of a feudal system. We believe that society cannot evolve without developing wholly and, as far as possible, equally. On the other hand, feudalism doesn't allow a human being to step outside their circumstances. You can follow a capitalistic economic model, but the feudalistic social set-up must be dismantled. In many northern states of our country, we see that instead of breaking down these oppressive systems, the political set-up has turned feudal and caste associations into vote banks. Capitalism cannot save people whose daily lives are frozen by caste strictures.

At the administration level, decentralized governance is an integral part of our system. Accelerated land reform and decentralized planning went hand in hand in the initial years. Local self-governments are now extremely strong in our state, and there is a fundamental belief that local problems can be best understood by local people. An offshoot of that same principle is decentralized public healthcare. Even though the central government's public health policy says a family welfare health subcentre with a nurse and junior health inspector must be present in any place with a 5,000-strong population, PHCs like that do not exist in many states. Whereas in Kerala, this directive has been enforced effectively. From its humble beginnings, the primary healthcare sector in the state has had incremental improvements, with the most dramatic changes beginning in 2016. And in our integrated decentralized healthcare system the public has choices because every panchayat also offers alternative medical care. People can also choose between Ayurveda, homoeopathy, Unani and Siddha lines of treatment.

With health and land reforms, together with education, the social development index in Kerala improved. People are more aware and understand how to take care of their health, and so life expectancy in Kerala today is seventy-six years, in contrast to the national average which is below seventy years. One element works with another for overall enhancement of the quality of life. Health is only one part of social development. If poverty is rampant, there is no point focusing on health. The health department does not stand in isolation, and infrastructure alone does not guarantee a healthy population. But all of that begins with intention, and if the intention is the overall betterment of a population, you will get somewhere.

Critics of socialistic thinking believe the government should not be trying to do everything, producing everything from meat to oxygen, both of which are part of government-run efforts in Kerala. But when a large portion of your population is disadvantaged and when that disadvantaged population is not a profitable consumer base for private companies, who should these people turn to? Private companies are motivated by profit. But governments cannot behave that way, especially in the health segment. If COVID has taught us anything it is that ensuring the safety and health of our population is an economic and financial necessity as much as a social and ethical one. This is part of the Kerala Model. It is about the structure and, yes, personality of the system that infuses our form of governance.

The benefits of thinking for the weakest sections of society are most evident in times of disasters. We can never truly progress by leaving behind the majority among us. No matter how many gated communities we build in this country, poverty and negligence are always going to be waiting just outside. Because of our history of caste bias and colonialism, a great many among us have been left behind for centuries – and need a leg-up. So, increasing access to public services, especially healthcare, is really the only option. No matter how much support and tax breaks a government provides the private sector, it doesn't translate to social commitment. Private healthcare is important, but it won't treat a pandemic, infectious diseases or a natural disaster as a priority, because these do not come with high-value treatment protocols. Afflictions like tropical diseases are not profitable to treat, plus these ailments take long and intense care to heal, so there's little motivation for private hospitals to focus on them. Which is why in places like Kerala, having a solid public healthcare system is so important. As author Arundhati Roy says, 'for the greater common good' the government must invest in the public healthcare system. That is the Kerala difference.

In our socialistic model, essential services and tools for the public healthcare system are provided by the state itself. Kerala's self-sufficiency model has saved it in times of crises. The central government's policies promote privatization, and while there is a case for that too in certain situations, as far as we are concerned, the Left believes in government ownership. And in crisis situations, such as a public health catastrophe, socialist thinking saves lives. Nothing illustrates this better than Kerala's handling of the COVID crisis.

There are many examples of subsidiary institutions under the state government which do crucial work that keeps this system as fair and egalitarian as possible. Or which help the public healthcare system function efficiently. An example is the KMSCL, the role of which I've mentioned before. Till it was set up in 2007, the health department and each public health institution had to negotiate individually with companies in a time-consuming process, procuring essentials without quality assurance or standardization across the public healthcare system. Now KMSCL conducts negotiations on behalf of the entire public healthcare system, standardizing the process and quality of things that are bought. It is also a publicly audited entity, so any irregularities are quickly caught.

When the COVID crisis began we couldn't get adequate PPE kits in the market; there was a huge shortage. At the time a PPE kit cost about Rs 1,500. Kerala had some stock amassed from the Nipah crisis, but when we found it was running low we decided to buy 50,000 kits for Rs 1,500 each. By the time 15,000 of that order was delivered, the price had gone down. So, we cancelled the order and bought the rest at the lower price. In the Assembly there was a submission asking if these differently priced kits indicated some sort of corruption. We bought them at a higher price because we didn't want to risk running short while waiting for the price to fall. Without this kit in stock, we'd be jeopardizing our public health staff's lives. We entrusted the work of maintaining these stocks to KMSCL. KMSCL is also in charge of all the construction work requirements at public health institutions; it set up all the catheterization labs and dialysis units installed as part of the public healthcare system revamp.

Similarly, managing oxygen capacity in the state required the collaborative effort of three government entities: the Petroleum and Explosives Safety Organization (PESO), the state's commerce and industries ministry, and of course KMSCL. On 23 March 2020, Dr R. Venugopal, Deputy Chief Controller of Explosives at PESO and nodal officer for oxygen supply, issued an advisory to all medical oxygen filling plants in the state that they should ensure continuous supply of medical oxygen during the ongoing COVID crisis. In this advisory he wrote presciently, 'A rise in the number of patients admitted with coronavirus in Kerala will lead to an increased demand for medical oxygen at hospitals, and someone needs to deliver it. I request all oxygen filling plants and licensed medical oxygen suppliers [and] gas distributors to adjust their production plans according to the development of the epidemic, focusing on the production of medical oxygen and ensuring adequate transport capacity.' With falling oxygen saturation being one of the critical signs of an active COVID infection, it was only logical that we needed to ensure adequate ventilators and oxygen supply. And looking at what was going on in other countries at the time, it was clear that the demand for oxygen could increase exponentially if patient numbers increased. Some of the oxygen produced in Kerala was being sent to Tamil Nadu since it is a neighbouring state. And if that was to continue, we had to produce enough to suit potentially increased needs in Kerala itself. At the time, even though the state's daily usage was only around 150 tonnes, with cases projected to increase, we decided to make arrangements for at least 240 metric tonnes of production per day by increasing the capacity of the existing oxygen plant; we would then expand oxygen coverage to ICU beds.

Today most beds at medical college hospitals in the state have direct oxygen supply. In addition to that, as part of our public health infrastructure development plan, we included independent oxygen plants at large hospitals at the district and taluk levels. This will ensure self-sufficiency in oxygen production for these public hospitals within two to three years. It was widely reported in 2021 that our state was unlikely to face a medical oxygen crisis unlike Delhi, because oxygen was in plentiful supply here. That is because the Kerala government planned for a catastrophe. I think the oxygen crisis example illustrates my larger point that it is not money that ensures a government executes its responsibilities properly, it is intention.

During my term we also set up a permanent State Health Agency (SHA) to carry out activities related to the implementation of the Karunya Arogya Suraksha Padhathi (KASP), an insurance scheme in the state. The intention of this scheme was to provide health cover of Rs 5 lakh to more than 41 lakh families in the most vulnerable segments of the population who availed secondary and tertiary care hospitalization. It would benefit more than 64 lakh people at the bottom 40 per cent of the state's population. When we invited expressions of interest from private insurance companies to conduct and manage this insurance scheme, we received a good offer from Reliance General Insurance, which already manages the central government's insurance schemes. In Kerala, being a free scheme, the premium was to be paid by the government, not the individual covered. Reliance quoted Rs 1,725; the closest other quote was Rs 3,000. So, we opted for Reliance, and for one year, Reliance managed this insurance scheme.

But we found that during this period there were tremendous delays in reimbursements. The company would deny most claims on some flimsy pretext or the other. Since the government was paying the premium, we expected that when people submitted claims, the company would make the payouts. However, they were refusing to pay the hospitals, usually with the excuse that the treatment availed was not part of the scheme. Whenever I spoke to the company, they were very reassuring, but nothing would change. It became a huge problem for us, because if we don't receive the reimbursement, the finance department does not pay out the rest of the money. It was an utter mess. I realize that the fundamentals of the insurance industry are based on turning down claims, but as a government-supported scheme, it was completely pointless to continue that way.

Perhaps we could have a government entity, like KMSCL, to manage this insurance scheme? When Rajeev Sadanandan was the health secretary and we discussed this option, he was quite against the idea. He was very clear about it: 'You think the government can do anything, but there are some things it shouldn't get into. Only an expert agency should do it. Who would be able to manage this? Certainly not doctors.' I didn't want to pressure him because there was some truth in what he was saying. But then it wasn't working with our so-called 'expert agency' either. Rajan, the succeeding health secretary, had a greater understanding of finance and understood his way around tax structures, and so was more supportive of the idea of creating such an agency. But it was Dr Rathan U. Kelkar, Kerala's Mission Director of the National Health Mission, who was able to create a framework to set up what we named the State Health Agency.

We thought we could give the SHA the responsibility of conducting this insurance scheme, which would be carried out in tandem with the National Health Agency. We only needed to pass an executive order for this. I said, 'Let's take this to the cabinet; if the cabinet passes it, the SHA can be created in the same form as KMSCL and developed.' I spoke to the chief minister, and he said, 'If you're enthusiastic about it, then do it.' He always speaks like that. I told him I was confident that with some efficient officers, and headed by an IAS officer, it could be done. Taking the final proposal to the cabinet, I got its approval. That's how the SHA came into being in 2018, with Dr Kelkar as the executive director, Dr Bijoy as general manager, and the minister for health as the chairman of the organization. During COVID – since the insurance scheme was directly under the government, which offered free COVID treatment to all – we were able to easily empanel private hospitals under this scheme and pay them directly.

Two other key drivers of the state's approach to recent crises that can be said to form part of the Kerala Model have been technology and communication. With Nipah, from the start we'd decided that we would give people information, directly and regularly. One part of that was the daily press conference every evening, when we announced the major changes and decisions of the day. There was much less room for fake news if information came straight from the government. During the first COVID wave, I did the briefing and then later, when more departments of the government became involved, the chief minister did it, and it became an important part of the day for people. The head of government taking questions directly during a crisis, speaking with people eye to eye, as it were: that was a show of confidence and reliability.

The other element of communication we had during the COVID crisis was our reporting system. From the bottom to the top and the top to the bottom, every section of government connected with the other in a systematic flowchart, allowing communication and information to move smoothly. In public health crisis situations, identification of ailments, communicating it through the chain, and alerting all stakeholders makes all the difference. With Nipah, the timing saved us. Two doctors in one hospital, identifying a virus as unusual, saved lives. In so many other places in the time gap between alerting and identification, hundreds of lives have been lost. The independence of our rural self-government system, which empowers the lowest rungs of government but also makes it accountable up the chain of command, allows decision-making that is more accurate and appropriate for specific populations. A panchayat president and medical officer working together, the transformation of grassroots FHCs, and a network of field staff who know their populations inside out – all these elements build up into a strong web of communication.

When you're armed with ground-level information and there's technology to amplify or corroborate it, you have a genuinely winning combination. In late 2021, I gave a talk to the students at the Indian Institute of Management, Bangalore, on the topic 'How technology was used to deal with COVID'. For Kerala, technology was a key component from the beginning. The COVID dashboard run by the

Kerala government at that time had up-to-date data and statistics related to the pandemic, the Arogya Jagratha portal was always open for people to find information. The health department control rooms that functioned at the district levels allowed for hospitals to manage their inventory and for the administration to have a constant feel of what was going on. The crisis management cells at the chief secretary's office in Thiruvananthapuram and district collectors' offices, and the 24-hour disaster management cells were all tech-enabled. No one had to go hunting for information, updates were in real time, and we knew where we stood. Data relating to bed strength and oxygen capacity were critical elements of the dashboard of information.

Technology also allowed us to efficiently conduct contact-tracing investigations, without which we would have been in a blinding fog in many situations. The health department worked very closely with the IT department to make this happen. The state had a war room to deal with emergency situations during the lockdown, such as people not having food or housing, so citizens wouldn't be inconvenienced. When a citizen rang the control room and made a complaint, the war room informed the district collector's disaster management cell which in turn got in touch with the panchayat president and figured out a solution. We also used artificial intelligence and robotic technology to disperse medicine in isolation wards. Telecommunication was essential in keeping in touch with people who were in COVID wards. There was a connection from the superintendents' rooms at the medical colleges to all patients' beds.

While I am sure there have been slip-ups, that there were gaps in day-to-day practice, what I hope we've been able to prove is that money doesn't beget a great system. Intention and hard work on the other hand can close the financial gap quite a bit. From the start we followed some very simple principles to manage our healthcare system and various crises. We listened to the science, used technology to effectively monitor the situation, and communicated directly to people. It was intuitive as well as scientific.

Kerala is a small state with a perpetually insufficient exchequer, so if this had been a battle that hinged on expensive equipment and resources, we would have failed dismally. What worked for us was the long-standing social contract between the government and our people which prioritizes their quality of life, the bottom-up structure of administration, community-based reporting, the importance placed on medical intervention, and the willingness of people to work together. The methods we employed required only that we be quick, consistent and thorough.

14

Ministering to the Most Vulnerable

I am often simply described as Kerala's former health minister. The two public health crises we dealt with often give the impression that the health department was the entire focus of all my activities during the years between 2016 and 2021. Even in this book, the descriptions of my work as a minister have mostly related to the Aardram Misson, Nipah and COVID. This might cause the reader to assume that other departments I was responsible for – Women and Child Development (WCD) and Social Justice – didn't get the attention they deserved. When in fact those subjects were dearer to me in many ways.

When I became minister in 2016, my portfolio was called Health and Family Welfare and Social Justice. At the time, the social justice department dealt with issues related to women, children, senior citizens, the disabled and the transgender community. Over the years there had been a clamour by women's groups for women's and children's issues to be dealt with separately by a department dedicated to that segment. And so, in 2017, a year after I became minister, the LDF government decided to form a new department for women and children and so my portfolio was bifurcated anew into Health and Family Welfare, Women and Child Development, and Social Justice. Having a department dedicated to a particular subject has several benefits. The issues that come under its jurisdiction get better funding from the government; a host of bureaucrats are then singularly focused on that topic; there's more freedom to create programmes dedicated to those groups. Having said that, splitting a department creates several jurisdictional and practical issues. The bureaucratic division must be done from top to bottom down the chain of the administration, starting from the state level and going to the district and all the way down till the local level. Unfortunately, due to COVID this administrative bifurcation wasn't completed, though that didn't stop the overall work from moving forward while I was there.

As a political activist, most of my career before becoming an MLA was focused on women's and children's rights. In the earliest part of this book I've spoken of the type of work I did back in those days, campaigning in my own community to increase political awareness and participation among women. Those experiences and an understanding of the realities women face gave me ample insight into the issues that the WCD department must focus on.

On the one hand, Kerala is almost like a promised land for women's emancipation. The state has undergone many revolutions when it comes to women's rights, and today we know that Malayali women have better access to education, employment and health facilities than most of their counterparts in other parts of the country. The societal changes brought on by the Leftist movement against untouchability and caste-based discrimination also significantly buttressed women's rights. Then there was the vast poverty alleviation and small-scale entrepreneurship scheme of the Kudumbashree movement, which brought women from all sections of society into the ranks of the employed. Kudumbashree, with a membership of more than 43 lakh women, is the largest network of women in the world. This organization of neighbourhood groups of women in Kerala is based on the fundamental belief that the empowerment of women is closely linked to economic empowerment. Through the Kudumbashree network women can unify and work on a range of issues while also being able to engage in income-generating activities and access reliable microcredit.

The Kudumbashree movement has its foundations in the Left ideology of women's empowerment, particularly the emphasis communism has laid on their freedom from domestic work burdens. During the Russian Revolution, revolutionary socialists like Alexandra Kollontai and Clara Zetkin discussed women's brutal living conditions with Vladimir Lenin. After the Russian Revolution Lenin announced that women would be enlisted to work in the economy, administration, legislature and other government businesses. All courses and educational institutions were open to them so that they could improve their professional training. And to further alleviate the domestic pressures on women, he promised to open facilities like creches, public laundries and common kitchens.

Kerala, with its socialistic leanings and as the site of the first democratically elected communist government in the world, has many realities to contend with. On the one hand, the state has gone a long way in shedding its feudal heritage but at the same time it sits within a feudal, capitalist country. Its inclinations and reactions can sometimes seem self-contradictory, and especially now as religious fundamentalism rises all over the country, in our state, issues like women's rights cannot be allowed to slide backward. As Malayalis, we must face the reality that women's educational status has not resulted in equal representation in all ways and places, especially in the workforce in Kerala. We've also not been able to completely remove the shackles of superstitions and patriarchal belief systems. Violence against women, which is endemic throughout the country, is also endemic in Kerala. Women are so enveloped by domestic chores that they are not visible enough in public life, particularly in decision-making positions. Even women who have managed to build careers for themselves are still expected to bear household responsibilities, often entirely, and so become doubly burdened. People have strong opinions on these topics based on their cultural and religious systems. They have the right to that, of course. But it is the government's job to set the standard.

The government's role is to keep repeating through word and action that every citizen, regardless of gender, has certain unassailable rights. It cannot ensure that every household will abide by these laws within its four walls. We often see that they don't. When it comes to dowry, domestic violence and many malevolent social practices, we know that people behave in a complicit manner, allowing these things to go on. Yet, the government must persevere, campaign loudly, put legal guarantees in place, and enforce them when malpractices and discrimination come to light. The main goal is to change social mindsets. When I write about the things that our departments did to combat our society's worst ideas, it may seem like a whole lot of sloganeering, but what is a public campaign but a form of communication of governance ideals and principles. When I took charge of these departments my team and I looked at smaller, nuanced problems that different groups faced and tried to address those with the belief that progress is made with small steps.

For instance, in our culturally conservative society, there is an assumption that a woman who is out late in the evening is 'asking for trouble'. It is a frightening sexist notion that has often had brutal consequences for women. My team and I were very keen to address this problem. Of course, women have equal rights to public spaces.

Of course, we must be able to walk where we want when we want without the harassment of society's biases or even its patriarchal protectiveness. In 2017, one of Kerala's most celebrated actresses was attacked while she was returning from her workplace one night. I know women and their families shuddered at the fact that such a thing had happened in our state. It created an even more chilling atmosphere for women. Why should one half of the population be expected to curb their daily activities because of the malfeasance of a few? We needed to address the issue.

The WCD department announced a campaign called 'Sadharyam munnottu' – Be brave, go ahead – comprising a series of activities that were meant to reinforce women's right to be present in public spaces at whatever time of day and night they chose. The first major event was a series of Night Walks that encouraged women to occupy streets late at night, buoyed by the slogan 'Pothu idam entethum' (Public space is mine too). The first of these walks was organized on 29 December 2019. The date was very significant, because it was Nirbhaya Day, commemorated as the death anniversary of that brave young woman who was gang-raped in Delhi back in 2012. It was a message to our society that women don't need to keep to particular hours. I am very encouraged by the fact that thousands of women, including many who don't usually participate in public campaigns of this kind, continue to organize and participate in these Night Walk events even today. (If you recall, another Night Walk event in January 2020, in which I participated, became the backdrop of a significant development during the early days of COVID.)

We also wanted to create a safe space for women travellers who needed a temporary economical place to stay overnight in Kerala's towns and cities. The solution was Ente Koodu (My Nest), a group of air-conditioned rooms and dormitories, usually located near Kerala State Road Transportation Corporation (KSRTC) bus stands and railway stations, maintained by the WCD department. The first one was inaugurated in Thiruvananthapuram in 2019.

The safety and rehabilitation of sexual assault victims was of particular concern for the government. On the one hand, survivors were given Rs 2 lakh immediate financial aid and they had the option of living in one of the many government-run safehouses called Nirbhaya homes. But we also wanted to ensure that they would be able to reclaim their lives beyond their circumstances. So we set up a programme called Tejomaya in order to identify and support survivors who wanted to pursue higher education. Several women made use of this opportunity and eventually joined the workforce, and one person in particular became a lawyer.

I have mentioned the increasing influence of religious and political conservatism. One example of that was the extreme reaction in Kerala to the Supreme Court verdict allowing women's entry into the Sabarimala temple. Historically, women were free to visit this very important temple located in Kerala's central district of Pathanamthitta. However, at some point, women of reproductive age were barred from entering Sabarimala, which was given legal sanction by a Kerala High Court ruling. In September 2018, in a judgment on a Public Interest Litigation that challenged the custom, the Supreme Court overruled the High Court and declared that all pilgrims, regardless of gender, could enter the temple. Of course, the Kerala government had a legal responsibility to abide by the court's judgment and protect women who chose to visit the temple. This raised a massive outcry against the government among religious fundamentalists. As an offshoot of that controversy there was a sudden spike in discussions that described menstruation as 'impure'. The WCD department immediately started a campaign against this piece of misinformation. Positing menstruation as a matter of purity was pure superstition, so without wading into any debates on the topic of temple entry, our department sought to prevent the issue leading to a comeback of long-forgotten misrepresentations.

We knew of course that economic upliftment and visibility were crucial to improving the situation for women in the state. As I mentioned earlier, women are not equally represented in all sections of the workforce in Kerala. While there are a considerable number of women at the lowest and mid-levels, there aren't enough women entrepreneurs, business leaders and senior management. In that direction, one of the significant things we were able to do was create a master plan for an International Women's Research and Trade Centre, as part of the Kerala Gender Park in Kozhikode. It has been designed as an inclusive incubation space for women from all sections and different capabilities. For students, it will serve as a resource centre and a venue for the exchange of ideas with experts; for women entrepreneurs, it will be a place to seek help with specific activities to scale their businesses, while for women from the poorest sections of society, the centre will offer skill development opportunities. The plan for the centre kicked off with a Rs 25 crore grant from the government and the signing of an MoU between the Kerala government and UN Women, which agreed to set up its southern zone office at the Gender Park. Of course, all these plans and programmes must be pushed forward and completed for the full potential to be realized. Malayali women are a strong workforce abroad, and the intention with these plans is to aid and help the women who want employment elsewhere or to build businesses and careers in Kerala itself.

Another key area tackled by the WCD department was the state's network of Anganwadis, the childcare centres under the national Integrated Child Development Scheme which serve children from the poorest sections of society. While Anganwadis exist throughout the country, most are in a deplorable condition. In Kerala 80 per cent of these government-run childcare centres are at least working out of their own buildings, even though most are not very spacious. The government decided to upgrade these buildings and refashion them with modern facilities. We created a master plan for a string of contemporary Anganwadis we called 'Smart Anganwadis', taking the best ideas from the Montessori and home-grown Jodo Gyan method, which focuses on learning through play using special tools and kits. These improved Anganwadis would be created in existing ones that were located on at least three to five cents of land. We began this project by allocating funds for at least one Smart Anganwadi in each of the fourteen districts. Today, five have been completed by the government. At the same time, several panchayats have mimicked this model on their own, and that way many improved Smart Anganwadis have emerged in the state.

Something I am particularly proud of is the effort the department put into addressing the mental health of children. We increased the coverage of counselling services in government schools, particularly focusing on teenagers. During COVID and the difficult time when online schooling became the norm, counselling services became an especially important aid for children. There was constant focus on mental health in all sorts of situations related to COVID, with the department offering these services to people in quarantine, patients and others alienated by the crisis. I firmly believe this was invaluable, that without this intervention we would have seen a heartbreaking increase in cases of suicide. There are many more things that were done: when I rummage through my memory, more and more of these details tumble out. Yet, as I said at the beginning, so much cannot be put down here, or you will be burdened with a listing of anecdotes.

The last of the three departments that were part of my portfolio was Social Justice, which oversaw issues pertaining to some of the most vulnerable and discriminated populations in the state: the disabled, the transgender community, senior citizens, ex-convicts and the destitute. I like to think of the Social Justice portfolio as a place for empathy, an opportunity for that ambiguous entity we call a government to behave with kindness and care. The government's role here is critical also because its attitude affects the way society itself behaves with alienated communities. The issues you don't address say a lot about one's biases.

The work related to the social justice department provided me with some of my most reassuring and treasured memories of my time as a minister. I'd like to share two stories here. The first is about a little girl whose face and name are etched in my mind. Eleven-year-old Sonamol. She was admitted to a private hospital in Thrissur to treat epilepsy, and later developed a condition called toxic epidermal necrolysis, which caused her to go completely blind. Her parents didn't have the financial wherewithal to pursue further treatment, and so she was living through the trauma of sudden blindness.

The Kerala Social Security Mission, which is a part of the social justice department, was manned by Dr Mohammed Asheel. As executive director of the Mission, he was passionate about this work, and when a bureaucrat has this combination of qualities, great things happen. Dr Asheel read Sonamol's story in the newspaper and he believed we could help her. When he brought the matter to my notice, I discussed it with the department secretary, Biju Prabhakar, another dedicated officer who was especially focused on dealing with children's issues. The department organized for the little girl to meet several experts, but every single one said it would be difficult to restore her eyesight. Then we heard about specialists at the L.V. Prasad Institute in Hyderabad. The Social Security Mission used funds from the We-Care scheme, a registered charity under the social justice department which collects funds from the public to help the poor, and arranged for Sonamol and her family to go to Hyderabad for her treatment. We also dispatched a young doctor called Dr Rahul from the Thrissur Medical College to accompany the family to help them with communication and coordination. It took more than two months of treatment for this little girl to get her eyesight back. But she did.

When the family was ready to return to Kerala, she said she wanted to come meet me first thing. I still remember the day I met Sonamol at the ministerial bungalow in Thiruvananthapuram. As a public servant, I've been lucky enough to have had many moments of exceptional satisfaction. Yet when it's about a child, I feel an immense amount of gratitude for being able to do what I can. Knowing that little girl had a renewed ability to see the world, thinking of the possibilities that had opened up for her again – it gave me a feeling of deep calm and conviction. As a mother and grandmother, I could imagine the trauma her parents had gone through. Gaining Sonamol and her parents' love and gratitude was one of the many high points of my professional life.

The second story I'd like to relate is also about children and parents in difficult situations. They were the people whose lives were touched by a programme called Anuyatra that was run by the social justice department to explore ways in which disabled people could be empowered. The Anuyatra team particularly worked with children who had various developmental issues, from autism to cerebral palsy. The department focused on educating families on how to deal with their children's challenges and on projects that would create interesting opportunities for these kids. One day Dr Asheel came to my office with a celebrity: Kerala's most famous magician and motivational speaker, Gopinath Muthukad. Muthukad had an interesting idea. He wanted to teach magic to disabled children: he believed this unusual intervention would build the children's confidence and create an opportunity for their parents to see these little ones being creative. Who doesn't love to watch their kids perform on stage. It was a chance that low-income parents with disabled kids would probably never get. When I spoke to doctors and other experts, they were doubtful this unusual exercise would yield results, especially in children facing serious motor development problems because of cerebral palsy. I knew Muthukad wanted to partner with the government on this experimental project. While it might have been simpler to say no, seeing the belief in those two men I felt it was worth a try and gave them the go-ahead.

In 2018 Muthukad's Magic Academy, supported by the Kerala State Social Security Mission, selected twenty-three children to undergo training in magic and formed them into a team called MPower (Magic Power). I was there the first day these children started their practice sessions. I remember the trainer distributed two strings to each of us, before instructing us on the way to tie a magic knot that could be untied without using our fingers. Out of the twenty-three children, ten followed the instructions perfectly and did exactly as they were told. It was a great revelation to everyone who was involved in the project. We realized that despite their many difficulties each child had varying levels of capacity and this activity allowed each of them to shine in their own way. In just four months, the children were ready for their first public performance.

Thrilled at the prospect, we wanted the children and parents to have a special audience. The department invited then Vice President of India, Hamid Ansari, former Kerala governor Retd. Chief Justice P. Sathasivam, and Chief Minister Pinarayi Vijayan to attend. On their big day, for forty-five minutes these little performers had the audience in the palm of their hands. Governor Sathasivam was visibly emotional watching the performance, while Vice President Ansari expressed his awe of the kids and congratulated the department for championing the idea.

The kids were such a success that the Magic Academy set up

a permanent performance platform called the MPower Centre supported by UNICEF and the Kerala State Social Security Mission. The older children who are now trained here are also given professional opportunities with Muthukad's team, which has turned them into earning members of their families. But even more importantly, we know from testing and anecdotally through the parents that this programme had an immense positive impact on the kids. It offered them opportunities to identify talents that would have otherwise gone completely unexplored. It also gave the kids something fun and interesting to look forward to every day. It was a public–private partnership that we couldn't have envisioned without Muthukad's enthusiasm. He was so buoyed by the experience that he set up a larger initiative called the Different Arts Centre, which is focused on identifying and training disabled children in various art forms. The social justice department was able to do many things because of people like Muthukad. Many such well-wishers came forward to join hands with the government to set up facilities, including a network of rehabilitation centres. I couldn't be more grateful for their philanthropy. It really helped plug the government's resource deficiencies in this critically important area.

One of the quirks of my portfolio was that within its special focus groups, there were people on the opposite ends of the age spectrum: kids on the one hand and senior citizens on the other. Almost 15 per cent of our population is over sixty years of age, and many of the oldest among them live solitary lives because their children and other relatives live abroad or in other cities. At the same time, there is an increasing number of cases of elder abuse and abandonment. As a government agency the only thing we could do was offer more and better places of succour to abandoned older folks. So, we began work on improving the condition of government-run old age homes and pushed local tribunals to settle complaints of elder abuse. We also had a system in place that ensured older patients with mobility issues received medication at home.

With all these groups of people, from the disabled to the senior citizens, we had a front-seat view of the complicated nature of the family unit. It could be both terrifyingly apathetic and unbelievably supportive. Which end of that care spectrum one ended up on was just a matter of one's destiny. My own home had always been filled with people of varying age groups, and as I wrote earlier, our mothers and my aunt were part of my household at the end of their lives. So for me it always seemed like a terrible loss of opportunity when older people were left out. The intergenerational nature of a home can be very beneficial for all age groups. I understand that requires everyone at home to behave with some amount of wisdom and be willing to make adjustments; unfortunately, that is not always the case.

But of all the various groups of people represented by the social justice department, perhaps none needed as much backing and protection of the government as the transgender community. We began various programmes that increased opportunities for education, skill development and employment among them. When the Kochi Metro began, the chief minister announced that the transgender population must be given jobs and a certain percentage of jobs were kept aside for the transgender community and it certainly impacted both visibility and their earning power. The department also organized the Varnapakittu cultural festival specially for transgender people to show their talents. The two-day festival had 189 contestants from across Kerala. We understood that the most important thing for the transgender population was visibility: it was important for these citizens to claim their space in public life. There were many things that needed to be done for that, of course. We believe we made some progress by adding 'transgender' as a gender option on all government application forms. The government also issued special identity cards for the transgender population and spearheaded a literacy programme so they could complete their education.

For all that I relate here and all the work that I know is being done on these matters, the fact remains that in India, social justice for all is still a utopian dream. Yet, it is important to keep trying, to keep fixing, making small improvements to a broken system so all of this will finally add up to a transformation. In Kerala, I am proud of the effort our government makes. We don't always get it right, but we try. I was extremely lucky to have had a team of people who believed in our purpose as a department as much as I did. A quirk of the department, or rather a discipline, was ensuring every phone call was answered. As a minister, I couldn't often take calls myself but someone on my team always would. We follow this principle even today. Everyone on my team was empowered enough to make sure that every caller was heard and reassured they'd get an answer. We can't help everyone at once, but we can at least listen.

When you look at these portfolios, the challenges and problems they encompass could be overwhelming. But far from paralysing my team, it acted as a spur for them; they were always creative and solution oriented, I am proud to say. They were my eyes and ears out there, hearing and learning on my behalf, always ensuring that people understood that the system cared. That 'we' feeling helped us deal with many frustrations, heartbreaks and disappointments. When you're in government you hear so many difficult stories that sometimes the burden can be staggering. This is also why fighting for social justice is the ultimate endeavour, especially at a time when fascist tendencies are on the rise. We must do our best.

Epilogue: Onward

From the moment I accepted the job of minister for Health, Women and Child Development and Social Justice in Chief Minister Pinarayi Vijayan's government in 2016, I was conscious of the responsibility I was taking on. Especially as a woman. Because if one of us does a bad job, people criticize our entire gender. So, I felt this strong conviction that I had to make sure these portfolios made a significant contribution while under my watch, and that we put science – rather than biases and fears – at the forefront.

When I started my work, I had a plan. I would comprehensively study every part of each portfolio, starting at the very bottom of the structures on which they rested. I had more than thirty-five years of public service behind me, and over those decades I had built up an understanding of the system from its lowest rungs. I knew the stories of the people and the realities of their lives from personal experience, and as a minister my desire was to effect changes that could make a real difference. And I was able to do much of it only because I was working within the people-centric LDF government. Its focus on people is self-evident in its manifesto and gave me a grounding for the work we had to do.

I began with this intense desire to make an impact, and that motivated me throughout those five years, despite the many crises and obstacles we faced. I personally felt the pressure of each of the difficult situations we went through, particularly the public health crises of Nipah and COVID. But on the positive side, it was a term filled with immense professional satisfaction. When you get to solve problems that have existed for a while, when you can help a patient recover, or make improvements to a system, the sense of fulfilment is beyond any award, any recognition.

When we went into the 2021 election campaign season, from February to April, we were still dealing with the pandemic, but Kerala had outperformed every other state on all measurable counts throughout the crisis. As a state we'd combated historic problems and people understood the effort it had taken to get through it all. There was an unusual positive sentiment in the air at the time. Malayalis are very politically engaged and ruthless when it comes to roasting their politicians, but in 2021 there was a feeling that the government had truly done its best. As a representative of the health department, I believed that despite the day-to-day crises of the bulk of my ministerial term, my team had managed to start building anew on the foundation we'd inherited. You can't create a healthcare system in five years; you can only improve upon the existing set-up, and that's what we did. We'd started a process that would be complete only years after.

The LDF government had come to power in 2016 with an ambitious goal to remodel the state for a new century, so every branch of government stepped up to make that happen. The health department, for instance, had an exceptional amount of support from the cabinet, particularly from the finance department. Without the KIIFB, of which I've spoken earlier, we wouldn't have had the resources to fund many of the projects we initiated. K.M. Abraham, the CEO of KIIFB and the current chief principal secretary to the chief minister, advised us accurately each time we needed it. Meeting after meeting, yelling, cajoling, refining project reports, and with a dedicated team that would go back and forth as many times as required, we were able to see things through. For that matter, the chief minister's continuous appraisal of our projects helped maintain our momentum and push forward.

On the election trail I felt that people realized the effort that had gone in and appreciated the results. There was a feeling that ours was a people-friendly government that had done its best. There was less cynicism; on the other hand, there was fandom from very unexpected sources. I remember meeting one gentleman during my campaign in Mattanur, who said, 'I am a lotus man [BJP supporter], but this time, Teacher, I'll vote for you.' So, going into the election, I felt quite positive. I thought my own result could be above 49,000 votes, which was the existing record in the state.

Indeed, it turned out to be a historic summer. In May 2021 the LDF, headed by the CPI(M) and Comrade Pinarayi Vijayan, was voted back to power for an unprecedented consecutive second term, securing 99 seats out of 140 Assembly constituencies. In Kerala's election history, that has never happened. In this state, election results have always pushed out parties – either the LDF or the UDF, led by the Congress – like a swivel door, one coming in, the other going out, term after term. Till this last election. For me, the election season was the culmination of five years of exceptional highs and lows, the pinnacle of a career I'd never expected for myself. I was re-elected to my seat in the Mattanur constituency with the largest mandate in Kerala's election history: a margin of 61,000 votes.

The approval of your own people matters much more than any

award. So, when the results came, I was happy of course, but I always feel in such situations – maybe because of the way I grew up – somewhat tense, a little worried. A sense of foreboding. Perhaps people expected me to be part of the new cabinet, but that wasn't the Party's decision. To foster another generation of leaders, the new cabinet had a crop of fresh faces, including former journalist Veena George as the new health minister. My new mandate was to be the party whip of the CPI(M) and the chairman of the Estimate Committee, one of the four financial committees in Kerala's Legislative Assembly. It is the first time a woman has held either position.

I've been asked many times since that election whether I was disappointed about not being part of the second LDF cabinet in 2021. I wasn't particularly surprised or concerned about the seat in the cabinet, but it had been my dream to complete the process of renewing the health sector, and I was concerned that perhaps those changes would be left incomplete. It takes more than one term to finish a task as large as the one we'd undertaken. How can you revamp an entire system in less than five years on a shoestring budget whilst also fighting multiple public health crises? You can't, but you can start and hope that others keep the process going, follow the plan and finish the job. These are essential societal changes and a governmental responsibility. Since Kerala still has an LDF government the modernisation drive we started in 2016 will continue and a vast metamorphosis will occur in Kerala's public healthcare system.

Generally, I don't feel possessive about positions, or any circumstance of my life. Everything changes, and you must adapt. If I didn't adapt, I wouldn't be where I am today. I am an ordinary woman, but my philosophical roots are very strong. They are not shaken by the actions of others and the ebb and flow of politics. I understand that people are perplexed by my reaction or lack thereof. But my perspective is entirely different. When I was a college student my central concern for my life was whether it would have purpose. I come from loving yet difficult circumstances, with a history of family members whose lives were extinguished before their ambitions could be fulfilled. From one angle that is an invaluable legacy to inherit but, from another, knowing that my family sacrificed so much makes me feel a sense of tremendous responsibility. So today, when I think of the opportunities that have come my way, I am truly grateful that I could be useful. I believe all political workers have stories like this. I put down my experiences in the hope that new people coming into the world of political work will find something of use in my anecdotes.

I also feel exceptionally lucky that my family had the intellectual foresight to choose and fight for communist beliefs. I believe this political philosophy, which puts the group above self, has made all the difference to our state. It is what enabled our system to work together to beat an invisible enemy. We work as a group for the greater good. We believe that the weakest need to be put at the forefront. It gives us clarity and focus. One good-intentioned individual can only do so much in government but a group of well-intentioned people … well, that's real strength.

As the face of the 2016–21 health department in the Kerala government, I am proud of the work we did and the accolades we're offered, even when I turn them down. As happened with the Ramon Magsaysay Award. On 29 July 2022, I received an email from the Magsaysay Award committee in the Philippines, telling me I had been chosen as one of the four award winners for 2022. As a member of the Party Central Committee of the CPI(M), I discussed this development with my colleagues, and it was decided I should turn down the award for various political reasons. So, indeed, that is exactly what I did. In situations like that, when public and political considerations seem to pull in opposing ways, I like to remember what Mother Teresa once said: 'If you are humble, nothing will touch you, neither praise nor disgrace because you know what you are.'

Now my attention is entirely focused on my Party work and the constituency, Mattanur, that I represent. I have spent my entire life in the district of Kannur. This region and people are the foundation of my personal and professional life. And there is so much to be done here. In Subroto Bagchi's book *Go Kiss the World*, the entrepreneur and advisor to Odisha Chief Minister Naveen Patnaik talks of meeting his mother when she was sick and couldn't see him because she'd lost her eyesight. When he kissed her forehead, she said, 'Why kiss me, go kiss the world, there's much to do.'[1] Indeed, in public life there are many obstacles to overcome and much to get done.

I am not a scholar, and I don't have high educational qualifications. I have a basic degree, and I am a schoolteacher, that is all. I studied Marxist philosophy and accepted it deeply, and that is what has impacted my life. Socialist ideology talked about having a scientific temperament, and pushing forward for equality and egalitarianism. What are communism and socialism after all? Broadly they stand for the belief that everyone should work according to their capacity and take according to their needs. Whichever field you are in, you can apply this principle.

The magic of public service is impact, and it can keep you going and going – and going. I've heard people remark about the longevity of politicians' careers, how remarkable it is that most of us never retire. I think that energy and renewal come from that ability to make a difference. New challenges give new purpose.

So, my life as a comrade continues . . .

Notes

Preface

1. Alexandra Kollontai (translated by Salvator Attansio), *The Autobiography of a Sexually Emancipated Communist Woman*, Herder and Herder, 1971. Citation refers to the Herder and Herder edition.

1. An Intertwined History

1. Jawaharlal Nehru, *Glimpses of World History*, Penguin Books, 1934.
2. Sheeba P.K., 'A Peep into the History of Kottiyoor Migration', *International Journal of English Literature and Social Sciences*, vol. 6, no. 2, March–April 2021, https://ijels.com/upload_document/issue_files/68IJELS-104202154-APeep.pdf.

2. Communism Comes Home

1. 'Formation of the Communist Party of India at Tashkent (1920)', cpim. org. https://cpim.org/history/formation-communist-party-india-tashkent-1920.
2. EMS Namboodiripad, 'The Congress Socialist Party and the Communists', cpim.org. https://www.cpim.org/content/congress-socialist-party-and-communists.
3. 'Red Salute to Salem Jail Martyrs!', *Peasant Struggle*, 11 February 2018,

https://kisansabha.org/aiks/movements-and-struggles/red-salute-to-salem-jail-martyrs/.

3. Winds of Change

1. 'Recalling AKG's Tryst with Amaravathi', *The Indian Express*, 16 May 2012, https://www.newindianexpress.com/states/kerala/2011/jun/07/recalling-akgs-tryst-with-amaravathi-260400.html.

8. A New Chapter Begins

1. Robert M. Wolfe and Lisa K. Sharp, 'Anti-vaccinationists Past and Present', *The BMJ*, 24 August 2002, https://www.bmj.com/rapid-response/2011/10/29/history-vaccination-and-anti-vaccination-programmes-india.
2. B.A. Prakash and Jerry Alwin (eds), *Kerala's Economic Development: Emerging Issues and Challenges*, Sage Publishing, October 2018.

11. Taming Nipah

1. 'Emerging and Re-emerging Zoonoses', World Organisation for Animal Health News, 18 November 2004, https://www.woah.org/en/emerging-and-re-emerging-zoonoses/#:~:text=An%20emerging%20disease%20is%20defined,previously%20unrecognised%20infection%20or%20disease.
2. Jonathan H. Epstein, Simon J. Anthony, Ariful Islam and Peter Daszak, 'Nipah Virus Dynamics in Bats and Implications for Spillover to Humans', *Proceedings of the National Academy of Sciences of the United States of America*, vol. 117, no. 46, 2 November 2020, https://doi.org/10.1073/pnas.2000429117.

12. A Deadlier Virus Strikes

1. Laura Spinney, 'The Coronavirus Slayer! How Kerala's Rock Star Health Minister Helped Save It from Covid-19', *The Guardian*, 14 May 2020, https://theguardian.com/world/2020/may/14/the-coronavirus-slayer-how-keralas-rock-star-health-minister-helped-save-it-from-covid-19.

2. 'Covid: Sarkar Kanakinnu Purame 16 Maranam Koodi' [Covid: 16 Deaths Above the Government Count], *Malayala Manorama*, 27 September 2020.

3. Manju Sara Rajan, 'KK Shailaja on Being in the Thick of Things during COVID-19: "More than Fear, I Feel an Enthusiasm to Get Involved"', *Vogue India*, 9 November 2020, https://www.vogue.in/culture-and-living/content/kk-shailaja-kerala-minister-interview-vogue-india-november-2020-cover-story.

Epilogue: Onward

1. Subroto Bagchi, *Go Kiss the World: Life Lessons for the Young Professional*, Penguin Books, 2006.

Select Bibliography

Bagchi, Subroto. *Go Kiss the World: Life Lessons for the Young Professional.* Penguin Books, 2006.

'Covid: Sarkar Kanakinnu Purame 16 Maranam Koodi' [Covid: 16 Deaths Above the Government Count]. *Malayala Manorama.* 27 September 2020.

Epstein, Jonathan H., Simon J. Anthony, Ariful Islam and Peter Daszak. 'Nipah Virus Dynamics in Bats and Implications for Spillover to Humans'. *Proceedings of the National Academy of Sciences of the United States of America*, vol. 117, no. 46, 2 November 2020.

'Formation of the Communist Party of India at Tashkent (1920)'. cpim.org. https://cpim.org/history/formation-communist-party-india-tashkent-1920.

Kollontai, Alexandra. *The Autobiography of a Sexually Emancipated Communist Woman*, trans. Salvator Attansio. Herder and Herder, 1971.

'Martyrs Remembered'. *The Hindu*, 13 February 2016.

Nabae, Koji. 'The Health Care System in Kerala: Its Past Accomplishments and New Challenges'. *Journal of the National Institute of Public Health* [Japan], vol. 52, no. 2, 2003.

Namboodiripad, E.M.S. 'The Congress Socialist Party and the Communists'. cpim.org, January 1984. https://www.cpim.org/content/congress-socialist-party-and-communists.

Nehru, Jawaharlal. *Glimpses of World History*. Penguin Books, 1934.

Prakash, B.A. 'Agricultural Backwardness of Malabar during the Colonial Period (1792–1947): An Analysis of Economic Causes'. *Social Scientist,* vol. 16, November 6–7, June–July 1988). Republished by Thiruvananthapuram Economic Studies Society, September 2017.

Prakash, B.A. and Jerry Alwin (eds). *Kerala's Economic Development: Emerging Issues and Challenges.* Sage Publishing, October 2018.

P.K., Sheeba. 'A Peep into the History of Kottiyoor Migration'. *International Journal of English Literature and Social Sciences,* vol. 5, no. 2, March–April 2021.

Rajan, Manju Sara. 'KK Shailaja on Being in the Thick of Things during COVID-19: "More than Fear, I Feel an Enthusiasm to Get Involved"'. *Vogue India,* 9 November 2020.

'Recalling AKG's Tryst with Amaravathi'. *The Indian Express,* 16 May 2012.

'Red Salute to Salem Jail Martyrs!'. *Peasant Struggle,* 11 February 2018.

Spinney, Laura. 'The Coronavirus Slayer! How Kerala's Rock Star Health Minister Helped Save It from Covid-19'. *The Guardian,* 14 May 2020.

Spinney, Laura. 'How KK Shailaja and Her 'Covid Brigade' Won a Victory Against the Virus'. *The Guardian,* 22 December 2020.

Wolfe, Robert M. and Lisa K. Sharp, 'Anti-vaccinationists Past and Present', *The BMJ,* 24 August 2002.

World Health Organization (website). 'Nipah Virus Disease – India'. 24 September 2021. https://www.who.int/emergencies/disease-outbreak-news/item/nipah-virus-disease---india.

World Organisation for Animal Health News (website). 'Emerging and Re-emerging Zoonoses'. 18 November 2004. https://woah.org/en/emerging-and-re-emerging-zoonoses/#:~:text=An%20emerging%20disease%20is%20defined,previously%20unrecognised%20infection%20or%20disease.

Acknowledgements

For some time now I've been meaning to write a book about my grandmother, but I never got around to it because of my busy work schedule. This book has given me a chance to remember her and to talk about the many stories I'd been carrying in my mind for so long. My heartfelt thanks to Juggernaut Books, especially Chiki Sarkar, for encouraging me to work on this book.

I didn't have any diaries or notes to share when we began working on this, so I owe no small debt to my dearest Manju Sara Rajan, who listened to my experiences that came out all mixed up like a kaleidoscope. But she was able to organize, arrange and then craft everything beautifully in English. Due to my schedule while I was a minister, then during the election campaign and later in the midst of so many distractions, I was never able to give as much time or attention to this project, but Manju was always patient and she threaded everything together piece by piece. One of the cherished experiences to come out of our work together is the wonderful time I spent in Kottayam at Manju's house with her family. My team and I will always remember the lovingly made and presented meals, long conversations walking through the garden and in her library and the sound of the birds everywhere. That quiet and peaceful environment by the Meenachil river contributed greatly to the making of this book and it was a lovely background to our writing partnership.

I must also thank Bhaskarettan and my children Shobith, Sinju, Lasith and Megha, who continuously reminded me to work and finish this book. It was another one of the many things I couldn't have done with all my heart without their support.

It was my personal assistant and disciple Pramod who deliberately planned and set aside time from my schedule to focus on working on this memoir. Otherwise I don't know how I would have managed to do it. I have to also mention here the other members of my staff – Shiju, Vimal and Shajahan, who have, over the years, become like family to me.

I want to mention here comrades Brinda Karat and Subhashini Ali. Both have always been a source of inspiration and support in my political career. And now I also realize that though I was able to mention the names of some of the many people I worked with during the course of my career, there are many who I couldn't talk about. I must emphasize here that despite that omission, I am aware of the importance of each person's role in different aspects of my life. I am a product of my community and for that, I am most grateful.

K.K. Shailaja

I began working on this book in early 2021 during what we all now call 'COVID time'. That year and the following turned out to be critical years for Shailaja Teacher, me and our families. There were moments when I didn't think we would get to the finish line, because so much seemed to be happening around us and to us. Now when I look back at the two years it took for this book to take shape, the years during which we worked on it were also seminal points in our personal and professional lives.

The greatest gift that has come to me from this book is the relationship I've formed with Teacher and her team. I've been lucky enough to be at the receiving end of her empathy and care many times. In January 2021, after weeks of coordination, when Shailaja Teacher arrived at my home, for what was meant to be an intense few days of writing, I was diagnosed with COVID and she had to leave. For the next ten days, every morning hers was the first call of the day. On days when she missed the check-in, her assistant, Mr. Pramod, would be on the phone, asking if I needed anything. Our friendship and camaraderie is an unintended and a most welcome result of this time spent together and all that happened while working on the book.

During the writing of *My Life as a Comrade*, there were many days when the blank page was so scary that I just blocked it off. My friend of more than a decade and incessant cheerleader, fellow journalist and author Madhavankutty Pillai, was always the phone call I made during those moments. From suggesting author-friendly software and tips to reading the first few chapters, he was my writing helpline, and I am most grateful for his wisdom and encouragement with regard to this book and so much more. A special mention to Susan Cherian, who helped me copyedit the book before I submitted my first draft and shared stories about her own family's relationship with communism.

The lesson I learned from hearing Teacher's story was about the power of family. The family unit is our constant learning ground and – for good and sometimes bad, consciously and unconsciously – impacts choices, often over generations. Teacher's story made me reflect on my own family, and while some no longer remain, they all have left an impact on me as a writer. I wrote most of this book at my home in Kottayam, Kerala, during the same time that my boys, Mark and Samir Mathew, were housebound and attending online school. In mid-2022 the two of them would head off for boarding school, and as it turned out, our days at home for the previous two years were a gratifying bookend to seven years together in Kerala. Their entry into my life changed me forever, and this book and everything I do is dedicated to my boys.

There are two people forever watching over me, checking my flight arrival and departure times, cajoling me to drink enough water and travel a bit less: my parents. Molly and Rajan Abraham have survived immense heartbreaks with optimism and forgiveness and have taught me a great deal about how to live life. Thank you for your acceptance, care and support – it means everything to me. My late brother Manoj Rajan, who stood in line for hours so Jeffrey Archer could sign a copy of *Twelve Red Herrings* for my eighteenth birthday, always supported my love of books and read everything I wrote.

My friends Sunita Namjoshi, Namita and Alex Kuruvilla, Murielle and Joe Ikareth, Ruby Jacob, Sunil Eapen, Reema Gupta, Rachana Nakra, Wei Leng Tay, Shameem Akhtar, Malini Mathew, Divya Varughese: in word and deed, you helped me profoundly during the making of this book. You listened, held my hand, nurtured, counselled and supported me in every way that I needed so I could get to the finish line. Please know that I am immensely grateful.

Manju Sara Rajan

A Note on the Author and Co-Author

K.K. Shailaja is a member of the Legislative Assembly of Kerala from the Mattanur constituency and a CPI(M) Central Committee Member. She is the former minister for Health, Social Justice, Women and Child Development of Kerala. Popularly known as 'Shailaja Teacher', she is the author of several books on gender, communism and public health in Malayalam.

Manju Sara Rajan is a writer, editor and arts manager, who is presently the editor-in-chief of beautifulhomes.com, India's largest design and décor content platform, by Asian Paints, where she also serves as an advisor. She is the former CEO of the Kochi Biennale Foundation, where she oversaw the management of Kochi-Muziris Biennale 2016. She was the founding editor of the Indian edition of *Architectural Digest* and contributing editor for *Vogue*. MSR began her career in 2002 as a reporter in *Time* magazine's Asia bureau in Hong Kong, before moving to India and other media publications like *Indian Express*, *Mint Lounge* and *Open* magazine. In 2020, she wrote several profile pieces on K.K. Shailaja for *Vogue* India's coverage of the COVID pandemic and its management. This book was the outcome of her cover profile of Shailaja Teacher in the November 2020 edition, in which Shailaja Teacher was named 'Leader of the year'.

Index

Aardram Mission, 138–9, 142, 149, 154, 158, 160; Award, 171

Abdul Rehman Sahib, Mohammad, 27

Abraham, K.M., 273

Abu Bakkar (Kayyur martyr), 67–8

access: to education, 245; to healthcare, 131, 132

accountability, 128

accredited social health activist (ASHA), 165, 190

Achuthanandan, V.S., 47

agitations: against to evictions, 27; of farmers, 26, 28; for India's Independence, 27; against Salem jail massacre, 33–4

AIIMS *see* All India Institute of Medical Sciences (AIIMS)

Ajanya (nursing student infected with Nipah), 201–3

AKG, 23–5, 27, 38, 46, 96, 98; hunger strike for land acquisition drive, 45–6

Alappuzha, 212, 220, 225

All India Institute of Medical Sciences (AIIMS), 162

Alma-Ata declaration of 1978, 132

Amaravathi, 45–6

America, COVID-19 mitigation methods in, 223

American upma *see* yellow upma

AMR *see* antimicrobial resistance (AMR)

Amrutham Arogyam project, 165

amshamadhikari, 32

Anganwadis, 104–5, 263–4

Anoop (doctor), 181

Ansari, Hamid, 267

antibiotics misuse, 167

anti-caste revolution, 244

anti-communist groups, 44

antigen test for COVID-19, 223–4

antimicrobial resistance (AMR), 166–7

Antony, A.K., 118

Antony, Mini, 129

Anupama, T.V., 210, 225

Anuyatra programme, 266–8

Apex Trauma and Emergency
    Learning Centre, 163
Appanu yajamanan, 32, 41–2
Appu (Kayyur martyr), 67–8
Aralam, 97
Arogya Jagratha (Health Vigilance),
    180; Facebook page and mobile
    app, 204; portal, 254
arranged marriages, 51, 53, 78, 105
artificial intelligence, 254
Arun (head of MIV), 182, 183, 198
Arya Vaidya Sala hospital, 134
ASHA see accredited social health
    activist (ASHA)
Asha (doctor), 198
Asheel, Mohammed, 162, 225, 226,
    265–6
Assembly elections: Kuthuparamba
    constituency, 110–13, 124;
    Peravoor constituency, 118–19,
    122–4
Astana declaration in 2018, 132
asymptomatic, positive, stable
    patients, 222, 231
atrocities, 22; caste, 42; of Malabar
    Special Police (MSP), 67
Australia, treatment for Henipavirus
    infection in, 200–1
Ayappancoil, land acquisition drive
    in, 45
Ayurvedic systems, 134
Ayush, 129

Baby Memorial Hospital in
    Kozhikode, 181
Balakrishnan, Kodiyeri, 101

Balan, A.K., 120–1
Balaram, N.E., 38
Balwadis, 104. see also Anganwadis
Bangladesh, Nipah virus in, 184, 186,
    187
basic life support (BLS) ambulances,
    163
BEd education of Shailaja, K.K., 86,
    106
Beena (doctor), 225
Bhagawati (local goddess), 16
Bhaskaran Master, K., 74–82, 85–9,
    110, 111, 119, 125
Bhaskarettan see Bhaskaran Master,
    K.
Bhattacharyya, Lord Sushanta
    Kumar, 164, 165
Bhattathiripaadu, V.T., 76
Bhoi, Sanjeev Kumar, 162
Bijoy (general manager, SHA), 252
BLS ambulances see basic life
    support (BLS) ambulances
BMC see Brihanmumbai Municipal
    Corporation (BMC)
Bolshevik Party, 22
bourgeoisie, 47, 128
brahmarakshassus, 61–2
'Break the chain' campaign, 222, 226
Brihanmumbai Municipal
    Corporation (BMC), 230
British administration of Malabar,
    8–13
BSc degree of Shailaja, K.K., 99
bureaucracy, 127–8
bureaucrats, 139; ministers and, 128

Calicut, 152
Cancer Control Board, 167
Cancer Strategic Action Plan, 167
cancer treatment, 161
capitalism, 246
capitalistic economic model, 246
cardiology care, 159
castes: atrocities, 42; bias, 25,
    247; and clothing, 35, 40–1;
    discrimination, 41–2, 47;
    eliminating barriers, 244; in
    Malabar, 5, 8, 9; and religion, 244;
    role in smallpox, 37–8
caste system: in Malabar, 5, 8, 9;
    practice, 19–20
casualty departments, 158
Chahal, Iqbal Singh, 229–30
Chandran (son of Shailaja's
    grandmother), 18, 29, 34, 59
Chandran Master, K.T., 83
Chandrika (daughter of Shailaja's
    grandmother), 18, 29, 59, 69
Chanduettan (veteran leader), 112
Chathukutti (local committee
    member), 109
CHC see Community Health Centre
    (CHC)
CHD see congenital heart disease
    (CHD)
Chemmaruthi, 152
Chengarothu, Nipah virus in, 183,
    189–91
Chennithala, Ramesh, 198
Cheriyamma of Kavumbayi, 20–1
Chief Minister's Distress Relief
    Fund (CMDRF), 177, 221

chikungunya, 184
children: Anuyatra programme for,
    266–8; counselling services for,
    264; girl, 59; Muthukad's magic
    programme for, 266–8
Chirukandan (Kayyur martyr), 67–8
Christian educational institutions,
    44; mission hospitals, 135
Chua Kaw Beng, 185
clothing, caste and, 35, 40–1
cluster management strategy at
    Poonthura, 228–30
CMDRF see Chief Minister's
    Distress Relief Fund (CMDRF)
cobalt machine, 161
Cochin, 133
Cochin Cancer Research Centre,
    179, 184
colonial administration, 8–13, 19
colonialism, 247
communalism, 44–5
communalist forces, violence of, 96
communism, 3, 46; ban of, 27;
    bureaucracy and, 128; influence,
    42; in Malabar, 7, 22; and
    women's empowerment, 259
Communist Party of India (CPI),
    22–4, 31, 33; egalitarian
    approach, 2, 131; establishment
    of, 22; health classes for smallpox,
    38–9; sixth National Council of,
    47; socialist revolution, 46–7;
    voted to power, 43, 273
Communist Party of India (Marxist)
    (CPI(M)), 47, 72, 90, 98, 101,
    113, 122, 179

Community Health Centre (CHC), 137

community transmission of COVID-19, 230

congenital heart disease (CHD), 165–6

Congress government *see* United Democratic Front (UDF) government

Congress Socialist Party (CSP), 23, 24

construction of bridges, 115–16

contact-tracing: COVID-19, 209, 216; of Nipah virus, 191–2; technological investigations, 254

control rooms, 254; for COVID-19, 208

Corporate Social Responsibility (CSR) scheme, 152

Cotiote Wars, 10

counselling services for children, 264

Covid Care Centres (CCCs), 222, 232

Covid First Line Treatment Centres (CFLTCs), 222

COVID-19 in Kerala, 155, 161–3; antigen test for, 223–4; asymptomatic, positive, stable patients, 222, 231; bed capacity/strength, 222, 228, 231; cases per day, 230–2; cluster management strategy at Poonthura, 228–9; community transmission of, 230; contact tracing, 209, 216; control room for, 208; daily updates, 218; dashboard, 253–4; death analysis, 239, 241; Europe as a hotspot, 214–15; health emergency declaration, 220–1; help desk for, 214, 215; hiding death count as fake news, 238–41; identifying the first positive case, 210; increase of testing numbers, 223, 224; incubation period, 213, 221; infection rate, 223, 230, 233; insurance scheme for, 250–2; isolation at home, 231; from Italy, 214–15, 218; maintaining hygienic isolation, 231; mismatching the results of RT-PCR tests, 225; mitigation method for, 213–14, 223; mobile ambulance units for, 226; mortality rate, 207, 214, 223, 227, 232, 234; national lockdown for, 161, 220, 222, 227, 234, 254; in NRI Malayali, 220; oxygen capacity management, 249–50; peak of, 230; personal protective equipment (PPE), 249; Plan A, Plan B and Plan C strategies, 227–8, 231; prevalence of variants, 232–3; progress in mitigation of, 227; quarantine for, 212–13, 215, 221–3, 226–7, 231; rapid response team for, 208; reporting system, 253; RT-PCR test, 224, 225; rumours and fears about, 231–2; scanning people at airport, 213; state assembly election of 2021 and, 233; technology use, 253–4; test and results, 212, 214–16, 224; testing

passengers from Italy, 214–15;
three-pronged strategy to control,
222–6; total shutdown, 229–30;
treatment and quarantine of
British tourists in Idukki, 218–19;
uncooperative patients and, 216,
217; vaccines, 234–6; worst-case
scenario, 231
COVID RNA, 224
Covid Second Line Treatment
Centres (CSLTCs), 222
CPI *see* Communist Party of India
(CPI)
CPI(M) *see* Communist Party of
India (Marxist) (CPI(M))
cremation of Nipah patients, 199–
200
crisis management cells, 254
CSLTCs *see* Covid Second Line
Treatment Centres (CSLTCs)
CSP *see* Congress Socialist Party
(CSP)
CSR scheme *see* Corporate Social
Responsibility (CSR) scheme
Cuban medical system, 138
cultivation, 50–1
Cyclone Ochki, 173–4. *see also* floods
of August 2018; rescue operation
for, 174–5; survivors of, 175

Damayanthi (aunt of Shailaja, K.K.),
17, 29, 49, 55, 59–60, 65, 124
Damodaran, M.K., 4, 23, 28–30, 32,
51, 52
death cases of Nipah patients, 201–2
decentralized governance, 246

decentralized public healthcare, 246
Delta virus, 233
democratic centralism, 101
democratic revolution, 47
dengue, 144, 171, 180, 184
Devaki (great-grandmother of
Shailaja K.K.), 4, 5
Dharavi (Mumbai), 229–30. *see also*
cluster management strategy
diabetes, 164, 165, 237
dialysis units, 159
Different Arts Centre, 268
digitizing patient care, 168–70
disabled children, Anuyatra
programme for, 266–8
discrimination, caste, 41–2, 47
District Committee, 102, 110, 117
district hospitals, 159–60. *see also*
medical colleges; taluk hospitals
redevelopment
district medical officer, 210, 211
doctor–patient ratio, 138
Domicile Care Centre, 231
doxycycline tablets, 176, 177

Eachara Warrier, T.V., 100
East India Company, 7–8, 10
Ebola virus, 185, 195
education, 71–2; privatization of, 90;
reform, 43, 44; women, 42, 71,
103–4
egalitarian, 2, 7, 42, 87, 102, 131, 244,
248, 276
e-Health project, 168–70
Ekbal, B., 214
Elankulam Manakal Sankaran
Namboodiripadu *see* EMS

elder abuse and abandonment, 268
electricity connection, 116–17, 119–22
emergency areas of a government hospital, 158
emergency learning centre, 164
Emergency on 25 June 1975, 98–100
EMS, 23–5, 27, 38, 47, 136, 243–4; first communist government under, 43–4
Engels, Friedrich, 24, 276
Ernakulam, 170, 229
Ernakulam Medical College, 138, 219
Europe as hotspot for COVID-19, 214–15
evictions, 43, 45–6
Ezhava, 4, 8; women, 21

Family Health Centres (FHCs), 139–40, 142, 166; creation of new posts for, 153, 154; doctors' protests, 154; inaugurating in the Chemmaruthi, 152; people's fund for, 152–3
family welfare subcentres, 137
farmers: agitations of, 26, 28; demonstrations, 26
father–daughter Malayali doctors, 135
Father Pious, 119–22
feudalism, 47, 95, 102, 244–6, 259
FHCs see Family Health Centres (FHCs)
first communist government, 43–5
floods of August 2018, 175–7; chlorination and spraying, 177;

outbreaks of disease prevention, 176–7; rescuing people from flooded areas, 176; worth of damages, 177
food for all, 245
Food for Peace programme, 65
Forder, Robert, 200
free education, 44
fruit bats, 185–6, 190, 203

Gafoor (microbiologist), 183
Gandhi, Indira, 98
Gandhi, Mahatma, 68
Ganesh (superintendent), 219
George, Veena, 274
Ghosa, Navjot, 196
Gopakumar, R.S., 199
Gopalan, A.K see AKG
Gopalan Nambiar, K., 23
Gopalan, Susheela, 104
Gopal, Vipin, 159
go-to spirit chase, 107
government hospitals, 139, 143–7. see also district hospitals; taluk hospitals redevelopment; casualty departments, 158; development fund, 146; emergency areas of, 158; funding for, 168–70; Punalur, 156–7; radiation treatment, 161; redevelopment, 155–8; total number of beds, 137
Govindan Master, M.V., 74
Gowri Lakshmi Bai, Maharani Ayilyam Thirunal, 133
The Guardian, 227
Guru, Narayana, 76

Health and Family Welfare, 129
health emergency, 220–1
help desk for COVID-19, 214, 215
Henipavirus infection treatment in
    Australia, 200–1
herbal medicine, 134–5
Hindus-Muslims violence, 96
Hospital Development Committee
    Fund, 145–6
Hridyam scheme, 166
human monoclonal antibody
    (m102.4) medication, 200, 201
hunger strike of AKG, 45–6
Hunger Watch India, 221
Hyder Ali, 7
hypertension, 165

ICMR see Indian Council of
    Medical Research (ICMR)
IDC see infectious disease control
    (IDC)
Idukki: land acquisition for hydro
    project, 45; medical college, 160
Imbichi Bava, E.K., 47
IMR see Infant Mortality Rate (IMR)
INC see Indian National Congress
    (INC)
India, 22–3; agitations for
    Independence of, 27
Indian Council of Medical Research
    (ICMR), 188, 224, 225, 232;
    sero-surveillance study of, 230
Indian National Congress (INC), 23,
    24, 46
Indu (epidemiologist), 188
Infant Mortality Rate (IMR), 160, 166

infectious disease control (IDC), 165
infrared thermometer scanning, 213
inner-party democracy, 101
insurance scheme, 250–2
Integrated Child Development
    Scheme, 104, 263
International Women's Research and
    Trade Centre, 263
Irikkur, 14
Iritty, 6, 26, 29, xvi
Isaac, Thomas, 142, 272
isolation wards, for Nipah virus
    patients, 192, 194–8
Italy, COVID-19 from, 214–15, 218

jackfruits, 63–4
Jaleel, K.T., 172
Janaki Teacher, 66
jaundice, medicinal herbs for, 134
Jayakrishnan (doctor), 181
Jayakumar (superintendent), 217
Jayashree (district medical officer
    (DMO)), 180, 181, 182, 198
jenmi, 5, 6, 8–14, 19, 21, 42
Jilla Council election, 109–10
Joseph (COVID patient), 216, 217
Joseph, P.J., 115
Joseph, Sunny, 123
Jose, U.V., 188, 189, 199

Kadar, B.K., 98
kallappara (false measure), 12
Kalliatt Nambiar, 5–6, 14
Kalliatt yajamanan, 6, 32, 41–2
Kalyani, Chooliyat, 40–1
Kalyani, Edwompally, 108

Kalyani, M.K. (grandmother of
    Shailaja, K.K.), 4–5, 14, 16–18,
    22, 25, 27, 29–32, 34–6, 49–50,
    52, 54, 55, 60, 62–6, 73; anti-
    police and anti-Congress, 34;
    care of smallpox affected people,
    38–9; as go-to spirit chaser, 107;
    storytelling of, 58, 67–8, 72;
    upper-caste Nair women and,
    40–1
Kalyasseri, 4
Kanakathidam family, 23–4
kanakudian (land lease), 11
Kanaran, C.H., 26, 47
Kannur, 3, 4, 6, 46, 90, 134, 225, xvi;
    District Hospital, 224
Karivellur, 28
KARSAP see Kerala Antimicrobial
    Resistance and Stewardship
    Action Plan (KARSAP)
Karthika Thirunal Maharaja, 134
Karunya Arogya Suraksha Padhathi
    (KASP), 250–2
Karutha (neighbourhood of Shailaja,
    K.K.), 21, 67
KASP see Karunya Arogya Suraksha
    Padhathi (KASP)
Kayyoor, 28
Kayyur martyrs, 67–8
Keezhoor, 26
Keezhooridam Vazhunnavar, 23
Kelkar, Rathan U., 252
Kerala: connection with Wuhan, 208;
    COVID-19 in (see COVID-19
    in Kerala); as internationalist
    multicultural region, 133; non-

communicable lifestyle diseases,
    165; public healthcare system
    (see public healthcare system in
    Kerala)
Kerala Antimicrobial Resistance
    and Stewardship Action Plan
    (KARSAP), 167, 168
Kerala Clinical Establishment
    (Registration and Regulation)
    Act, 2018, 204–5
Kerala Education Bill, 44
Kerala Gender Park in Kozhikode,
    263
Kerala Infrastructure Investment Fund
    Board (KIIFB), 142–3, 161, 272
Kerala Medical Services Corporation
    Limited (KMSCL), 196, 248–9,
    252
Kerala Model: defined, 243; Karunya
    Arogya Suraksha Padhathi
    (KASP), 250–2; oxygen capacity
    management, 249–50; primary
    healthcare sector, 246; public
    healthcare system (see public
    healthcare system in Kerala);
    social development, 245–7;
    technology and communication
    use in Nipah and COVID-19,
    252–4
Kerala Pradesh Congress Committee
    (KPCC), 27
Kerala's Economic Development:
    Emerging Issues and Challenges,
    136–7
Kerala Simham see Pazhassi Raja,
    Veera Kerala Varma

Kerala Socialist Youth Federation
    (KSYF), 74
Kerala Social Security Mission, 265,
    267
Kerala State Drugs and
    Pharmaceutical Limited
    (KSDPL), 235
Kerala State Electricity Board
    (KSEB), 120–2
Kerala Stay of Eviction Proceedings
    Act, 43
Kerala Students' Federation (KSF),
    100–1
Kerala weddings, 41
Khobragade, Rajan N., 205, 208, 211,
    225, 252
KIIFB see Kerala Infrastructure
    Investment Fund Board (KIIFB)
KMSCL see Kerala Medical Services
    Corporation Limited (KMSCL)
Kollontai, Alexandra, 259, xv
komaram (person possessed by a
    spirit), 37–8
Kottayam, 7, 14' Medical College,
    161, 217
Kottiyoor, 46
Kozhikode, 3, 180–4, 187, 188, 192,
    193, 194, 195, 196, 197, 198, 201,
    263; Baby Memorial Hospital in,
    180, 181; Medical College, 180,
    183, 188, 191, 192, 197, 198, 199,
    224, 225, 232
KPCC see Kerala Pradesh Congress
    Committee (KPCC)
'Krishibhoomi karshakanu'
    ('Farmland for a farmworker'), 245

Krishnan, Karayi, 17
Krishnan, M.K., 4, 23, 28–30, 77;
    incarceration in Salem jail, 32–3
KSDPL see Kerala State Drugs
    and Pharmaceutical Limited
    (KSDPL)
KSEB see Kerala State Electricity
    Board (KSEB)
KSF see Kerala Students' Federation
    (KSF)
KSYF see Kerala Socialist Youth
    Federation (KSYF)
kudiyettam (intra-state migration), 14
Kudumbashree movement, 258–9
kulathozhil (inherited occupation), 8
Kumar, Dileep, 196
Kumar, Kesavendra, 129
Kumar, Sunil, 211
Kundan (father of Shailaja K.K.),
    51–3
Kunhambu, A.V., 47
Kunhammavan see Sahadevan
Kunjummavan (grand-uncle of
    Shailaja, K.K.), 99
Kuriakose, Moni, 179, 197
Kuthuparamba constituency, 152;
    election, 110–13
kuzhikanam (land lease), 11

Lancet magazine, 201
land: acquisition, 45–6; laws, 8, 9;
    lease system, 11–13; reforms, 136,
    246; rights, 43
Land Reform Act, 96
Lasith (son of Shailaja, K.K.), 84,
    88–9, 91, 92

Left Democratic Front (LDF), 119, 123, 124, 273

Left Democratic Front (LDF) government, 234; dealing Storm Ockhi and floods, 173–8; election manifesto on medical colleges, 133; forming new department for women and children, 257–8; power in 2016, 127, 271–4

Lenin, Vladimir, 5, 22, 128, 259

leprosy, elimination of, 165

leptospirosis, 176

Level 3 Calamity, 175

Liberation Struggle (Vimochana Samaram), 44

life expectancy, 244, 247

Linear Accelerator (LINAC), 161

Lini Sajeesh (nurse infected with Nipah), 193–5, 199, 217

liver transplant surgery, 161

Local Committee, 102

Logan, William, 9

Lookose, Mary Poonen, 135–6

love marriage, 77

lower-caste: dehumanizing the human beings of, 19–20; denial of access to school, 135; woman, 20–1, 41

Maathuettathi (doula), 57–8, 64

Madathil, 5, 6, 17, 14, 16, 29, xvi

Madathil branch of CPI(M), 72, 102

Madhavan Nambiar, K., 23

Madhavan, N.S., 239, 240

Madras Presidency, 8, 134

Mahila Federation, 74

Mahila Samajam, 104

Malabar, 3, 6–8, 14–15, ix, xvi; Ayurvedic and plant-based treatment, 134–5; British administration of, 8–13; castes in, 6, 8, 9; communism in, 7, 22; migration to, 14, 16; rebellious and egalitarian sensibility, 7; social structure, 8

Malabar Manual (Logan), 9

Malabar Special Police (MSP), 23, 24, 28–32, 67

Malappuram: district, 152; Nipah infections in, 193, 197–9, 201–2

Malayala Manorama, 238

Malaysia, Nipah virus in, 184–7

Manipal Institute of Virology (MIV), 181, 182

Mariam (COVID patient), 216, 217

Mariyam (Nipah patient), 180, 198

Mariyam (tale of a woman), in traditional childbirth, 58

marriages, 78–9, 105; arranged, 51, 53, 78, 105; love, 77

martyrdom, 42

Marxism, 72

Marx, Karl, 24, 95, 108, 276; bureaucracy, 128; cemetery, 125–6; scientific socialism of, 108

Marychettathi (neighbourhood of Shailaja, K.K.), 67

maternal mortality rate, 160

Mathew, Joseph, 115

Mathew, Thomas, 219

Mathrubhumi, 199, 205

matrilineal systems, 52

Mattanur, 6, 27, 90; constituency, 122

medical colleges, 160; creation of new, 160; superspeciality, 160–1; trauma care, 162-163

medical education, 136

medical officer of the panchayat, 150, 151

medical tourism sector, 138

Meena, Amit, 196

Menon, A.R., 136

Menon, Madhava, 32–3

Menon, Sivadasa, 116

Menon, Vinod, 164

MERS *see* Middle East Respiratory Syndrome (MERS)

midday meal, 65–6

Middle East Respiratory Syndrome (MERS), 207

migration to Malabar, 14, 16

Minimum Guarantee proposal, 116–17, 121

ministers and bureaucrats, 128

mitigation method for COVID-19, 213–14, 223

MITTAYI initiative, 166

MIV *see* Manipal Institute of Virology (MIV)

mobile ambulance units, 226

Moideen, A.C., 172, 211

Moopen, Azad, 196

Moosa (Nipah patient), 180, 198

mortality rate: COVID-19, 207, 214, 223, 227, 232, 234; Nipah virus, 187, 197

MSP *see* Malabar Special Police (MSP)

Mundassery, Joseph, 44

Munroe, Thomas, 10

Muthanga Adivasi demonstrations, 90

Muthukad, Gopinath, 266–8

Mysore occupation, 7–8

Nadda, J.P., 178, 198, 200

Nair, Edasseri Govindan, 76

Nair, Kunjambu (Kayyur martyr), 67–8

Nair, Kunjiraman, 14, 50

Nair, M.T. Vasudevan, 142, 155

Nair, Rairu, 14, 50

Nair, Sardar Chandrothu Kunjiraman, 24

Nambiar, Raman, 26, 27

Narayanan Mooss, E.T., 134

national bourgeoisie, 47

National Health Mission, 252

National Health Service (NHS), 138

National Institute of Virology (NIV), 182–4, 225

national lockdown for COVID-19, 161, 220, 222, 227, 234, 254

National Quality Assurance Standards (NQAS) certification, 168

Nava Kerala Mission, 130, 138

Naveen (doctor), 187, 198

Nayanar Academy, inauguration of, 179

Nayanar, E.K., 47, 68, 117, 179, 181

NCD *see* noncommunicable disease control (NCD)

'nCorona Guidelines', 209, 237

Nehru, Jawaharlal, 45, 46; writing to Indira Gandhi, 4–5
new education programme, 117
'New Kerala', 127
NHS *see* National Health Service (NHS)
'Night Walk' programme, 209–10, 261–2
Ningalenne Communistaki (You Made Me a Communist), 245
'Nipah belt', 187
Nipah virus, 182, 184–5, 211, 212; in Bangladesh, 184, 186, 187; in Chengarothu, 183, 189–91; contact-tracing of, 191–2; cremation of bodies, 199–200; death cases, 201–2; defence, 193; emergency care units, 198; false message spread, 203; first infection in Malaysia, 185; free of, 202; in fruit bats, 185–7, 190, 203; high risk of infection of medical college staff, 193; incubation period of, 186, 192, 193; infection rate, 200; infections in Malappuram, 193, 197–9, 201–2; information for the people, 252–3; isolation wards, 192, 194–8; in Malaysia, 184–7; medicine for, 200–1; misinformation, 204; mortality rate, 187, 197; personal protective equipment (PPE) for, 192, 195–6, 200, 202; in pigs, 186, 187; plan of action to combat the spread of, 197–8; prevention and containment, 191; Ribavirin for, 200–1; safety kits and N95 masks for patients, 196; in Siliguri (India), 184, 187; in Singapore, 184, 186; source of the infection, 189–90, 197; study of, 186–7; symptoms, 186; testing, 201–2; 24/7 call centres, 188, 189, 198; viral in social media and WhatsApp, 204; WHO recommendation of deep burial, 199 (*see also* COVID-19 in Kerala)
Nirbhaya Day, 261
NIV *see* National Institute of Virology (NIV)
N95 masks, 196
noncommunicable disease control (NCD), 164–5
Nooh, P.B., 216
Noorani, A.G., 45
NQAS certification *see* National Quality Assurance Standards (NQAS) certification

October Socialist Revolution of 1917, 4, 5, 22
old age homes, 268
One Health approach, 203–4
Onnekalkodi Malayalikal (1.15 crore Malayalis, Namboodiripadu), 243, 244
oxygen capacity management, 249–50
oxygen crisis, 250

Padmanabhan, M.O., 111, 114

Padmanabhan Nambiar, K., 23

panchayat, 150

Panchayati Raj Act of 1992, 141

panchayat presidents, 142, 150–2

Pappettan *see* Padmanabhan, M.O.

Party branch, 101–2

Pathanamthitta, 14; district, 159, 161, 215, 216, 262

Paul, Babu, 205

Payam, 5, 6, 23, 26, 28

Pazhassi, 6, 28

Pazhassi Raja, Veera Kerala Varma, 7–8, 10

Perambra, 180, 193

personal protective equipment (PPE), 192, 195–6, 199, 202, 249

perumazhakkalam (season of relentless rain), 175

Petroleum and Explosives Safety Organization (PESO), 249

PHC *see* Primary Health Centre (PHC)

Pillai, Krishna, 38

Pillai, Ramakrishna, 24

Plan A strategy in COVID-19, 227

Plan B strategy in COVID-19, 227, 231

Plan C strategy in COVID-19, 227–8, 231

plant-based treatment, 133–4

planting and harvesting paddy, 50

Police Association, 146–7

Police Officers' Association, 146

Politburo, 102

politics, Shailaja, K.K., 2–3, 85, 100–1, 109

Poonen, T.E., 135

Poonthura, cluster management strategy at, 228–9

'Pothu idam entethum' (Public space is ours too) slogan, 261

PPE *see* personal protective equipment (PPE)

Prabhakar, Biju, 225, 265

Pramod, P., 91, 127, 210–11, 284

President's Rule, 45

preventive healthcare, 165

primary healthcare system, 132–3, 137, 139, 140, 143, 155, 159, 246

Primary Health Centre (PHC), 136–7, 139, 141–3, 149–50, 152, 168, 188, 236, 246

private hospitals, 137, 143, 159, 161, 188, 204, 219, 248

privatization of education, 90

Proceedings of the National Academy of Sciences of the United States of America (PNAS), 186–7

protests: against Congress government, 45–6; against to join World War II, 26–7

public healthcare system in Kerala, 131, 246–8; Aardram Mission, 138–9, 142, 149, 154, 158, 161, 171; awards and certification, 167–8; cancer care, 167; casualty departments, 158; central government funding, 169–70; child care, 166–7; crisis, 155, 178; data for beginnings and

development of health sector,
136–7; digitizing patient care,
169–70; district hospitals, 159–
60; doctor–patient ratios, 138;
e-Health project, 168–70; Family
Health Centres (FHCs), 139–40,
142–3, 149–50, 152–3, 167, 236;
KIIFB funding for, 142–3, 160;
Malabar, 134–5; medical colleges
(*see* medical colleges); medical
tourism sector, 138; medicinal
herbs and plants, 134–5; Primary
Health Centre (PHC), 136–7,
139, 141–3, 149–50, 152, 236;
secondary level of, 137, 139, 143,
257; spending for, 142; state
government funding, 170; taluk
hospitals redevelopment, 155–9;
tertiary levels of, 139, 143; three
levels, 137; trauma care, 161–3;
Travancore, 133–4
public health nurses, 165, 190
public hospitals *see* government
hospitals
public money, 146
public vilification campaign, 217
Public Works Department (PWD),
115
Punalur Taluk Hospital, 156–7
PWD *see* Public Works Department
(PWD)

quality of healthcare delivery, 131
quarantine for COVID-19 patients,
212–13, 215–16, 221–3, 226–7,
231

radiation treatment, 161
Raghavan, M.V., 110
Rajan, P., 100
Ramakrishnan, T.P., 180, 181, 189
Raman Mestri, Madavalapil, 3–6, 23,
25, 32
Raman, M.K., 4
Ramon Magsaysay Award, 275
rapid response team for COVID-19,
208
Rashtriya Swayamsevak Sangh
(RSS), 96
Raveendranath, C., 211
Ravunni, M.K., 4, 23–7, 29, 42;
incarceration, 26, 27
RCCs *see* Regional Cancer Centres
(RCCs)
Regional Cancer Centres (RCCs),
167
Reliance General Insurance, 251
religious fundamentalism, 259
remarriage, 5
reporting system for COVID-19, 253
rescue operation for Cyclone Ochki,
174–5
reverse quarantine, 222, 226–7
Ribavirin, 200–1
right to free education, 44
road accident treatment, 161–2
robotic technology, 254
Roy, Arundhati, 248
RSS *see* Rashtriya Swayamsevak
Sangh (RSS)
RT-PCR test (Reverse Transcription
Polymerase Chain Reaction Test),
224, 225

Russian Revolution, 128, 259
ryotwari system (land revenue
　　collection), 10–11, 19

Sabarimala temple entry of women,
　　216, 262
Sabith (Nipah patient), 180, 189,
　　191, 192, 201–3
Sadanandan, Rajeev, 129–32, 139,
　　155, 181, 182, 201, 205, 206, 251
'Sadharyam munnottu' campaign, 261
safety kits for Nipah patients, 195, 196
Sahadevan (uncle of Shailaja, K.K.),
　　18, 29, 44, 51, 59, 69, 77, 85,
　　96–101
Sajeevan, Chandini, 188
Salem jail massacre, 32–4, 77
Salih (Nipah patient), 180, 181, 184
Samrajya Virudha Samaram, 27
Sarada Teacher, 117
Saritha, R.L., 144, 181–4, 187, 188,
　　198, 228
SARS see Severe Acute Respiratory
　　Syndrome (SARS)
SARS-CoV-2 (SARS coronavirus
　　2), 207
Sarvodaya College, 78
Sathasivam, P., 267
Scheduled Caste (SC), 120
Scheduled Caste and Scheduled
　　Tribes Development Department,
　　120
Scheduled Tribe (ST), 120
schizophrenia, 107
scientific socialism of Marx, Karl,
　　108

SDGs see Sustainable Development
　　Goals (SDGs)
secondary healthcare system, 137,
　　139, 143, 251
self-quarantine, 220
seroprevalence study, 224
sero-surveillance study of ICMR,
　　230
Serum Institute, 234
Severe Acute Respiratory Syndrome
　　(SARS), 207
sexual exploitation of lower caste
　　women, 20
SHA see State Health Agency
　　(SHA)
Shabna (panchayat president), 152–3
Shahirsha, R., 156, 157
Shailaja, K.K.: activities as an of
　　MLA, 114–17; awards for
　　COVID-19 prevention and
　　control, 241; balancing the house
　　and family–school–politics,
　　83–4; becoming MLA, 88; BEd
　　education, 86, 106; Bhaskaran
　　Master's proposal for marriage,
　　76–7; birth of, 57; birth place,
　　xiii–xiv; bonding of family, 93;
　　BSc degree, 99; childhood,
　　61; construction of bridges,
　　115–16; desire to haircut as
　　Baby Jayalalithaa, 69; education,
　　71–2; family, 3–6, 16–18, 93;
　　finance department support to
　　health department, 272; first
　　public failure, 123; first trip to
　　London in 2018, 125; full-time

politics, 87–8; given birth to two babies, 84; handwriting, 86; husband's support, 85–6, 111, 125; identification of officers to work in the ministry, 129–30; improvements to the primary healthcare, 132–3; involvement in politics and social work, 54; job at the Shivapuram High School, 82–3, 106–7; lacking to care of the sons, 87–9; leaving home after marriage, 79–80; life story, 1–3; living with joint family, 58–9; living with mother-in-law, 80–2; loss of father, 53–4; marriage, 78–9; Marxism, 72; mission as representatives of KSYF's District Committee, 75; mother's love, 49–55; Muthanga Adivasi demonstrations, 90; 1996 Kuthuparamba constituency election, 110–13; organizing the women's groups, 102–5; participating the Summit for Vaccine Internationalism, 236; as a Party member, 72, 73; as a Party's Central Committee member, 2, 124, 275; as a party whip of the CPI(M), 274; as a Party worker, 2, 3, 73, 110, 118; 2006 Peravoor constituency election, 118–19; 2011 Peravoor constituency election, 122–4; politics, 2–3, 85, 100–1, 109; professional satisfaction, 272; provision of electricity, 116–17, 119–22; response to the Opposition leader in COVID-19 crisis, 223; responsibility in COVID-19, 236–7; restrictions to eat midday meal in school, 65–6; reticence about public speaking, 75–6, 109; Social Justice portfolio, 264–9; speech at Pazhassi Reading Library, 75–6; studies and careers of the two sons, 91–2; teacher career of, 82–3, 106–7, 117; turn down of Ramon Magsaysay Award, 275; 2016 Kuthuparamba constituency election, 124; unannounced visit to public hospital, 144–7; voluntary retirement, 118; voluntary retirement from teaching profession, 118; Women and Child Development (WCD) portfolio, 258–64; working with Sadanandan, Rajeev, 129–31, 139, 204

SHAILI *see* State Health Application for Intensified Lifestyle Intervention (SHAILI)

Shalini (daughter of aunt Damayanthi), 59–60, 65

Shankaranarayan (Finance Minister), 118

Shantha (mother of Shailaja, K.K.), 17, 49–50, 60; death of, 55, 124; decision on husband's first wife, 53–4; marriage, 51–2; strength and resilience, 54

Sharmad (Trivandrum Medical College superintendent), 163

Shijitha (Nipah patient), 200

Shobha Teacher, 106–7

Shobith (son of Shailaja, K.K.), 84, 88, 91–2

Shyamala (daughter of Shailaja's grandmother), 18, 29, 59, 60, 69

Siliguri (India), Nipah virus in, 184, 187

Singapore, Nipah virus in, 184, 186

Singh, S.K., 188

SIRAS see Stroke Identification Rehabilitation Awareness and Stabilisation, (SIRAS)

'Sister Lini Memorial' award, 194

slavery, 13

smallpox, 36; Communist Party's health classes about, 38–9; precautions, 38; public vaccination programme for, 134; role of caste in, 37–8; superstition and, 36–7; turmeric for, 37–9

'Smart Anganwadis', 263–4

social development, 245–7

socialism, 245

socialistic model, 248

socialist revolution, 46–7

social justice department, 257, 264–9

social media, 204, 216

social revolution, 244

societal change, 108

Sonamol (patient of blindness), 265–6

SOPs see standard operating procedures (SOPs)

soul, 62

Spinney, Laura, 227

spirits, 62

Sreehari (nodal officer), 166

Sreejayan (doctor), 197

Srikanth (doctor), 162

standard operating procedures (SOPs), 209, 211, 221

State Committee, 102

State Health Agency (SHA), 250, 252

State Health Application for Intensified Lifestyle Intervention (SHAILI), 166

State Health Systems Resource Centre, 140

Stay of Eviction Proceedings Act, 96

storytelling, 58, 67–8, 72

Stroke Identification Rehabilitation Awareness and Stabilisation, (SIRAS), 159

stroke unit, 159

Subbaraiah (police officer), 68

Sudhan, Preeti, 198

Sugunan (doctor), 225

Summit for Vaccine Internationalism, 236

superspeciality facilities, 159

superspeciality medical colleges, 160–1

superstitions, 16, 61, 105–8; and smallpox, 36–7

Sustainable Development Goals (SDGs), 132

Sweet Health, 165

taluk hospitals redevelopment, 155–8

tapioca, 64

Tata Trusts, 164
teacher career of Shailaja, K.K.,
    82–3, 106–7, 117
technology use during COVID-19,
    253–4
telecommunication, 254
tertiary healthcare system, 139, 143
'Test, test, test', 223
Thalassery–Coorg road, 5, 6, 10, xvi
thali (mangalsutra) of Shailaja, K.K.,
    79
Theyyam performance, 16
Thillankeri, 28
Third Anglo-Mysore War, 8
Thiruvananthapuram, 3, 152, 228–9
Thomas (branch secretary), 119, 121–2
Thrissur, 134, 210–11; Medical
    College, 161, 212
thrombolysis treatment facilities, 159
Tipu Sultan, 7, 8
Tope, Rajesh, 229
total shutdown, COVID-19, 229–30
Total Trauma Care project, 162
'Trace, quarantine, test, isolate, treat'
    strategy, 222–5
traditional childbirth, 57–8
transgender population, 269
transgressions, 42
trauma, 174, 175; care, 161–3
Travancore, 3, 14–15; healthcare
    system, 133–4
Trivandrum: General Hospital, 174;
    Medical College, 138, 162, 239
tropical diseases, 180
tuberculosis, elimination of, 165
turmeric for smallpox, 37–9

24-hour disaster management cells,
    254
Type-1 diabetes, 164

Ubeesh (Nipah patient), 201–3
United Democratic Front (UDF),
    118, 124, 273
United Democratic Front (UDF)
    government: grant for e-Health
    project, 168; protests against,
    45–6, 90
untouchability, 19, 135, 258
UN Women, 263
upper-caste women, 40–1
Uruppumkutti, provision of
    electricity to, 119–22
Utility Certificate, 170

vaccines for COVID-19, 234–6
Varkeychettan (neighbourhood of
    Shailaja, K.K.), 63, 67
Varnapakittu cultural festival, 269
vasoori see smallpox
Vayalil, Shamseer, 196
Vazhunnavar, Narayanan, 26
Vengad panchayat, 115
Venugopal, R., 249
Venu, V., 205
verum paattam (land lease), 12
Vijayan, Pinarayi, 23, 86, 96–8, 110,
    124, 138, 173, 210, 267, 271, 273
violence: of communalist forces, 96;
    against women, 260
Vivekananda, Swami, 20, 76
voluntary retirement, 118
VPS Healthcare, 152

Warrier, Vaidyarathnam P.S., 134
war room, 254
Wayanad, 3, 10, 43
We-Care scheme, 265
Wellington, B., 46
WhatsApp, 203, 216–17
women: after Russian Revolution,
    259; education, 42, 71–2, 103–4;
    educational status, 259–60;
    empowerment of, 259; equal
    rights to public spaces, 261;
    Ezhava, 21; government's role
    on, 260; inequality in workforce,
    262–3; lower-caste, 20–1, 41;
    marriages, 105; pressure on,
    73; rights, 258–60; Sabarimala
    temple entry of, 216, 262; and
    superstitions, 105; upper-caste,
    40–1; violence against, 260

Women and Child Development
    (WCD), 257, 261–3
World Health Organization
    (WHO), 138, 167, 199;
    recommendation of the burial of
    Nipah patients, 199; 'Test, test,
    test', 223
World Organisation for Animal
    Health, definition of Nipah, 184
World War II, 9, 26
Wuhan, 207–8

yajamanan, Kalliatt, 6, 32, 41–2
Yechury, Sitaram, 179
yellow upma, 65–6
Yusuff Ali, M.A., 222

Zetkin, Clara, 259